Revise
PE
for OCR

second edition

by

Dennis Roscoe
Jan Roscoe

AS/A1 Revise PE for OCR

second edition

by

Dennis Roscoe
Jan Roscoe

AS/A1 Revise PE for OCR second edition

by

Dennis Roscoe
Jan Roscoe

Jan Roscoe Publications Ltd

An imprint of Heath Books Ltd

First edition published in 2009 by Jan Roscoe Publications.
Second edition December 2016.

Heath Books Ltd
Willow House, Willow Walk
Sutton
Surrey
SM3 9QQ
United Kingdom

tel: 020 8644 7788
fax: 020 8641 3377
email: orders@heathbooks.co.uk

A Catalogue record for this book is available from the British Library.

ISBN   978-1-901424-91-1.

Cover designs by Helen Roscoe-Rutter and David Roscoe-Rutter.

Published via Adobe InDesign, CorelDraw 10.410, Adobe Illustrator 9.0, Smartdraw 6.0, laid out and typeset by Dennis Roscoe

Printed and bound by

Hobbs the Printers Limited
Brunel Road
Totton
Hampshire
SO40 3WX
United Kingdom

tel: 023 8066 4800
fax: 023 8066 4801

email: estimating@hobbs.uk.com

INTRODUCTION

This 'A' level PE book has been written to address the changes in content and style of the OCR Level 3 Advanced Subsidiary GCE Level Physical Education (8PE0) and OCR Level 3 Advanced Year 1 GCE Level Physical Education (9PE0) syllabuses which commenced in September 2016. The 2016 AS syllabus will be first examined in June 2017, and has been designed to be able to be co-taught with the first year of the 'A' Level course to be first examined in June 2018. This means that students taking the AS Level in June 2017 can be taught in the same group as the first year of the two year 'A' Level course to be examined in 2018.

These Physical Education syllabuses are multi-disciplinary in nature, covering applied anatomy and exercise physiology, skill acquisition and sports psychology, and historical and contemporary studies. These subject areas have generated a substantial quantity of specialist literature each with its own specific language. At times you may be overwhelmed by the amount of material covered, however this book addresses the problem of dealing with copious notes by summarising the content of the subject matter and attempting to explain in simple language what are sometimes complicated concepts or issues.

Questions are provided throughout the text and exam style questions are provided at the end of each chapter. Answers can be downloaded by going to the following link: http://www.jroscoe.co.uk/downloads/as_a1_revise_pe_ocr/ on the JRP website. The answers will amplify the subject matter and provide clues as to how the exam itself should be approached. A new feature this time is the requirement that the final exam questions on each section of the syllabus shall include an essay type answer. This allows students to express their ability and knowledge in the context of properly written language (prose) with attention to grammar and punctuation. Question assessment guidelines and use of terminology are included immediately before the index section in this book.

Materials are presented in a concise and visual approach for effective and efficient revision. Modern terminology, nomenclature and units have been used wherever possible. At the end of the book there is a comprehensive index for easy reference.

HOW TO USE THIS REVISION GUIDE

The ideal use of this revision guide would be to purchase it at the start of the course and relate each of the summary pages to the specific areas of the syllabus as an aide memoire. The inclusion of specific questions and full answers (to be found on the following link: http://www.jroscoe.co.uk/downloads/as_a1_revise_pe_ocr/ provide a means of self-testing. Each chapter has its own link specified on the questions pages. Don't be tempted to find out the answers before attempting a question.

In reality, whole examination questions contain a much broader content than those given in this guide. Examiners will attempt to examine more than one small area of the syllabus within the context of one full question and therefore it is important that you revise all aspects of your syllabus.

The main use of the revision guide should be during the final revision period leading up to your examinations, as it should help you to understand and apply concepts i.e. link summary content with examination question.

The aim of this revision guide is to provide an aid that enhances syllabus analysis, and to raise your level of success in examinations.

THE QUALITY OF AUTHORS

The authors are experts in the physical education field and have considerable experience in teaching 'A' Level Physical Education. They have written examination syllabuses, and have set and marked examination questions within this subject area and taught at revision workshops throughout the UK. Much of the material within this book has been thoroughly student tested.

The authors hope that this revision guide will prove useful to staff and students. Jan Roscoe Publications will welcome any comments you would wish to make about the book's utility or layout. Thank you for using this work.

Dennis Roscoe
Jan Roscoe

ACKNOWLEDGMENTS

The authors wish to thank Bob Davis for his contribution in the Historical and Contemporary Issues elements of this book. Thanks are also due to Helen Roscoe-Rutter and David Roscoe-Rutter for their contributions as cover designers and photographers and Lois Cresswell, Jenny Pacey, Helen Roscoe-Rutter and Osian Jones for their patience as photographic models. Very many thanks are also due to Debbie Francis of Heath Books for proof reading the text. The authors wish to thank members of the Belgian Olympic Athletics Squad for permission to use their images.
Dennis Roscoe - *Editor*

ACKNOWLEDGMENTS FOR GRAPHICS

Figure
1.7 Simone Biles, Rio Olympics 2016, A. Ricardo/Shutterstock
1.22 Actionplus
1.28 Physical Education and the Study of Sport 5e, ISBN 978072343750
1.33 Toby Cramer/istock
5.7 Birgitte Magnus/istock
5.15 Sport Development Centre, Loughborough University
6.10 The Stretching Institute
6.19 Ed Hidden/istock
8.14 Caterine Ibarguen, Rio Olympics 2016, Erik Van Leewen/Wikipedia
10.2 Physical Education and the Study of Sport 5e, ISBN 9780723433750
10.3 Rich Legg/istock
10.4 Bradley/istock
11.2 Sir Chris Hoy, John the scone/Wikipedia, Creative Commons
11.11 Laura Trott, Jason Kenny, Rio Olympics 2016, J Ernesto/Alamy
12.5 GNU free documentation/Richard Giles
12. 7 Thailand hockey, Mooinblack/Shutterstock
13.1 Albo/Shutterstock
13.2 LTA Wimbledon
13.8 GB men's team pursuit Rio Olympics 2016, Stanislav Krasilnikov/Alamy
13.10 Vladmir Wrangel/Shutterstock
13.12 Jack Laugher, Chris Mears, Rio Olympics 2016, Xinhua/Alamy
15.4 Denise Lewis, Featureflash/Shutterstock
15.11 Dafne Schippers, Erik Van Leeuwen/Wikipedia
15.5 South Nottingham Academy, Afshan McKay, Bond Bryan Architects
16.10 Laura Trott, Rio Olympics 2016, J. Ernesto/Alamy
16.10 Max Whitlock, Rio Olympic Games 2016, Iilyana Vynogradova/Shutterstock
16.10 Jack Laugher, Rio Olympics 2016, Mitch Gunn/Shutterstock
16.11 Game makers, London Olympics 2012, Gary Knight/Flickr
16.12 GB Women's hockey team Rio Olympics 2016, BOA/Andy Ryan
16.14 The Olympic Park Hatters/Flickr
16.15 English, Russians and French football fans UEFA 2016, Alberto Girotto/Shutterstock
16.16 Birds' Nest, Beijing, Anwar El Bizanti
16.18 Empty seats, Rio Olympics 2016, Ilnitsky/Alamy
16.20 IOC, Sport for Hope Programme

All other photographs or graphics are by Helen Roscoe-Rutter, Jan Roscoe, Dennis Roscoe, Bob Davis or from other free sources.

A Level year 2 Revise PE for OCR

JRP

HIGH QUALITY PHOTOS

QUALITY GRAPHS

REVISION SUMMARY NOTES

Factors affecting leader effectiveness

The following **leadership qualities** will determine a leader's effectiveness:
- Ability to communicate.
- Respect for group members.
- Enthusiasm.
- High ability.
- Deep knowledge of the sport and techniques or tactics.
- Charisma.

REVISION SUMMARY CHARTS

ANSWERS TO QUESTIONS are found on the JRP Website

3)   b) Why is blood doping an illegal ergogenic aid?
     3 marks
Answer
- WADA bans any means of artificially *enhancing performance* such as $\dot{V}O_{2max}$.
- Using chemicals or blood substitutes, and also blood doping can be *detrimental* to the athlete's health.
- Such as risk of infection from the reinfusion process.
- And high blood pressure.
- Because of a higher concentration of red blood cells, a much greater chance of thrombosis or blood clotting (possibly causing stroke or heart attack).
- Blood doping is in conflict with the general *spirit of sport*.

For **full listings** see the **JRP Catalogue** or visit **www.jroscoe.co.uk**

ROSCOE et al
A2 Revise PE for OCR
ISBN   978-1-911-24106-5

A2 Revise PE for OCR
second edition

Dennis Roscoe
Jan Roscoe

Jan Roscoe Publications Ltd

2016 Specification

This new Revise Series covers all aspects of the examinable 'A' Level year 2 OCR syllabus commencing September 2017.
The book consists of student notes, full colour illustrations, photographs, exam questions and full answers. Key concepts are clearly defined with examples that can be used in answers to exam questions, enabling the student to self-test. This student revision guide supports a comprehensive revision plan and will enhance student grades (due in spring 2017).

HOW TO ORDER

tel   **+44(0)208 644 7788**
(open 9am-5.30pm)

fax   **+44(0)208 641 3377**
(open 24 hours a day)

email **orders@heathbooks.co.uk**

by post to: **Heath Educational Books, Willow House, Willow Walk, Off Whittaker Rd, Sutton, Surrey, SM3 9QQ**

CONTENTS

AS/A1 Revise PE for OCR

Part 1

Applied anatomy and physiology

Part 2

Exercise physiology

CONTENTS

Part 6

Sport and society

APPLIED ANATOMY AND PHYSIOLOGY

CHAPTER 1: Skeletal and muscular systems

> **STUDENT NOTE** Knowledge and understanding of the skeletal system is required and includes structure and functions of bones, joints and connective tissues.

Joints, movements and muscles

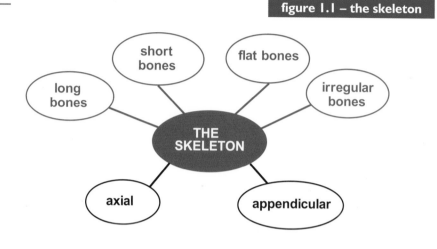

figure 1.1 – the skeleton

The skeletal system

- **The appendicular skeletal system** (figure 1.1) consists of the shoulder girdle, skull, hip girdle, leg and arm bones.
- **The axial skeleton** consists of the skull, vertebral column, ribs and sternum.

The functions of the skeletal system are to act as a lever system, as surface area for attachment of muscle, tendons and ligaments, and to give shape and support to the body. Also, red and white blood cells are manufactured within bone marrow, and bones store fats and minerals.

Types of bones and principal functions

- **Long bones**, for example, the femur (which acts as a lever).
- **Short bones**, for example, carpals (which have strength and lightness).
- **Flat bones**, for example, the pelvis (which has a large surface area for muscle and tendon attachments), the cranium (has the function of brain protection).
- **Irregular bones**, for example, the vertebrae (which protect the spinal cord), the patella (a sesamoid bone) which increases the mechanical advantage of the quadriceps tendon.

> **STUDENT NOTE**
>
> You need to familiarise yourself with the names of bones in figure 1.2 in relation to joints when you answer movement analysis questions.

figure 1.2 – the human skeleton

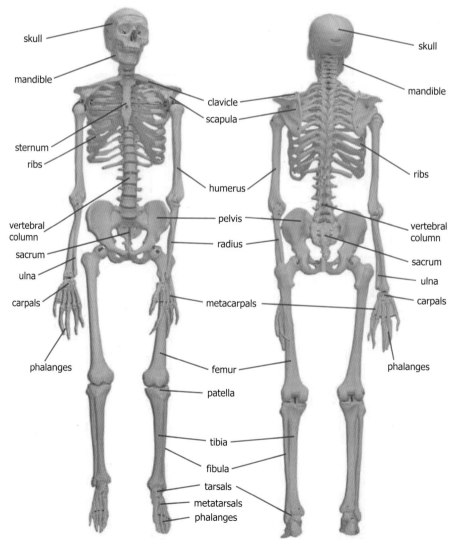

Bony features

Protrusions and **depressions** act as the places on bones at which ligaments and muscle tendons attach (their shape increases the surface area on the bone available for attachment).

Cartilage

- **Hyaline (articular) cartilage** has a smooth, solid matrix which sits on the ends of bones, and forms the exact surfaces which are in contact and move across one another when a joint is used.
- **White fibro-cartilage** is tough and slightly flexible and exists between vertebrae.
- **Yellow elastic cartilage** is soft and elastic and exists in the ear lobes.

The structure and function of bone tissue

- The **periosteum** is an outer protective covering of bone which provides attachment for muscle tendons and ligaments. The deeper layers of the periosteum are responsible for growth in bone width.
- The **epiphyseal disc** or growth plate is the segment of a bone in which an increase in bone length takes place.
- **Compact bone** consists of solid bone tissue, located down the shaft of a long bone and the outer layers of short, flat and irregular bones. Its dense structure gives strength and support.
- **Cancellous bone** has a lattice-like or spongy appearance. It is light-weight and is located at the ends of a long bone, in addition to providing the internal bone tissue in short, flat and irregular bones.

The articular system

Joints

Articulation is defined **'as a place where two or more bones meet to form a joint'.**

Joint types (figure 1.3) are:

- **Fibrous or immovable** – for example, between bones of the cranium.
- **Cartilaginous or slightly moveable** – for example, vertebral discs.
- **Synovial or freely moveable** (classified in table 1.1, page 17).

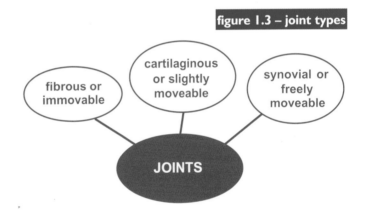

figure 1.3 – joint types

Synovial joint (figure 1.4)

- The **synovial fluid** reduces joint friction by lubrication, and maintains joint stability.
- The **synovial membrane** encloses fluid and secretes fluid.
- The **joint capsule** is a sleeve of tough, fibrous tissue surrounding the joint.
- A **ligament** is an extension of the joint capsule consisting of strong, fibrous connective tissue that provides stability by joining bone to bone.
- **Articular cartilage** prevents friction between bones, and cushions the ends of bones.
- **Bursae** prevent friction and wear.
- **Pads of fat** cushion the joint.
- **Menisci** help bones fit together and improve stabilisation of the joint.

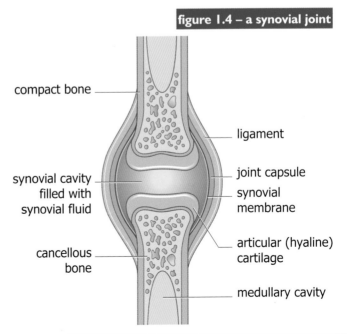

figure 1.4 – a synovial joint

Joints movement and muscles **13**

Planes of movement

STUDENT NOTE

The axes of the body shown in figure 1.5 are explained in the A Level Year 2 book in this series.

Terms used in movement analysis

Terms of movement consist of three main sections:

* Planes of the body.
* Axes of the body.
* Movement patterns.

To help analyse movement, it is possible to imagine a series of lines and surfaces that divide the body into sections – the lines are called **axes** and the surfaces called **planes**.

Planes of the body

The term **body plane** is defined as '**an imaginary flat surface running through the centre of gravity of the body**', and is used to assist in the understanding of movement of body segments with respect to one another. Within each plane an axis can be identified in association with a particular joint about which the movement takes place.

Three imaginary planes

Refer to figure 1.5.

* **Frontal (coronal) plane**

    * A vertical plane that divides the body into **front and back** sections.

    * Movements in this plane include abduction and adduction, as for example in a cartwheel (figure 1.6).

    * And spinal lateral flexion, as for example in side flexion trunk bends.

* **Sagittal (median) plane**

    * A vertical plane that divides the body into **left and right** sides.

    * Movements in this plane include flexion and extension, as for example in somersaults (figure 1.7), biceps curl, pole vault take-off, sprinting, dorsiflexion, and plantarflexion.

* **Transverse (horizontal) plane**

    * A horizontal plane that divides the body into upper and lower sections.

    * Movements are rotational movement patterns which are supination, pronation, horizontal extension, horizontal flexion and spinal rotation.

    * Example movements would be twisting or turning, the spinning skater, discus, hammer (figure 1.8) or ski turns.

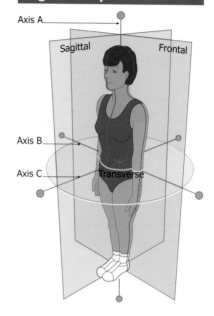

figure 1.5 – planes and axes

Axis A

Sagittal   Frontal

Axis B

Axis C   Transverse

figure 1.6 – a cartwheel in the frontal plane

figure 1.7 – a gymnast tumbling in the sagittal plane

figure 1.8 – a hammer thrower turning the transverse plane

Movement at joints – terminology (figure 1.9)

The possible ranges of movements within a synovial joint (see figure 1.4 page 13) vary according to the shape of the articular surfaces and therefore according to the joint type.

Movement in the frontal (coronal) plane

Abduction means to take away and so is characterised by movement away from the midline – for example, a cartwheel in gymnastics.

Adduction means to bring together and so is characterised by movement towards the midline – for example, bringing the lower legs back together from the inverted cartwheel.

Depression describes movement of the shoulders downwards – for example, the preparation for a dead lift, gripping the bar.

Elevation describes movement of the shoulders upwards – for example, a shoulder shrug.

Eversion is the joint action at the ankle characterised by the turning of the sole of the foot laterally outwards – for example, the kick action in breaststroke.

Inversion is the joint action at the ankle characterised by the turning of the sole of the foot medially inwards – for example, a football player inverts the foot to pass the ball with the outside of his or her boot.

Lateral flexion is sideways bending.

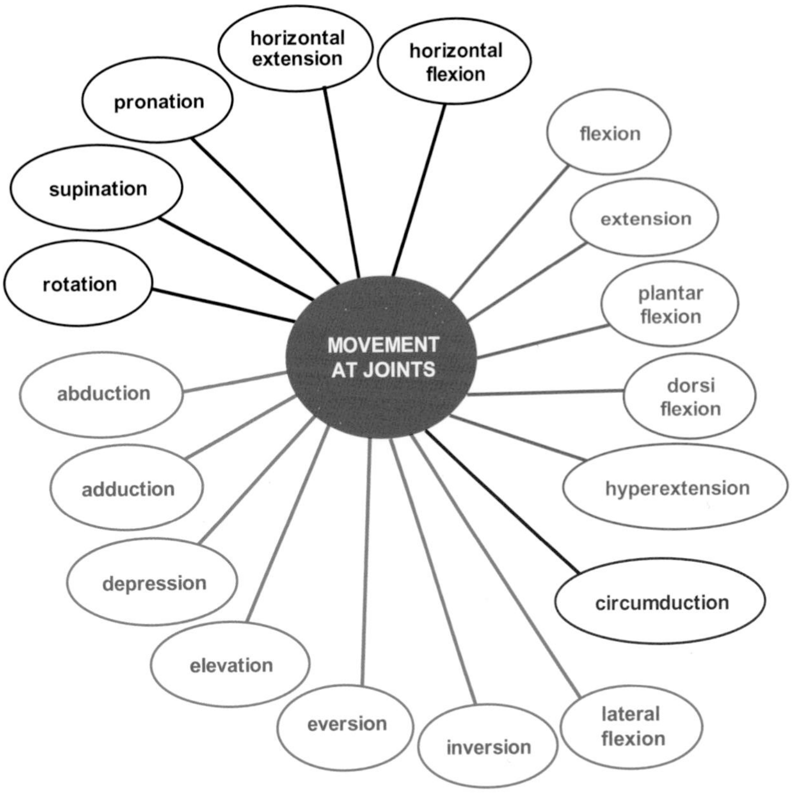

Movement in the sagittal (median) plane

Flexion means to bend, resulting in a decreased angle around the joint – for example, bending of the knee.

Extension means to straighten, resulting in an increased angle around the joint – for example, straightening of the knee from a bent-legged to straight-legged position.

Plantarflexion involves extending the toes thereby increasing the angle at the ankle – for example, standing on tip-toes.

Dorsiflexion describes movement of the foot towards the shin – for example, walking on one's heels.

Hyperextension is the forced extension of a joint beyond its normal range of motion – for example, the arched spine that is created in the flight phase of the Fosbury Flop high jump technique.

figure 1.9 – movement at joints

horizontal extension · horizontal flexion · pronation · flexion · supination · extension · rotation · plantar flexion · **MOVEMENT AT JOINTS** · abduction · dorsi flexion · adduction · hyperextension · depression · circumduction · elevation · lateral flexion · eversion · inversion

Circumduction is a combination of flexion, extension, abduction, adduction and rotation– for example, when the upper arm moves (arm circling) so that it describes a cone with the shoulder joint at the apex, involving all three planes of movement.

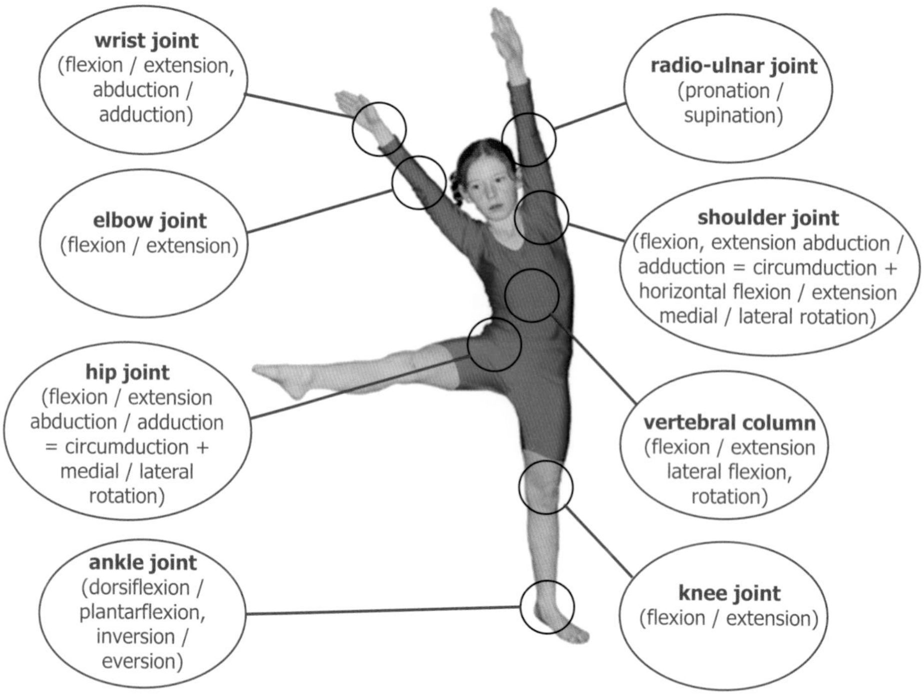

Movements in the transverse (horizontal) plane

Horizontal flexion (also known as horizontal adduction) occurs when the shoulder starts in a flexed position with the arm(s) parallel to the ground, followed by the shoulder joint moving towards the midline of the body – for example, during the press-out phase of a bench press, and the arm swing into the release phase of a discus throw.

figure 1.10 – major joints – movement patterns

wrist joint
(flexion / extension, abduction / adduction)

elbow joint
(flexion / extension)

hip joint
(flexion / extension abduction / adduction = circumduction + medial / lateral rotation)

ankle joint
(dorsiflexion / plantarflexion, inversion / eversion)

radio-ulnar joint
(pronation / supination)

shoulder joint
(flexion, extension abduction / adduction = circumduction + horizontal flexion / extension medial / lateral rotation)

vertebral column
(flexion / extension lateral flexion, rotation)

knee joint
(flexion / extension)

Horizontal extension (also known as horizontal abduction) occurs when the shoulder joint, with the arm(s) parallel to the ground, move away from the midline of the body – for example, a seated row as the elbows are pulled back as far as possible, and the preparatory swing of a discus throw.

Pronation is characterised by the rotation of the forearm medially so that the hand faces downwards – for example, a top-spin forehand in tennis.

Supination is characterised by the rotation of the forearm laterally so that the hand faces upwards – for example, the right hand action in a hockey flick.

Rotation is the turning of a structure around its long axis.
Rotation can be inwards, hence **medial rotation** of the humerus with the forearm flexed brings the hand towards the body – for example, in the breaststroke the humerus rotates medially as the hands enter the water.
Rotation can be outwards, hence **lateral rotation** of the humerus describes a movement whereby the hand moves away from the body – for example, the humerus rotates laterally in preparation for the forehand stroke in tennis.

Most movements that occur in physical activities are combinations of movements explained above.

STUDENT NOTE

In your movement analysis you will need to identify major skeletal muscles of the human body (figures 1.11 and 1.12 page 17) in relation to joint activity and muscle analysis in tables 1.2 (page 18), 1.3 and 1.4 (page 19). The muscles identified in these tables give you plenty of choice to select from. However, if you refer to your exam syllabus you may wish to focus on the muscles that your exam board has specified.

Table 1.1 – summary of synovial joint types and movement ranges

synovial joint types	movement range	example body place: articulating bones
ball & socket	3 axes, flexion / extension, abduction / adduction, rotation, circumduction.	**hip:** femur, acetabulum of pelvis. **shoulder:** scapula, humerus.
hinge	1 axis, flexion / extension.	**knee:** femur, tibia. **elbow:** humerus, radius, ulna.
pivot	1 axis, rotation.	**spine: atlas:** odontoid process of axis (turns head side to side). **elbow:** proximal ends of radius and ulna.
condyloid (modified ball & socket)	2 axes, flexion / extension, abduction / adduction = circumduction.	**knuckles:** joint of fingers: metacarpals, phalanges. **wrist – radio-ulnar joint:** radius, carpals.
saddle	2 axes, flexion / extension, abduction / adduction = circumduction.	**joint at base of thumb:** carpal, metacarpal.
gliding	a little movement in all directions.	**centre of chest:** clavicle, sternum. **spine:** articulating surfaces. **wrist:** carpals. **ankle:** tarsals.

figure 1.11 – superficial anterior muscles

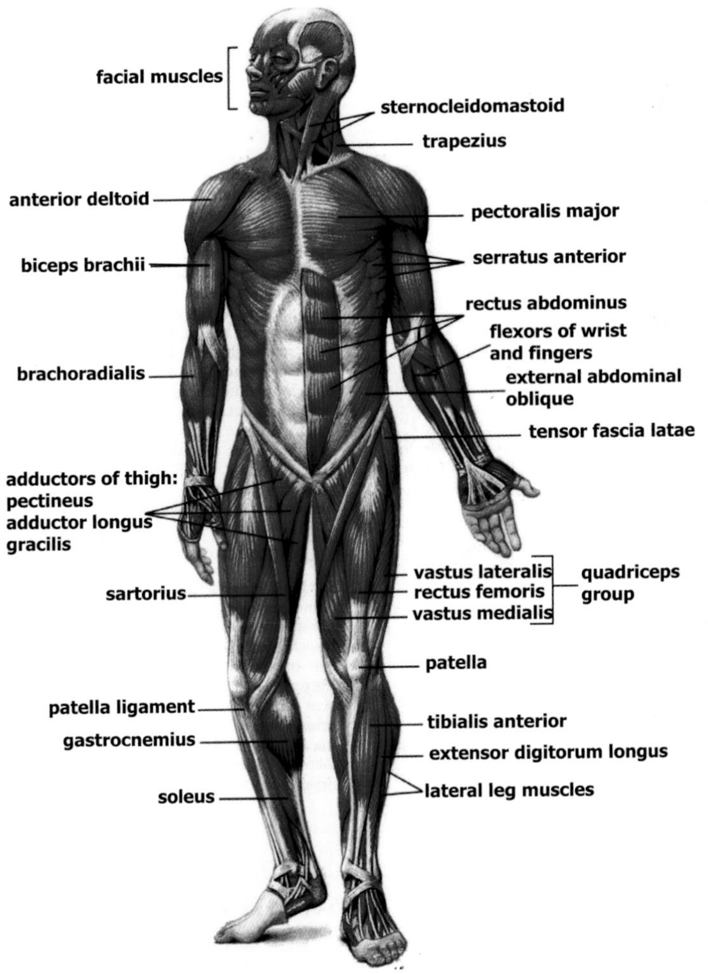

facial muscles
sternocleidomastoid
trapezius
anterior deltoid
pectoralis major
serratus anterior
biceps brachii
rectus abdominus
flexors of wrist and fingers
external abdominal oblique
brachoradialis
tensor fascia latae
adductors of thigh:
pectineus
adductor longus
gracilis
vastus lateralis
rectus femoris
vastus medialis
quadriceps group
sartorius
patella
patella ligament
tibialis anterior
gastrocnemius
extensor digitorum longus
soleus
lateral leg muscles

figure 1.12 – superficial posterior muscles

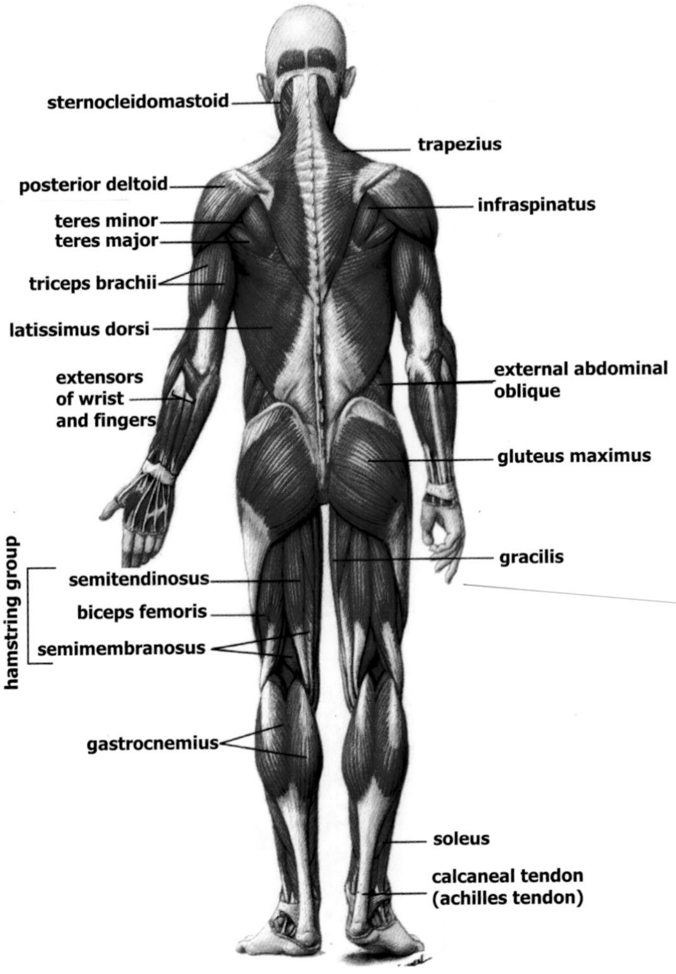

sternocleidomastoid
trapezius
posterior deltoid
infraspinatus
teres minor
teres major
triceps brachii
latissimus dorsi
external abdominal oblique
extensors of wrist and fingers
gluteus maximus
gracilis
hamstring group
semitendinosus
biceps femoris
semimembranosus
gastrocnemius
soleus
calcaneal tendon (achilles tendon)

Table 1.2 – **joints, movements and muscles in the wrists and arms**

body part / joint	movement pattern	active (agonist) muscles	movement examples
wrist	extension	**extensor carpi ulnaris**, extensor digitorum.	follow through in an over-arm throw.
	flexion	**flexor carpi radialis**, flexi carpi	dumbbell wrist curls.
arm / elbow	flexion	**biceps brachii**, brachialis.	bicep curls.
	extension	**triceps brachii**, anconeus (forearm).	follow through over-arm throw, bench press, triceps dips.
forearm / radio-ulnar (pivot)	supination	**supinator**, biceps brachii.	catching the bar during a clean.
	pronation	**pronator teres**, pronator quadratus.	putting top spin on a tennis ball.
shoulder joint	adduction	**latissimus dorsi**, anterior deltoid, teres major / minor.	recovery phase in overarm throw, triceps dips.
	abduction	**medial deltoid**, supraspinatus.	preparation phase shoulder pass.
	flexion	**pectoralis major**, anterior deltoid, coracobrachialis.	release phase in overarm throw, triceps dips.
	extension	**posterior deltoid**, latissimus dorsi, teres major.	shoulder position during javelin approach run.
	medial rotation	**latissimus dorsi**, posterior deltoid, pectoralis major, teres major, subscapularis.	forehand stroke / follow through at table tennis.
	horizontal flexion	**pectoralis major**, anterior deltoid.	arm swing into the release phase of a discus throw.
	horizontal extension	**trapezius**, posterior deltoid, latissimus dorsi.	preparatory swing (backward) of the arm in the discus.
	lateral rotation	**infraspinatus**, teres minor.	backhand stroke / follow through at table tennis.
shoulder or pectoral girdle (scapula + clavicle)	elevation	**upper fibres of trapezius**, levator scapulae, rhomboids.	a dumbbell shoulder shrug.
	depression	**lower fibres of trapezius**, latissimus dorsi, pectoralis minor, serratus-anterior (lower fibres).	preparation for dead lift when gripping the bar.
	protraction	serratus anterior.	recovery phase during breaststroke.
	retraction	rhomboids, trapezuis.	pull phase during breaststroke.
	upward rotation	**upper fibres of trapezius**, serratus anterior.	arm recovery phase during butterfly stroke.
	downward rotation	**rhomboids**	arm pull phase during butterfly stroke.

STUDENT NOTE

The main agonist muscle for each movement is in
red bold font type in table 1.2.

Table 1.3 – **joints, movements and muscles in the trunk and spine**

body part / joint	movement pattern	active (agonist) muscles	movement examples
trunk / spine	flexion	**rectus abdominus**, internal / external obliques.	sit ups.
core stability muscles	extension / hyperextension supports lower back	**erector spinae group** - sacrospinalis / - multifidu (deep lumbar portion).	extension - trunk position during netball shot at goal, hyperextension - flight phase of the Fosbury Flop.
abdominal wall	rotation	**external obliques**, rectus abdominus, erector spinae.	hammer throw swings, barani in trampolining / gymnastics.
	lateral flexion	**internal obliques**, rectus abdominus, erector spinae, quadratus lumborum, sacrospinalis.	side bends, twisting trunk / abdominal curls.

Table 1.4 – **joints, movements and muscles in the hip, knee and ankle**

body part / joint	movement pattern	active (agonist) muscles	movement examples
hip	flexion	**iliopsoas**, rectus femoris, pectineus, sartorius, tensor fascia latae, adductor longus / brevis.	squat start (low) position, high knee lift during sprinting, moving the knees up into a tuck position.
	extension	**gluteus maximus**, hamstring group, adductor magnus.	high jump take-off, rear leg drive during sprinting.
	adduction	**adductor longus / magnus / brevis**, pectineus, gracilis.	cross over phase during javelin run-up, side footing a football.
	abduction	**gluteus medius / minimus**, sartorius, tensor fascia latae, piriformis.	movement into the inverted phase of a cartwheel.
	medial rotation	**gluteus medius / minimus**, tensor fascia latae, iliopsoas, gracilis.	hip movement across circle during travel phase of a discus turn.
	lateral rotation	**gluteus maximus**, psoas major, adductors, piriformis, sartorious.	movement into a yoga stork position.
knee	extension	**quadriceps femoris group** - rectus femoris / vastus medialis / vastus intermedius, vastus lateralis.	high jump take-off, rear leg sprint phase.
	flexion	**hamstring group** - biceps femoris / semimembranosus / semitendinosus,	squat start (low) position, high knee lift during sprinting, moving the knees up into a tuck position.
ankle	plantarflexion	**gastrocnemius**, soleus, tibialis posterior, peroneus, flexor digitorum longus.	take-off phase during jumping.
	dorsiflexion	**tibialis anterior**, extensor digitorum longus.	landing phase from jump.

STUDENT NOTE

The main agonist muscle for each movement is in **red bold** font type in tables 1.3 and 1.4.

Functional roles of muscles and types of contraction

Antagonist muscle action

This term describes the fact that muscles work in pairs (see figure 1.13).

- The **agonist** is the active muscle, the muscle under tension or doing work and functioning as the **prime mover** of a joint during the desired movement.
- The **antagonist** relaxes to allow the agonist to work as movement occurs.
- For example, curling a bar, the agonist = **biceps brachii muscle**, and the antagonist = **triceps brachii muscle.**
- A **fixator muscle** holds the body in position so that an agonist muscle can operate, thus preventing any unwanted movements that might occur as the prime mover contracts. For example, the trapezius and deltoid muscles hold the shoulder in place during the bar curling exercise in figure 1.14.
- A **fixator** muscle is specifically referred to as a **stabiliser** when it immobilises the bone of the prime mover's origin, thus providing a stable base for the action of the prime mover. For example, the deltoid and trapezius muscles **stabilise** the scapula during a bar curl.

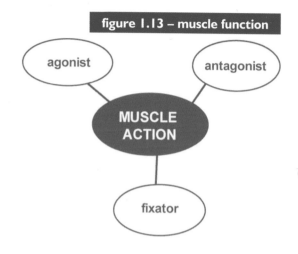

figure 1.13 – muscle function

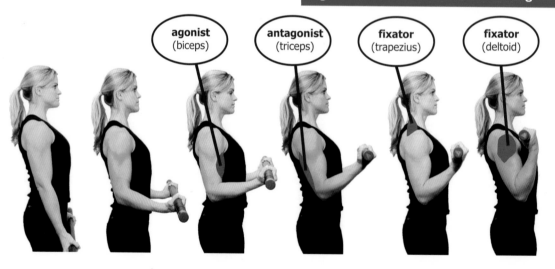

figure 1.14 – muscle function – curling a bar

agonist (biceps) antagonist (triceps) fixator (trapezius) fixator (deltoid)

Dynamic Muscle Contraction – isometric, concentric and eccentric contraction

During muscular contraction, a muscle may shorten, lengthen or stay the same. When a muscle changes its length, the contraction is classified as **dynamic**. When the muscle remains the same length, a **static** contraction occurs.

Static contractions – isometric muscle contraction

In **isometric contractions** (figure 1.15) the length of the muscle does not change, but the amount of tension **increases** during the contraction process.

In a training situation isometric work is done by exerting the maximum possible force in a fixed position for sets of 10 seconds, with 60 seconds recovery.

Isometric contractions are responsible for the constant length of postural muscles in the body and hence stabilise the trunk in many dynamic activities such as in sprinting.

figure 1.15 – isometric holds

Concentric muscle contraction

This type of contraction (figure 1.16) involves a muscle shortening under tension and is a form of **isotonic muscle contraction.** For example, in the driving upwards phase in a jump or squat, the quadriceps muscle group performs a concentric contraction as it shortens to produce extension of the knee joint.

Eccentric muscle contraction

This type of contraction (figure 1.17) involves a muscle lengthening under tension and is a form of **isotonic** muscle contraction. When a muscle contracts eccentrically it is acting as a brake, thus controlling the movement. This is called the **stretch shortening cycle**. For example, during the downward moving part of a jump or squat, the quadriceps femoris muscle group is lengthening under tension and so the work is labelled **eccentric** or **negative**. **Eccentric** muscle contraction produces the biggest overload in a muscle, thereby enhancing its development as far as strength is concerned. The chief practical use of eccentric muscle contraction is in **plyometric** or **elastic or explosive** strength work.

For eccentric contractions, the **agonist** muscle is the active muscle which in this case is lengthening. In the case of the landing from a jump or controlled downward movement in a squat, the quadriceps femoris muscle group lengthens under tension, and is therefore the **agonist**. To be the **agonist** in this situation, a muscle **must** be under tension. The **antagonist muscle action** during the example of a downward squatting movement would be the hamstring muscle group, which gets shorter and which relaxes or acts as a fixator for the hip joints.

Many muscle contractions involve a combination of dynamic and static work in which the muscles shorten by some amount, and the degree of tension increases.

figure 1.16 – concentric contraction

concentric muscle contraction (quadriceps)

figure 1.17 – eccentric contraction

eccentric muscle contraction (quadriceps)

Analysis of movement

figure 1.18 – high jump take-off and flight

figure b

figure a

STUDENT NOTE

In the following movement analysis examples not all agonist muscles have been listed. The main agonist muscle for each movement is in **red bold** font type in table 1.5. Refer to page 20 for the antagonist muscle action.

Table 1.5 – **the high jump**

After a continually accelerated run-up with a long penultimate stride, the jumper has a very fast last take-off stride before arriving at the position in figure 1.18 a.

physical activity	joint used	articulating bones	movement produced	agonist muscles	type of muscular contraction (isotonic)
high jump at take-off figure 1.18 a	ankle - take-off leg	talus, tibia, fibula.	plantarflexion	**gastrocnemius**, soleus, tibialis posterior, peroneus, flexor digitorum longus.	concentric
	knee - take-off leg	tibia, femur.	extension	**quadriceps femoris group:** rectus femoris / vastus medialis / vastus intermedius / vastus lateralis.	concentric
	shoulder girdle	clavicle, scapula.	elevation	**upper fibres of trapezius**, levator scapulae, rhomboids.	concentric
high jump in flight figure 1.18 b	hips	femur, acetabulum of pelvis.	extension	**gluteus maximus**, adductor magnus, assisted by: **hamstring group:** biceps femoris / semimembranosus / semitendinosus.	concentric
	spine	vertebrae.	extension / hyperextension	**erector spinae group**	concentric

physical activity	joint / type	movement pattern	plane
high jump at take-off figure 1.18 a	ankle - hinge	plantarflexion	sagittal
	knee- hinge	extension	sagittal
	shoulder - ball & socket	horizontal adduction	transverse
high jump in flight figure 1.18 b	hip - ball & socket	extension	sagittal
	spine - irregular	extension / hyperextension	sagittal

STUDENT NOTE

You **must** list all muscles in the quadriceps femoris and hamstring groups when you analyse the actions of the knee and hips during physical activity.

Table 1.6 – **sprinting leg action**

physical activity	joint type	movement produced	agonist muscles	antagonist muscles	type of muscular contraction
leg action in sprinting – figure 1.19 a left leg	ankle / hinge	plantarflexion	gastrocnemius, flexor digitorum longus.	tibialis anterior, extensor digitorum longus.	concentric
	knee / hinge	extension	quadriceps femoris group	hamstring group	concentric
action of hip joint figure 1.19 b - left leg	hip / ball and socket	flexion	iliopsoas, rectus femoris, adductor longus / brevis.	gluteus maximus, hamstring group, adductor magnus.	concentric
action of the trunk - figure 1.19 c	spine / cartilaginous	extension	erector spinae group	rectus abdominus	isometric

figure 1.19 – sprint – a full stride

figure a   figure b   figure c

figure 1.20 – over arm throw

figure a   figure b   figure c

Table 1.7 – **the arm action in an over arm throw**

physical activity	joint used	articulating bones	movement produced	agonist muscles	plane
arm action in over arm throw - figure 1.20	elbow	humerus, radius, ulna.	elbow joint extends as movement progresses.	triceps brachii, anconeus.	sagittal
	shoulder girdle	scapula, clavicle.	elevation, upward rotation.	**elevation:** upper fibres of trapezius, levator scapulae. **upward rotation:** upper fibres of trapezius, serratus anterior.	sagittal
	radio-ulnar (wrist)	carpals, radius, ulna.	supination to pronation.	pronator teres, pronator quadratus.	sagittal

STUDENT NOTE

The main agonist muscle for each movement is in **red bold** font type. The main antagonist muscle for each movement is in **blue bold** font type in table 1.6 and 1.7.

figure 1.21 – push-up – down then up

figure a

b

c

d

e

STUDENT NOTE

Note that during a very controlled downward phase in figures 1.21 a-c the **agonist** muscle at the elbow joint is the **triceps brachii** muscle. This is because the triceps brachii muscle is under extreme tension as it lengthens and so acts as a brake to control the downward phase of the action. The same explanation applies to the pectoralis major and anterior deltoid muscles, which act as the agonists at the shoulder joint.

STUDENT NOTE

The main agonist muscle for each movement is in **red bold** font type. The main antagonist muscle for each movement is in **blue bold** font type in table 1.8.

Table 1.8 – **the full action of the push-up - down then up**

physical activity	joint type	movement produced	agonist muscles	antagonist muscles	type of muscular contraction (isotonic)
arm action in push-up – down movement figure 1.21 a to c	elbow / hinge	flexion	**triceps brachii**, anconeus.	**biceps brachii**, brachialis.	eccentric
– up movement figure 1.21 c to e	shoulder / ball and socket	horizontal flexion	**pectoralis major**, anterior deltoid.	**trapezius**, posterior deltoid.	concentric

STUDENT NOTE

The main agonist muscle for each movement is in **red bold** font type in table 1.9.

STUDENT NOTE

As the ankle plantarflexes, during the foot strike of the ball, the tibialis anterior lengthens and is under extreme tension. Then as the ball leaves the foot this muscle will shorten (contract) and the foot will dorsiflex.

figure 1.22– a kick

Table 1.9 – **leg action in a kick**

This sequence covers the strike phase only for the kick.

physical activity	joint type	movement produced	agonist muscles	plane	type of muscular contraction (isotonic)
leg action in kicking (right leg) – figure 1.22	ankle / hinge	plantarflexion	**tibialis anterior**	sagittal	eccentric
	knee / hinge	extension	**quadriceps femoris group**	sagittal	concentric
	hip / ball and socket	flexion	**iliopsoas, rectus femoris, adductor longus / brevis.**	sagittal	concentric

figure 1.23 – squat – down then up

figure a   b   c   d   e

Table 1.10 – **the full action of the squat - down then up**

STUDENT NOTE

You **must** list all muscles in the quadriceps femoris and hamstring groups when you analyse the actions of the knee and hips during physical activity.

physical activity	joint used	articulating bones	movement produced	agonist muscles	fixator muscles	type of muscular contraction (isotonic)
leg action in squat - figure 1.23	knee – figures a to c	tibia, femur	extension to flexion	**quadriceps femoris group**	adductor magnus	eccentric
	hip – figures c to e	femur, acetabulum of pelvis	flexion to extension	**gluteus maximus, hamstring group, adductor magnus.**	erector spinae, transversus abdominus, gracilis.	concentric

Skeletal muscle contraction

The anatomy of the neuromuscular system

Skeletal muscle is caused to contract by **nerve impulses** sent from the **cerebellum** in the brain. These electrical impulses are sent down a specialised nerve called a **motor neurone** (figure 1.24). At the muscle fibre end of the motor neurone, this nerve terminates at a **synaptic end bulb**. The synaptic end bulb is the end of the nerve fibre at the junction with the muscle fibre. The muscle fibre side of this junction (between nerve and muscle fibre) is called a neuro-muscular junction or **motor end plate** (see figures 1.26 and 1.27 on page 27 for more details of this). A signal is transmitted between the motor end plate and a muscle fibre causing the muscle fibre to contract and exert force.

Further specialised nerves called sensory fibres relay information back to the cerebellum where information about the tension within the muscle and its rate of contraction is received.

The muscle motor unit

A motor neurone will terminate at several synapses (motor end plates) each linked to a number of muscle fibres. The block of muscle fibres and the nervous system which controls their contraction and relaxation is called a motor unit. A **motor unit** is therefore defined as '**a single block of muscle fibres and its neurone**'. Therefore when a motor neurone is stimulated, all fibres connected to that neurone are activated at once (the '**all or none law**'). A single neurone will control muscle fibres of the **same type**, either fast twitch **or** slow twitch. Figure 1.26 on page 27 shows a simplified diagram of a motor unit which is structurally enlarged in figure 1.27 also on page 27.

Structure of a motor neurone

See figure 1.24 for a diagrammatic view of a motor neurone. The **cell body** includes a nucleus and cytoplasm, but the cell membrane is receptive to stimuli from other neurones.

Dendrites are highly branched processes which extend out from the cell body and are specialised to receive stimuli from sensory organs or from other neurones. The **axon** conducts nerve impulses to other cells (nerve, muscle, gland cells).

Special structures include:
- **Myelin sheath** which electrically insulates the nerve.
- **Nodes of Ranvier**, which are gaps in the myelin sheath where the **action potential** jumps from node to node.
- **Axon terminal** which ends with a **synaptic end bulb** containing **neurotransmitter** substances.

These substances enable the **action potential** to be applied to adjacent cells.

figure 1.24 – structure of a motor neurone (nerve cell)

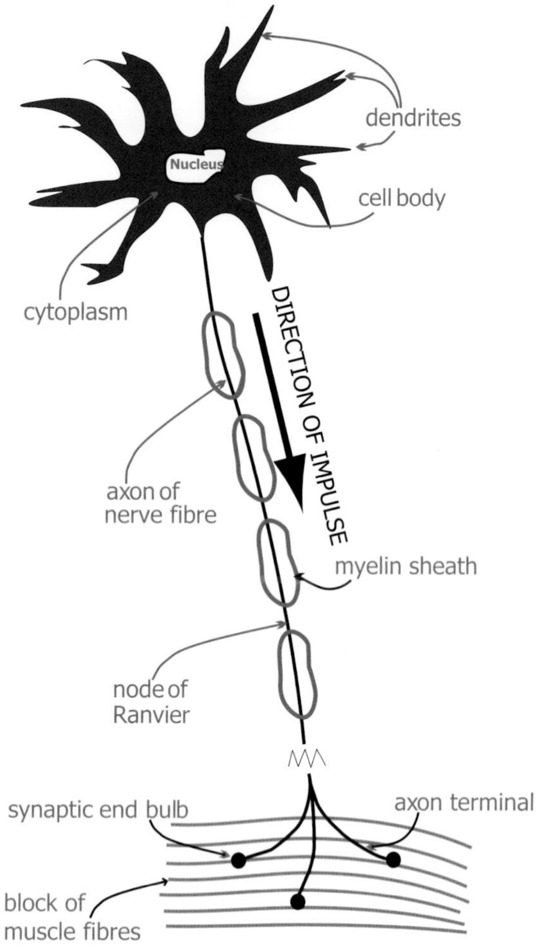

An action potential

Transmission of neural messages along a neurone is an electrochemical process. An **action potential** is initiated when sufficient numbers of sodium ions (Na^+) diffuse into the neurone. This depolarises the axon to a critical threshold level called the **all-or-none law**. This is followed by repolarisation back to the resting potential. This process forms an electrical impulse which then transmits itself down the neurone (see figure 1.25). In effect this electrical impulse is **conducted** down the axon. The **myelin sheath** insulates the axon, and the action potential travels from node to node in a wave like action, since ion exchange only occurs at the nodes of Ranvier.

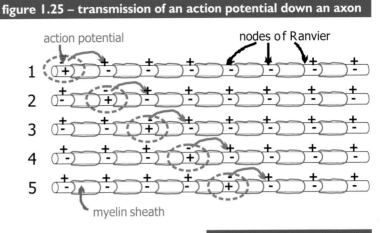

figure 1.25 – transmission of an action potential down an axon

The nerve action potential is followed by the muscle action potential. A delay of 0.5 milliseconds occurs due to release of transmitter substances (such as acetylcholine from synaptic knobs) which initiate the muscle action potential. The area of depolarisation travels down a muscle cell passing the entrances to 'T' vesicles which secrete calcium ions needed to initiate muscle contraction.

Each different muscle fibre type (slow twitch or fast twitch) is innervated by a separate and different type of motor neurone.

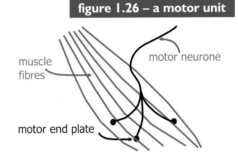

figure 1.26 – a motor unit

The motor end plate

The function of the motor end plate is to transfer an impulse from the motor neurones (see figure 1.26) to the muscle fibre block. This causes all muscle fibres attached to this end plate to contract.

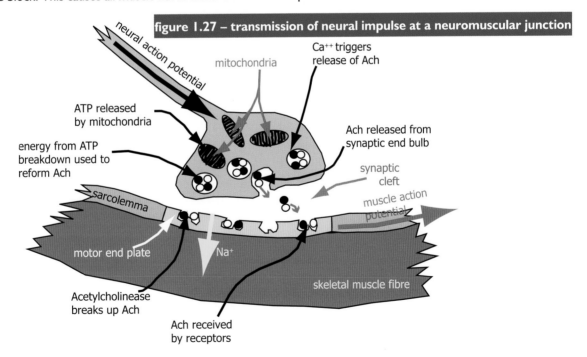

figure 1.27 – transmission of neural impulse at a neuromuscular junction

Synapse

- A synapse is a junction where the axon of one neurone interacts with another neurone. Figure 1.27 outlines the process whereby the nerve impulse is transmitted from the neurone via the synapse to the muscle bed.

- This process involves the use of calcium ions (Ca^{++}) to trigger the release of a substance called acetylcholine (Ach) which then jumps into receptor sites in the motor end plate attached to the muscle fibre.

- This in turn triggers release of sodium ions (Na^+) which re-establish the action potential within the muscle fibre itself (and eventually cause it to contract and use energy).

Muscle fibre structure and physiology

Skeletal muscle tissue

Skeletal muscle (also called striated voluntary muscle because microscopic bands or striations can be seen) attaches to bone and is responsible for the following functions:

- **Producing** movement by exerting force on its origin and insertion.
- **Maintaining** body posture and changing body shape.
- **Generating** heat to keep us warm.
- **Storage** of glycogen for energy.

Skeletal muscle tissue and tendons

Skeletal muscles are usually attached to bone on each end by tough connective tendons. When a muscle contracts it shortens, and this places tension on the tendons and attached bones. The muscle tendon tension causes movement of the bones at a joint, where one of the attached bones generally moves more than the other. The more movable bony attachment of the muscle, known as its insertion, is pulled towards its less movable attachment known as its origin.

A variety of skeletal movements are possible, depending on the type of joint involved (see table 1.1 on page 17) and the attachment of the muscles.

Figure 1.28 shows the basic structure of a muscle from the muscle belly down to the individual sarcomere. Each myofibril consists of filaments of actin (thin filaments) and myosin (thick filaments), the forces between which enable a muscle to shorten its length and hence contract and exert forces on its origin and insertion.

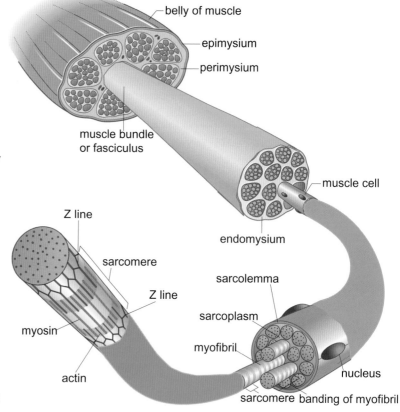

figure 1.28 – structure of skeletal muscle

belly of muscle
epimysium
perimysium
muscle bundle or fasciculus
muscle cell
Z line
endomysium
sarcomere
sarcolemma
Z line
sarcoplasm
myosin
myofibril
actin
nucleus
sarcomere banding of myofibril

Muscle contraction

- The process of muscle contraction is initiated when a **neural action potential** (electrical impulse form the brain) travels via a **motor neurone** to the **motor end-plate**, which creates a **muscle action potential** (see page 27).

Motor neural firing patterns

In order to control muscle contraction, the cerebellum innervates one or more motor units. Each motor unit controls a number of fibres, so that either **all** the fibres attached to the motor unit are activated at the same time, or **none** of these fibres are activated. This is called the '**all-or-none law**'. Different fibre groups (attached to different motor units) are fired at different times. Each firing produces a fibre '**twitch**'.

The force produced by a single fibre twitch follows the left hand graph in figure 1.29. Note that each twitch only lasts a short length of time, so that in order to prolong the force exerted by a twitch, the fibre group must be fired repeatedly.

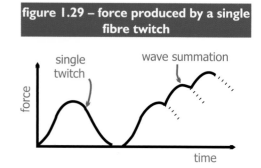

figure 1.29 – force produced by a single fibre twitch

single twitch
wave summation
force
time

The build up of force in a single fibre is represented in the right hand graph in figure 1.29. When a fibre is fired repeatedly in this manner, the way in which the force builds up is called '**wave summation**'.

Multiple fibre twitches

In order to activate fibres across a whole muscle body to produce force in a controlled manner, different fibre groups are fired in succession. The total force across the space of a muscle is the sum of the effect of different fibre groups, and is shown in figure 1.30. This is called 'spatial summation'.

In order to control very fine movements, it is necessary to be able to vary the total force produced by fibre twitches. **Gradation of contraction** refers to the ability of muscle to produce forces varying from very light to maximum force or tension.

This can be achieved in two ways:

- Increasing the frequency of stimulus (wave summation).
- Varying the number of motor units recruited.

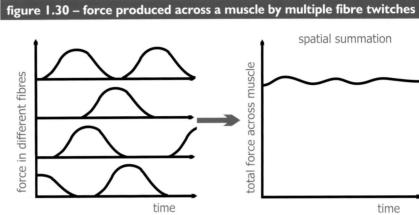

figure 1.30 – force produced across a muscle by multiple fibre twitches

For example in hockey, there would be fine control of movement required for a flick, as opposed to the maximum effort required for a full hit.

If there were no time for relaxation between motor unit firing, eventually (after a few seconds) there would be a complete lock up of muscle. This is called 'tetanine contraction' and happens when a muscle is used at maximum for too long.

The cerebellum

The balance of fine and gross control is under the control of the **cerebellum**. In order to produce smooth coordinated movement, the cerebellum compares the intended movement with the actual movement (from sensors within the moving structure – the proprioceptors). If a difference is detected, the cerebellum sends impulses to the appropriate motor units in the spinal cord which would produce a correction. In sport, the cerebellum is involved in the learning of **fine motor skills** (as in archery) or **gross motor skills** (as in weight lifting).

Gross movements use leg and arm muscles which have about 1000 muscle fibres associated with one motor unit, whereas fine movements (of the eyes and fingers for example) require muscles with far fewer (10-100) muscle fibres controlled by a single motor unit.

Control is achieved by increasing or decreasing the number of motor units in operation. Different motor units are activated in turn across a muscle and this gradation of contraction across a muscle enables very small forces to be maintained if required. The self-regulation of rhythmic movements between one muscle and its antagonist relies on control of movement which requires relaxation of antagonists during the dynamic activity of an agonist. This process is called 'reciprocal innervation'.

Short-term response of the neuromuscular system to exercise

Skeletal muscle is caused to contract by **nerve impulses** sent from the **cerebellum** in the brain. These electrical impulses are sent down a specialised nerve called a **motor neurone** (figure 1.24 on page 26). At the muscle fibre end of the motor neurone, this nerve terminates at a **synaptic end bulb** - as shown in figure 1.24 on page 26.

The synaptic end bulb is the end of the nerve fibre at the junction with the muscle fibre. The muscle fibre side of this junction (between nerve and muscle fibre) is called a neuromuscular junction or **motor end plate** (see figures 1.26 and 1.27 on pages 27 for more details of this). A signal is transmitted between the motor end plate and a muscle fibre, causing the muscle fibre to contract and exert force.

Further specialised nerves called sensory fibres relay information back to the cerebellum where information, about the tension within the muscle and its rate of contraction, is received.

Muscle contraction during exercise of differing intensities, and during recovery

Muscle fibre types

Not all skeletal muscle fibres have identical functional capabilities. Some muscle fibres contract quickly and fatigue quickly (known as **fast twitch** muscle fibres) whereas others contract more slowly and are resistant to fatigue (known as **slow twitch or type I** also called **S**low **O**xidative (**SO**) fibres). Fast twitch fibres are classified into 2 groups – **fast twitch type IIa** also called **F**ast-**O**xidative-**G**lycolytic (**FOG**) and **fast twitch type IIb** also called **F**ast-**G**lycolytic (**FG**) muscle fibres.

Table 1.11 - **major structural and functional differences** between **Slow-Oxidative (SO type I), Fast-Oxidative-Glycolytic (FOG type IIa) Fast-Glycolytic (FG type IIb)** muscle fibre types.

	SO – type I	FOG – type IIa	FG – type IIb
structural differences			
colour	red	red to pink	white
fibre diameter	small	medium	large
fibres per motor unit	10-80	300-800	300-800
sarcoplasmic reticulum development	low	high	high
myoglobin content	high	high	low
capillary density	high	midway / high	low
mitochondrial density	many	midway	few
energy stores (phosphocreatine (PC) / glycogen / ATP content)	low	high	high
functional differences			
myosin ATPase activity	low	high	high
glycolytic enzyme activity	low	high	high
oxidative enzyme activity	high	midway	low
motor unit strength	low	high	high
recruitment order	first	second	third
contractile strength	low	high	high
contractile time	long	midway	short
fatigue resistance	low	midway	high
aerobic capacity	high	moderate	low
anaerobic capacity	low	high	high
primary function	maintaining posture / endurance-based activities	running / sprinting	high intensity rapid activity

STUDENT NOTE

The **metabolism** of the different types of cell or fibre differs depending on the different way in which ATP is regenerated following dissociation to produce energy. The fast twitch muscle fibres tend to be anaerobic and do not require oxygen for production of energy. They have high storage of phosphocreatine but low myoglobin content. The slow twitch muscle fibres tend to be aerobic and have low phosphocreatine but high myglobin content. The myoglobin (see page 53) contains an immediate source of oxygen which is transferred across the cell wall, from blood haemoglobin to the mitochondrion for abundant energy release.

Short-term responses to exercise

Fibre type recruitment and force production

Fibre type usage (**recruitment**) is based on the intensity of exercise.

- **At low intensity, slow twitch** (ST or SO – slow oxidative) motor units are recruited first.
- **At higher intensity fast oxidative glycolytic** (FOG) type **IIa** motor units are recruited.
- **At greatest intensity fast glycolytic** (FG) type **IIb** motor units are recruited to produce powerful fast muscle contractions.

All available fibres are recruited for all high power activities as seen in the graph (see figure 1.31).

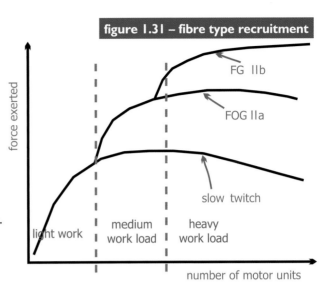

figure 1.31 – fibre type recruitment

Differences within individual muscles

The proportion of muscle fibre type differs within individual muscles. Most muscles have both fibre types, however the large postural muscles contain a high proportion of slow twitch fibres because postural muscles need to produce low forces over a long period of time.

The arms tend to consist of more fast twitch muscle fibres as they need to move quickly but over shorter periods of time. The percentages of muscle fibre types found in the legs determine whether the athlete is more suited to sprinting or endurance running.

Differences in fibre type distribution between different individuals (figure 1.32 page 32)

The average fibre type distribution within **sedentary** men and women and young children is between 45% and 55% slow twitch fibres, with fast twitch equally distributed between type IIa and IIb subdivisions. However, individual variation is large.

Elite sprinters have a greater percentage of fast twitch muscle fibres, whereas elite long-distance runners have a higher percentage of slow twitch muscle fibres in their leg muscles. As might be expected, elite men and women show similar trends.

Table 1.12 - **differences in fibre type proportion between different sports and type of event**

	average % ST	range of % ST
males		
marathon	81	50 - 98
cross country skiers	64	52 - 75
cyclists	59	52 - 72
800m runners	52	40 - 62
untrained	47	42 - 76
shot putters	39	19 - 57
sprinters	40	20 - 53
females		
cross country skiers	59	47 - 74
cyclists	54	37 - 66
800m runners	62	44 - 73
untrained	53	30 - 72
shot putters	53	50 - 55
sprinters	32	28 - 52

Nature or nurture?

- Proportions of fibre types are **genetically determined**, and this could account for specialisms of individuals such as whether a person becomes good at marathon running or weight lifting.
- On the other hand, researches have shown that a knowledge of a person's predominant fibre type is of limited value in predicting the outcome of specific exercise performances.
- This finding is not surprising because performance capacity is the end result of the blending of many physiological, biochemical, neurological and biomechanical 'support systems' – and is not simply determined by a single factor, such as muscle fibre type.
- Men have a greater tendency to be more muscular than women, due to the release of greater amounts of the hormone **testosterone** during adolescence and adulthood. But women can grow muscle in a similar way to men when exposed to high intensity training.

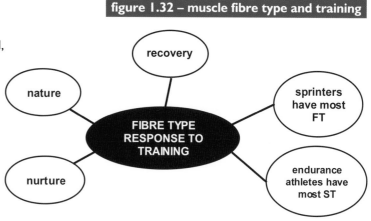

figure 1.32 – muscle fibre type and training

Muscle fibre type and recovery rates

The amount of recovery muscles need depends on the **intensity** of the workout in relation to fibre type recruitment, as illustrated in figure 1.31 on page 31.

Endurance athletes mainly train at **submaximal** workloads stressing **slow twitch motor units** which generally exhibit an asynchronous firing pattern (i.e. some motor units fire while others recover - known as **spatial summation**). This serves as a built-in recuperation period so performance continues with minimal fatigue as is the case during a continuous activity such as a marathon race.

During an aerobic interval training session, recovery between bouts of exercise is short, for example 6 x 1200 metre runs with half the running time as rest. This is because slow twitch (ST) fibres are working submaximally, there is less likelihood of fibre damage and so recovery between sessions is rapid. This means that endurance-based athletes are able to train on consecutive days.

In contrast, the synchronous firing of **fast twitch motor units** (i.e. many motor units recruited simultaneously) allows the weightlifter to generate a high force quickly for a desired lift or a sprinter to run a 100 metres race flat out. In short bursts of energy, such as sprint starting over 30 metres, there is little lactate accumulation, as the energy is supplied via the **alactic energy system**, and so recovery of fast glycolytic fibres progresses rapidly. This means that the athlete is able to perform 6 block starts over 30 metres with a 2 minute walk back recovery.

Brief, all-out physical activity interspersed with recovery represents a specific application of the interval training principle (see page 77) for anaerobic conditioning.

As the duration of the activity extends beyond 10 seconds, energy is provided predominantly by the lactic acid energy system, again stressing the fast glycolytic fibres. So repetition of an activity, for example 4 x 300 metres flat out with 15 minutes recovery, causes **lactate stacking**, resulting in a higher blood lactate than with just one exhaustive effort burst. Hence a longer recovery between each 300 metres is needed when compared with the recovery required between sprint starts.

figure 1.33 – all muscle action uses ATP

Muscle soreness is often felt during the latter stages of a strenuous exercise period, the following day and the day after, or at both times. This may be due to local muscle tearing of fast twitch muscle fibres and the presence of lactic acid acting on pain receptors. Muscle soreness felt the day after strenuous exercise is known as **delayed onset of muscle soreness** (DOMS). Recovery from muscle soreness will take longer and so the performer needs to have a minimum of two days recovery before exercising the same muscle groups, otherwise fatigue carries over and could hinder subsequent training sessions.

Practice questions

1) A prime mover, also known as the agonist muscle, of hip flexion is the:
   a. rectus femoris.
   b. Iliopsoas.
   c. vastus muscles.
   d. gluteus maximus.

2) Which of the following movements occurs in the transverse (horizontal) plane?
   a. flexion and extension of the hip joints during sprinting.
   b. spinal rotation observed during a discus throw.
   c. abduction and adduction of the legs during a cartwheel.
   d. all of the above movements.

3) Characteristics of isometric contractions include all but:
   a. shortening.
   b. increased muscle tension throughout the contraction phase.
   c. absence of shortening.
   d. used in resistance training.

4) In order to control muscle contraction, the cerebellum innervates one oR more motor units (each consisting of a single block
   of muscle fibres and its neurone). Which one of the following statements describes how a single motor unit produces a stronger stimulus?
   a. the motor neurone fires so much that there is no time for relaxation (tetanine contraction).
   b. by repeatedly increasing the frequency of the stimulus (wave summation).
   c. by increasing the number of motor neurones in succession (spatial summation).
   d. both answers b and c apply.

5) Muscle fatigue is a state of physiological inability to contract even though the muscle still may be receiving stimuli. Although many factors appear to contribute to fatigue, which one of the following statements is false during moderate exercise?
   a. it may result when ATP is no longer available for the cross-bridge cycle.
   b. it may be caused by a loss of muscle cell Ca^{++}.
   c. it may be caused by the accumulation of extracellular K^+.
   d. it may be the result of lactic acid production.

figure 1.34 – a shot putter

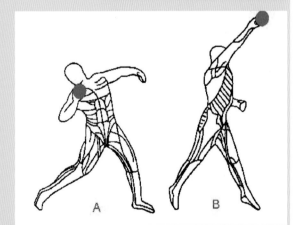

6) a) The diagram in figure 1.34 shows a shot putter during the delivery phase of the technique.
        List the bones that articulate in the shoulder joint.   2 marks

   b) Briefly explain the movement sequence of the right arm during the delivery phase of the shot put.   3 marks

7) Describe the following movement terminology, and give a physical activity for each movement:
    Abduction, circumduction, rotation and plantarflexion.
                                              8 marks

figure 1.35 – long jump take-off and flight

Practice questions

8) Figure 1.35 a-c shows an athlete during the final stride, take-off and flight phase of a long jump. Using these three figures, analyse the action of the left leg (foot in contact with the ground) to include joint type, movement patterns, type of muscle contraction, acting muscles and plane of movement. Identify factors that affect the maximal force required for long jump take-off.
10 marks

figure c

figure b

a

figure 1.36 – tennis forehand

9) Figure 1.36 shows a tennis player completing a forehand drive. Use the figure to help you complete the following joint analysis.

a) For the shoulder joint during horizontal flexion, identify the type of joint, the articulating bones, an agonist muscle, and the type of contraction for the agonist.
4 marks

b) Using the muscles that create flexion of the elbow during the forehand drive, explain what is meant by antagonistic muscle action.
4 marks

c) Identify the movement pattern produced and an agonist muscle responsible for the action on the right hand side of the trunk.
2 marks

d) For the right wrist, identify the articulating bones, a fixator or stabilising muscle, and the movement pattern at the completion of the forehand drive.
3 marks

10) Differentiate between concentric, eccentric and isometric muscle contraction, using practical examples to support your answer.
6 marks

11) Using figure 1.31 on page 31, describe the relationships between motor unit recruitment and exercise intensity.
3 marks

12) Identify and explain the function of the different regions of a motor neurone.
6 marks

13) a) What is a motor unit?
2 marks

b) Explain how a motor unit transfers a neural impulse into muscular contraction.
8 marks

c) The result of an electric impulse reaching the muscle fibres is a maximal contraction of those fibres. Explain this statement and describe how the force exerted by the muscle can vary significantly.
3 marks

d) Why is it that muscle fibres attached to different motor units will not necessary contract at the same time?
3 marks

14) Analyse how the characteristics of different skeletal muscle fibres help contribute to success in different sports.
10 marks

Practice questions

15) Table 1.13 shows the percentage of slow twitch muscle fibres in three muscle groups of elite male (M) and female (F) athletes and non-athletes. The percentage of fast twitch muscle fibre is calculated as the difference between 100% and the percentage of slow twitch fibres.
   (Data from research literature – source – 'Essentials of Exercise Physiology' 2e, McArdle, Katch and Katch)

Table 1.13 – percentage of slow twitch muscle fibres

athletic group	shoulder (deltoid)	calf (gastrocnemius)	thigh (vastus lateralis)
long distance runners		79% (M) 69% (F)	
canoeists	71% (M)		
triathletes	60% (M)	59% (M)	63% (M)
swimmers	67% (M) 69% (F)		
sprinters		24% (M) 27% (F)	
cyclists			57% (M) 51% (F)
weight lifters	53% (M)	44% (M)	
shot putters		38% (M)	
non-athletes			47% (M) 46% (F)

a) Compare and account for the differences in percentage distribution of slow twitch muscle fibres with respect to long distance runners and sprinters.   3 marks

b) Calculate the percentage of fast twitch muscle fibres for the long distance runners and sprinters.   2 marks

c) Data collected for male triathletes shows a fairly even distribution of slow twitch muscle fibres across all three muscle groups. Discuss two possible reasons for this trend.   3 marks

d) For shot putters, only the calf muscle is given a value in the table. What percentage distribution of slow twitch muscle fibres would you expect in the deltoid muscle for shot putters? Give a reason to support your answer.   2 marks

16) Describe some of the factors which determine muscle speed and tension characteristics.   4 marks

17) Skeletal muscle contains both slow and fast twitch muscle fibres but the proportion of each depends upon the function of a muscle as a whole. Table 1.11, page 30 lists some of the differences between slow and fast twitch muscle fibres.

a) Suggest why the muscles concerned in maintaining the trunk posture of the body of the sprinter might be expected to have a larger percentage of slow twitch muscle fibres.
   Using table 1.11 explain why fast twitch muscle fibres may build up an oxygen debt during a 400m sprint.   5 marks

b) Account for the difference in the speed of contraction between slow and fast twitch muscle fibre types.
   Fast twitch muscle fibres are divided into two types, IIa and IIb. Identify the major functional characteristic between these sub groups.
   In what sporting activities would the adaptation of fast twitch type IIb to type IIa fibres be relevant to a sportsperson?   6 marks

18) How can an understanding of motor unit recruitment recovery assist an athlete when planning training sessions?   6 marks

Answers link: http://www.jroscoe.co.uk/downloads/as_a1_revise_pe_ocr/OCRAS_A1_ch1_answers.pdf

CHAPTER 2: *The cardiovascular system*

Cardiac anatomy and dynamics

The heart (figure 2.1) is a muscular pump lying deep within the chest cavity and slightly to the left of the sternum.

figure 2.1 – heart structure

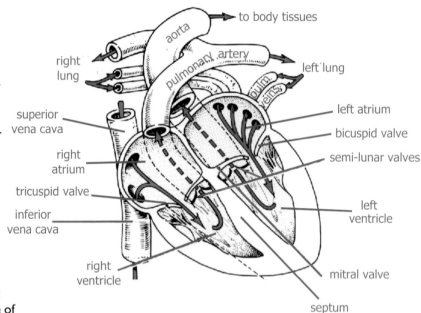

Heart layers

The **heart** consists of **three** layers:

- The **outer** layer, known as the **pericardium**, is a double layered bag surrounding the heart. The fluid between the two layers reduces friction between the heart itself and the surrounding tissue as the heart moves (beats). This layer also maintains the heart's shape.

- The **second** layer is called the **myocardium** or striped cardiac muscle tissue consisting of united fibres (united because they are all in one mass) joined by intercalated discs. This muscle tissue is activated by the 'all-or-none law'. The **cardiac impulse** is transmitted throughout the entire myocardium at the same point in time, and hence this muscle tissue is **all** activated at once. When there is no cardiac impulse, none of the heart muscle can be activated.
  Since the heart generates its own impulse it is said to be **myogenic**. The **septum** consists of myocardial tissue (muscle) and divides the heart into two sections, each of which acts as a pump.

- The **third** layer is an inner glistening membrane called the **endocardium**. Its function is to prevent friction between heart muscle and flowing blood.

Heart chambers

The heart consists of **four** chambers:

- **Two** are at the top (**atria**). Both the right and left atria have thin walls.
- **Two** are at the bottom (**ventricles**). Both ventricles have thicker walls than the atria. The left ventricle wall is the thickest, since this ventricle pumps blood to the main body mass, whereas the **right ventricle** pumps blood to the **lungs only**.

Heart valves

Heart valves **prevent back-flow of blood**, with the (**cuspid**) **mitral** or **bicuspid** valve sited between the left atrium and the left ventricle, and the **tricuspid** valve sited between the right atrium and the right ventricle. The **semi-lunar** valves prevent back-flow of blood into the heart from the pulmonary artery and aorta, and only allow blood to flow in one direction through the heart. This means that when the heart muscle contracts, it only pumps the blood out to the lungs (pulmonary artery) or body (aorta), and not back the wrong way.

Blood vessels

Blood vessels attached to the heart are the **venae cavae** and the **pulmonary artery** on the right side, and the **pulmonary veins** and the **aorta** on the left side.

Coronary blood supply

The coronary blood supply consists of arteries (within the cardiac muscle itself) which supply glucose and oxygen (O_2) to myocardial tissue, and coronary veins, which transport carbon dioxide (CO_2) and other wastes from the heart muscle.

How the heart works

The cardiac impulse

figure 2.2 – the cardiac impulse

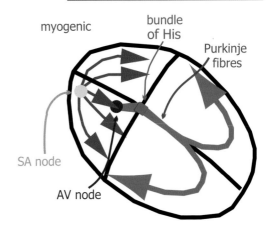

- The dynamic action of the heart (figure 2.2) is that of a dual-action pump in that both sides of the heart contract simultaneously, even though the functions of the two sides are different.
- Cardiac contractions are initiated by an electrical impulse (the **cardiac impulse**) that originates from the pacemaker or sinoatrial node (**SA node**). Because the heart generates its own impulses it is said to be **myogenic**.
- The electrical impulse travels down the atrial mycardium until it reaches the atrioventricular node (**AV node**) situated in the wall of the atrial septum. This is followed by the atrial walls contracting (atrial systole).
- The AV node conducts the impulse through the **bundle of His** to the branched network of Purkinje fibres located within the septum and the ventricular walls (both the bundle of His and the Purkinje fibres are modified cardiac muscle), causing both ventricles to contract (**ventricular systole**).

The heart's conducting system regulates the sequence of events that make up the cardiac cycle.

The cardiac cycle

The cardiac cycle (figure 2.3) is a sequence of events that make up one heart beat and lasts for about 0.8 seconds, thus occurring about 75 times per minute.

The cardiac cycle consists of a period of relaxation of the heart muscle, known as diastole (0.5 seconds), followed by a period of contraction of the heart muscle, known as systole (0.3 seconds). During systole the electrical impulse is initiated in a set-timed sequence.

figure 2.3 – the cardiac cycle

pulse

CARDIAC CYCLE

systole = 0.3s

atrial systole

ventricular systole

diastole = 0.5s

Cardiac diastole

During **diastole** (0.5 seconds), the relaxed heart muscle allows the chambers to fill with blood. This occurs with the cuspid valves open, and the semi-lunar valves closed.

Cardiac systole

During **atrial systole** (0.3 seconds), the SA node impulse causes a wave-like contraction over the atria forcing blood past the cuspid valves into the ventricles. The semi-lunar valves remain closed.

In **ventricular systole**, the impulse reaches the **AV node**, the cuspid valves close because the fluid pressure (of blood) in the ventricles is greater than in the atria, and rises further as the ventricles contract. The semi-lunar valves open (since now the fluid pressure in the ventricles is greater than in the main arteries) and blood is pushed out into the pulmonary artery (towards the lungs) and the aorta (around the body).

The **pulse** is a wave of pressure produced by the contraction of the left ventricle. This pressure wave transmits itself around the arterial system of the rest of the body. The frequency of the waves represents the number of beats per minute (heart rate).

Vascular anatomy and dynamics

The blood circulation systems

There are two systems circulating blood from the heart as in figure 2.4.

The systemic circulatory system

This system consists of all the vessels which carry oxygenated blood away from the heart via the aorta, the arteries and arterioles and on to the capillaries embedded in the working tissues of the body. Then after giving up the oxygen (to the working tissues), the deoxygenated blood returns to the heart via venules, veins and the venae cavae.

The pulmonary circulatory system

This system consists of the pulmonary arteries that carry this deoxygenated blood from the right atrium of the heart to the lungs, where the blood is re-oxygenated from the air breathed into the lungs. Oxygenated blood is then returned to the heart via the pulmonary veins.

Blood vessel structure

Blood vessels (see table 2.1 on page 39) have properties that help circulation and allow blood to perform many of its functions (see summary in figure 2.5).

Except for single-walled capillaries and venules, all blood vessels have 3 layers.

The thickness and composition of the layers vary with blood vessel type and diameter.

Smooth involuntary muscle, within the middle layer of blood vessel walls, regulates the diameter of blood vessels via **vasomotor** and **venomotor** control.

figure 2.4– the circulatory systems

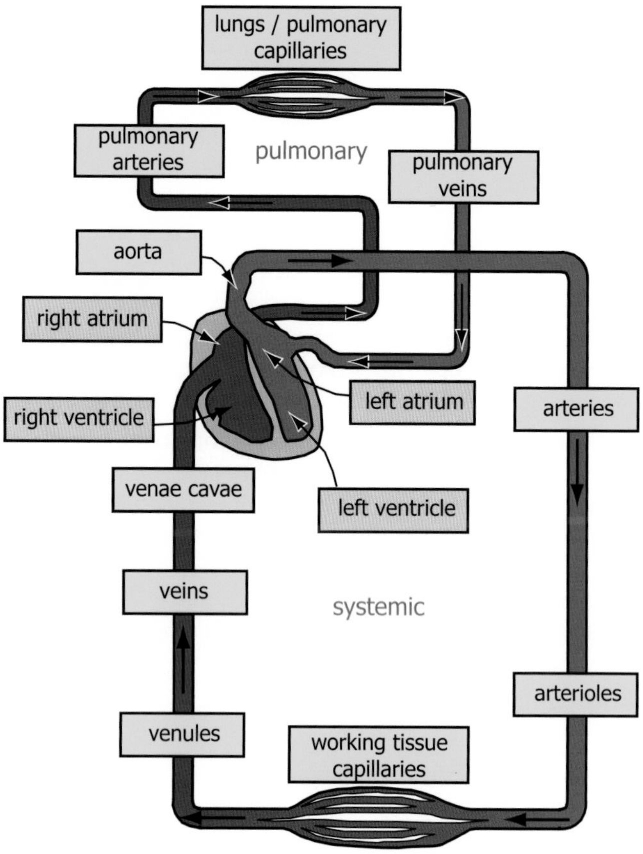

lungs / pulmonary capillaries

pulmonary arteries

pulmonary

pulmonary veins

aorta

right atrium

left atrium

arteries

right ventricle

venae cavae

left ventricle

veins

systemic

arterioles

venules

working tissue capillaries

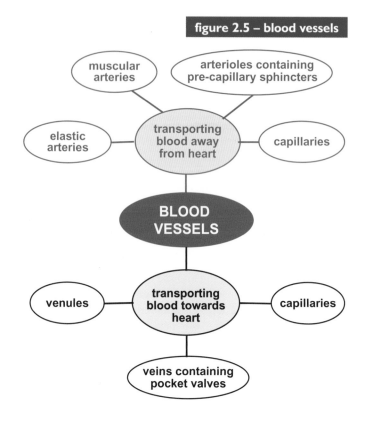

figure 2.5 – blood vessels

muscular arteries

arterioles containing pre-capillary sphincters

elastic arteries

transporting blood away from heart

capillaries

BLOOD VESSELS

venules

transporting blood towards heart

capillaries

veins containing pocket valves

Table 2.1 – **blood vessel structure and function**

type of blood vessel	vessel structure	vessel function / structure	vessel function	blood pressure in vessels
elastic arteries (aorta)	are thin-walled with large diameters.	middle layer (tunica media) contains a high proportion of elastic fibres and little smooth muscle.	during ventricular systole, these arteries extend with a rise in left ventricular pressure and recoil (contract) during ventricular diastole.	transport blood at high pressure away from the heart.
muscular arteries	thick-walled vessels with small diameters.	middle layer (tunica media) consists of some elastic fibres and lots of smooth muscle.	smooth muscle controls the shape of the central space or lumen via **vasoconstriction** and **vasodilation**.	transport blood at high pressure.
arterioles	reduce in size and muscular content as they get closer to the capillary bed.	smooth muscle (in the tunica media).	smooth muscle contracts (to reduce blood inflow) and relaxes (to increase blood inflow) to control inflow to their own capillary bed.	blood pressure reduces as vessel diameter reduces but total CSA of all vessels increases.
precapillary sphincters (contained within arterioles)	placed before capillary bed (within muscle or other tissue).		contract (to reduce blood inflow) and relax (to increase blood inflow) to control inflow to their own capillary bed.	
capillaries	tiny blood vessels whose walls are one cell thick, have semi-permeable walls or small spaces in the walls (tunica intima).	walls allow fluids rich in nutrients (O_2 & glucose) to be delivered to tissue cells, nutrients travel through the capillary walls into the tissue cells.	waste products (CO_2 and urea / lactate) are removed by travelling through the capillary walls from the tissue cells into the blood fluids. this is the opposite direction to the nutrients.	very low blood pressure as total vessel area reaches a maximum.
venules	walls consist of an inner wall (tunica intima), surrounded by a few smooth muscle cells.	positioned where several capillaries unite to collect outflow from a capillary bed at low pressure.	as venules approach the veins they develop a thin middle layer coat (tunica media).	blood pressure still very low as blood is transported towards the heart.
muscular veins	thin walled vessels contain less smooth muscle and fewer elastic fibres than arteries of same size.	have non-return valves, called pocket valves. positioned within the central space (or lumen) of these vessels.	sympathetic nerves causing **venoconstriction** activate the tunica media. The outer wall (tunica externa) is supported by collagen.	low blood pressure.
veins	thin middle layer supported by smooth muscle cells and collagen and elastic fibres.\n\nsome large veins are valveless e.g. hepatic veins.	blood flows in the veins because of muscular action in the surrounding skeletal muscle - **skeletal muscle pump**.	contracting muscle squashes veins forcing blood forwards towards the heart. since blood cannot flow back away from the heart due to the pocket valves within each vein.	low pressure blood reservoirs moving stored blood into general circulation during exercise.
venae cavae	are valveless and contain more smooth muscle in the middle wall.	smooth muscle acts to constrict or dilate the vessel (venomotor control).	deliver blood to the right atrium of the heart.	low blood pressure.

Venous return mechanism

The **venous return mechanism** (see figure 2.6) is the process by which blood returns to the right side of the heart. It depends on:

- **Gravity** that assists the flow of blood from body parts above the heart.
- The **skeletal muscle pump** in which contracting skeletal muscle squashes veins forcing blood forwards towards the heart (since blood cannot flow back away from the heart due to the pocket valves within each vein), as described above in table 2.1.
- The **respiratory pump** which relies upon the changes in pressure that occurs in the thoracic and abdominal cavities during inspiration and expiration. These pressure changes compress nearby veins and so assist blood flow back to the heart.
- **Valves (pocket valves)** which ensure that blood can only flow in one direction back towards the heart.
- **Venomotor control** which describes the limited capacity of veins to change their shape and therefore slightly increase venous return, due to **venoconstriction**. For a fuller description of this concept see page 41.

Hence the mechanism by which the bulk of blood returns to the heart during exercise is via the skeletal muscle pump, with the respiratory and cardiac pumps also helping.

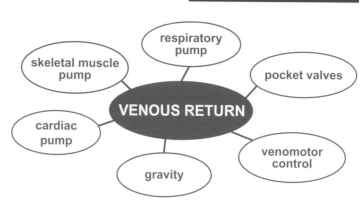

figure 2.6 – venous return

How is blood flow controlled?

Changes in blood vessel diameter depend upon the metabolic needs of body tissues. The vasomotor centre, located in the medulla oblongata of the brain, controls blood pressure and blood flow. This is an example of **negative feedback control**, in which an **increase** of blood pressure as sensed by baroreceptors causes a **decrease** in the blood pressure by changing blood vessel diameter.

As cardiac output increases, sensory receptors such as **baroreceptors** (responding to changes in blood pressure) and **chemoreceptors** (responding to changes in chemical composition of the blood) are stimulated.

Vasomotor control (figure 2.7)

Vasomotor control is concerned with the ability of muscular **arteries** and **arterioles** to change their shape. **During exercise**, the sensory receptors, baroreceptors and chemoreceptors, are stimulated. The vasomotor centre receives this sensory information. From here sympathetic nerves carry impulses to the smooth muscle walls of arteries and arterioles.

Non-active tissue

Within **non-active tissues**, these impulses cause **vasoconstriction** (tightening or narrowing) in the arteries, arterioles, and to the **pre-capillary sphincters** located at the openings of capillaries to the inactive tissue. The effect of this constriction is to **restrict blood flow** into the capillary bed of the non-active tissue.

Active tissue

In contrast, within **active tissue**, sympathetic stimulation to the smooth walls of arteries and arterioles and pre-capillary sphincters **is reduced**, and the muscles in the arterial walls and pre-capillary sphincters **relax**. Therefore these vessels dilate or open wider (known as **vasodilation**) and the **pre-capillary sphincters** open up, resulting in **additional blood flow** into active muscles.

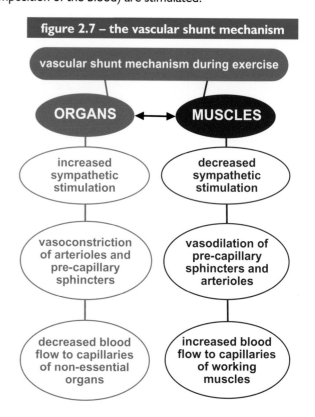

figure 2.7 – the vascular shunt mechanism

Capillary exchange and the vascular shunt

The flow of blood from an arteriole to a venule (that is through a capillary bed) is called the microcirculation. A **vascular shunt** (metarteriole-thoroughfare channel), is a short vessel that directly connects the arteriole and the venule at opposite ends of the bed (figure 2.8). When the **precapillary sphincters** are relaxed (open), blood flows through the true capillaries, and when the **precapillary sphincters** are contracted (closed), blood flows through the metarteriole thus bypassing the tissue cells.

figure 2.8 – the vascular shunt metarteriole

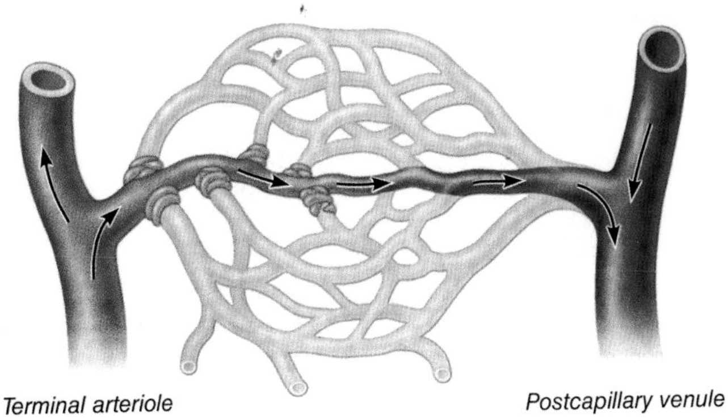

Vascular shunt mechanism

Hence, **as exercise begins**, as a result of vasomotor control, blood flow is diverted into active skeletal muscle where it is needed. This redirection of blood flow is called the **vascular shunt mechanism** and is illustrated in figures 2.7 (page 40), 2.8 and 2.9.

The vasomotor centre works in conjunction with the cardiac centre in maintaining blood pressure. Table 2.2 illustrates the redistribution of blood flow as exercise begins, away from the major organs of the body towards working muscle.

figure 2.9 – vascular shunt mechanism

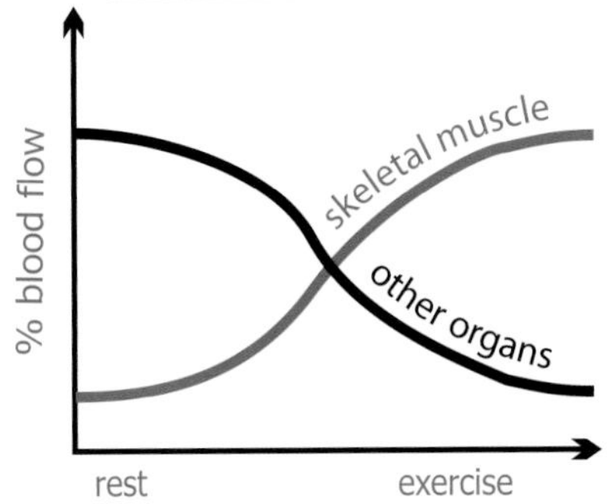

redistribution of blood during exercise

Table 2.2 – **comparison of the distribution of cardiac output at rest and during exercise**

	proportions of blood in various tissues			
tissue	**rest**		**maximal exercise**	
	%	**ml min⁻¹**	**%**	**ml min⁻¹**
liver	27	1350	1	300
kidneys	22	1100	1	250
brain	14	700	3	750
heart	4	200	4	1000
muscle	20	1000	88	22000
skin	6	300	2	600
other	7	350	1	100
total	100	5000	100	25000

STUDENT NOTE

Note the five-fold increase in total rate of blood flow at maximal exercise, and the fact that the brain maintains approximately the same blood flow – otherwise if the rate of flow to the brain reduced substantially, the sportsperson would faint and fall to the ground!

Venomotor control

Venomotor control describes the limited capacity of veins to change their shape. This is the result of venomotor tone, whereby the veins' muscular coat receives stimulation from the sympathetic nervous system. The effect of limited **venoconstriction** of veins causes a small increase in blood velocity and hence **an increase** in venous return.

Cardiovascular system during exercise of differing intensities and during recovery

Short-term cardiac responses to physical activity

See figure 2.10, page 42, for a summary of cardiac factors in short-term responses to exercise.

- **Heart rate** (HR) is defined as '**the number of beats of the heart per minute (bpm)**'.
- The average resting HR for males is 70 bpm, and for females 72 bpm.
- At rest, the HR for a trained athlete = 60 bpm or lower (heart rates of less than 60 is **bradycardia**), and the HR for an untrained person = 70-90 bpm (average 80).

Short-term cardiac responses to physical activity

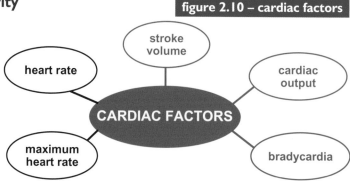

figure 2.10 – cardiac factors

- **Maximum heart rate** can be calculated using the
  formula: $HR_{max} = 220 - age$.
  So, for a 20 year old, $HR_{max} = 220 - 20 = 200$ bpm.
  Usually, maximum heart rates for untrained people
  are slightly less than for highly trained people, an
  example would be 190 (untrained) to 200 (trained)
  in the calculation outlined below.

- **Stroke volume** (SV) is '**the volume of blood pumped
  by the left ventricle of the heart per beat**' and
  is determined by venous return and elasticity and
  contractility of the myocardium.

- For example, the SV for a trained athlete = 110 ml at rest, and the SV for an untrained person = 70 ml at
  rest. The SV for a trained endurance athlete during maximal exercise intensity = 190 ml, and for an untrained
  person, during his or her maximum exercise intensity SV = 110 ml.

- **Cardiac output** $(\dot{Q})$ is '**the volume of blood pumped by the left ventricle of the heart in one minute**',
  and is the product of stroke volume and heart rate: $\dot{Q} = SV \times HR$

  Example figures are:
  For an untrained person at rest, $\dot{Q} = 70 \times 80$ = 5.60 l/min (or dm³ min⁻¹).
  For an untrained person during maximal exercise, $\dot{Q} = 110 \times 190$ = 20.90 l/min (or dm³ min⁻¹).
  For an endurance athlete at rest, $\dot{Q} = 110 \times 51$ = 5.61 l/min (or dm³ min⁻¹).
  For an endurance athlete during maximal exercise, $\dot{Q} = 190 \times 200$ = 38 l/min (or dm³ min⁻¹).

Short-term changes in heart rate, stroke volume and cardiac output

Heart rate response to exercise

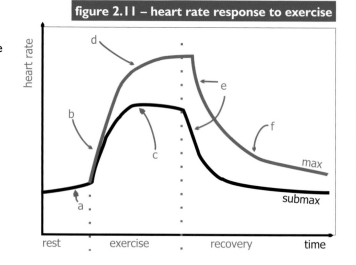

figure 2.11 – heart rate response to exercise

Referring to the graph in figure 2.11:

a = **Anticipatory rise** due to the hormonal action of adrenaline
and noradrenaline. This happens because the person tends
to get excited **before** the exercise starts, and hence heart
rate rises slightly.

b = **Sharp rise** during anaerobic work due to proprioceptor
sensory stimulation, and also due to continued release of
hormones and action of the skeletal muscle pump
(see page 54).

c = **Steady state** and some recovery of O₂ debt (aerobic).

d = **Continued high HR** due to maximal workloads which
continue to stress anaerobic systems, producing lactic
acid + CO_2 + K⁺, which stimulate chemoreceptors.
Additionally, intrinsic factors are also stimulated at maximal
level (refer to page 44).

e = **Rapid recovery** due to cessation of proprioceptive stimuli,
the skeletal muscle pump, and the withdrawal of hormones.

f = **Slow recovery**, clearance of metabolites such as lactic acid,
as systems return to normal resting values.

- Recovery is aided by an **active cool-down** which maintains the
  increased activity of the muscle and respiratory pumps and so
  assists increased venous return.

- An active recovery prevents blood pooling which occurs when
  the walls and valves of veins in human legs do not work effectively,
  thereby making it difficult for blood to return to the heart.

Stroke volume response to exercise

Referring to the graph in figure 2.12:

a = An increase in stroke volume, from a resting value of 60 ml beat^{-1} to 85 ml beat^{-1} prior to the start of the exercise period, and is due to the release of hormones such as **adrenaline** and **noradrenaline**. This effect is known as the **anticipatory rise**.

b = An increase in stroke volume as exercise commences. This is primarily due an **increased venous return** and **increased myocardial contraction during ventricular systole** (**Starling's Law of the Heart**) which causes the heart muscle to contract more forcefully, from 85 ml beat^{-1} to more than 110 ml beat^{-1} during submaximal work.

c = As work intensity increases during maximal exercise, there is a slight decline in stroke volume. At this point heart rate will rise rapidly to sustain the continued increase in cardiac output to meet exercise demands.

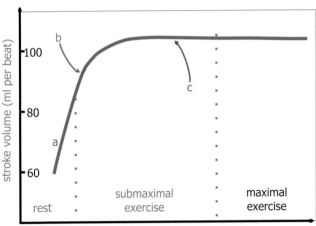

figure 2.12 – stroke volume response to exercise

STUDENT NOTE

Stroke volume increases to maximal values during submaximal work and does not increase further as work increases towards maximal effort. This is because once the heart is expanding and contracting utilising its fullest possible size, it obviously cannot get any bigger even though the energy needs of the body are greater. At this increased value, stroke volume is unable to increase any further since the overlap of the actin and myosin fibres during cardiac systole has reached maximum, and therefore stroke volume levels off.

Cardiac output response to exercise

Since **cardiac output** is the product of stroke volume and heart rate values $\dot{Q} = SV \times HR$, it will increase directly in line with exercise intensity.

Cardiovascular drift (figure 2.13)

- With **prolonged aerobic exercise**, at a constant exercise intensity, such as marathon racing or **aerobic exercising** in a **hot environment**, stroke volume gradually decreases and heart rate increases, and hence cardiac output remains approximately constant. During this process arterial blood pressure declines.

- These responses are due to the need to transfer excess heat produced by active tissues from deep in the body (known as the core) to the skin where it has access to the outside environment.

- This heat is moved by the blood during **vasodilation** of blood vessels directly underneath the skin. Evaporation is the primary route for heat dissipation and so as fluid or sweat evaporates heat is lost. Loss of fluid results in a reduced plasma volume and subsequent decreased venous return and stroke volume.

- A **reduced stroke volume** initiates a compensatory **heart rate increase** to maintain a **nearly constant cardiac output** as exercise progresses. All these circulatory responses are collectively referred to as the **cardiovascular drift**. See figure 2.13.

- It is important for athletes to **rehydrate** with sports drinks (water containing a little sodium and glucose) during prolonged exercise periods or whilst performing aerobic exercise in a hot environment. This will minimise the loss of fluids and thus reduce the effects of the cardiovascular drift.

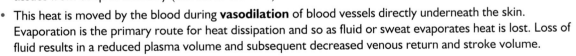

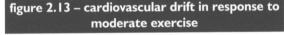

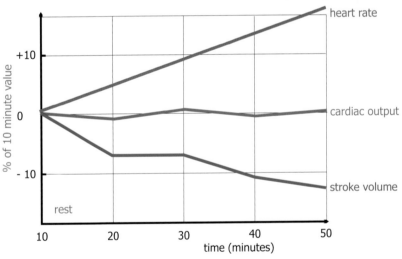

figure 2.13 – cardiovascular drift in response to moderate exercise

Regulation of heart rate

The cardiac control centre (in the medulla oblongata in the brain) regulates feedback that results in changes to heart rate from important **neural, hormonal** and **intrinsic** factors (figure 2.14).

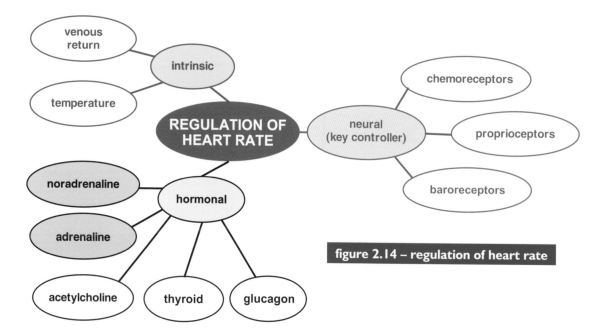

figure 2.14 – regulation of heart rate

Neural control factors

Neural control factors are the key controlling regulators and consist of:

- **Chemoreceptor reflexes** which involve receptors located in blood vessels such as the aortic arch and carotid sinuses.
  These reflexes detect chemical changes in blood O_2, CO_2, H^+ concentrations, and pH levels. Decrease in O_2 and pH levels, and increase in CO_2 and H^+ concentrations, all stimulate changes in heart rate via the cardiac accelerator nerve.
- **Proprioceptor reflexes** found in muscle spindles and Golgi tendons which respond to mechanical stimuli such as compression, bending or stretching of cells, detecting changes in movement. Increase in tension within cell structures will increase heart rate via the cardiac accelerator nerve.
- **Baroreceptor reflexes** which involve receptors located in blood vessels (such as the aortic arch and carotid sinuses). Their role is to detect changes in blood pressure. When blood pressure is too high the parasympathetic nerve releases acetylcholine, which decreases heart rate.

Hormonal factors

Hormones are released by the body in response to various stimuli. Those that affect heart rate are:

- **Noradrenaline** and **adrenaline** (the key hormonal regulators) which act to accelerate heart rate (tachycardia) and increase the strength of ventricular contraction which increases stroke volume.
- **Acetylcholine** which slows the heart (bradycardia) as described below.
- **Thyroid** hormone and **glucagon** which increase HR.
- **Increased glucagon** levels which assist in the breakdown of **glycogen to release glucose** into the circulatory system to fuel muscular contractions.

Intrinsic factors

Intrinsic factors account for changes in venous return:

- **Venous return** is **'the volume of blood returning to the heart during each cardiac cycle'**. This changes as a result of the actions of the skeletal muscle and respiratory pumps, and the electrolyte balance (Na^+, K^+) in muscular tissue.
- **Myocardial temperature** also affects venous return, in that the speed of nerve impulse transmission increases with temperature, and this will increase heart rate.
- **Starling's Law of the Heart** states that cardiac output is equal to venous return. An increase in venous return stretches the ventricular walls more and results in an increased strength of contraction and therefore an increase in stroke volume.

Neural control

- **Neural impulses** (resulting from feedback from neural, hormonal and intrinsic control) override the inherent rhythm of the heartbeat. Signals originate in the **cardiac control centre** (**CCC**) in the medulla and travel via the antagonistic actions of the sympathetic and parasympathetic nervous systems, to the pacemaker or SA node.

Sympathetic influence

- The **sympathetic nervous system**, the **SNS** (via the cardiac accelerator nerve), releases the neurotransmitters adrenaline and noradrenaline onto the SA node to **speed up** heart rate.

Parasympathetic influence

- The **parasympathetic nervous system**, **PNS** (via the vagus nerve), releases the neurotransmitter acetylcholine onto the SA node to **slow down** heart rate.

.

Practice questions

1) Heart rate is controlled by the cardiac conduction system. Which one of the following is the order of the cardiac conduction system?
   a.   atrioventricular node, sinoatrial node, bundle of His, Purkinje fibres.
   b.   atrioventricular node, sinoatrial node, Purkinje fibres, bundle of His.
   c.   sinoatrial node, atrioventricular node, bundle of His, Purkinje fibres.
   d.   sinoatrial node, atrioventricular node, Purkinje fibres, bundle of His.

2) The pulse is a wave of pressure produced by:
   a.   the contraction of the right atrium.
   b.   the contraction of the left ventricle.
   c.   the contraction of the left atrium.
   d.   the contraction of the right ventricle.

3) Which statement does not accurately describe veins?
   a.   have less elastic tissue and smooth muscle than arteries.
   b.   contain more fibrous tissue than arteries.
   c.   most veins in the extremities have valves.
   d.   always carry deoxygenated blood.

4) Which one of the following statements is false?
   a.   most of the total blood volume is contained in veins.
   b.   capillaries have a greater total surface area than any other type of vessel.
   c.   gas exchange between blood and tissue fluid occur across the walls of venules.
   d.   small arteries and arterioles present great resistance to blood flow.

5) Which one of the following would not result in dilation of the feeder arterioles and opening of the precapillary sphincters in systemic capillary beds?
   a.   a decrease in local tissue O_2.
   b.   an increase in local tissue O_2.
   c.   a local increase in CO_2.
   d.   a local increase in pH.

figure 2.15 – the cardiac impulse

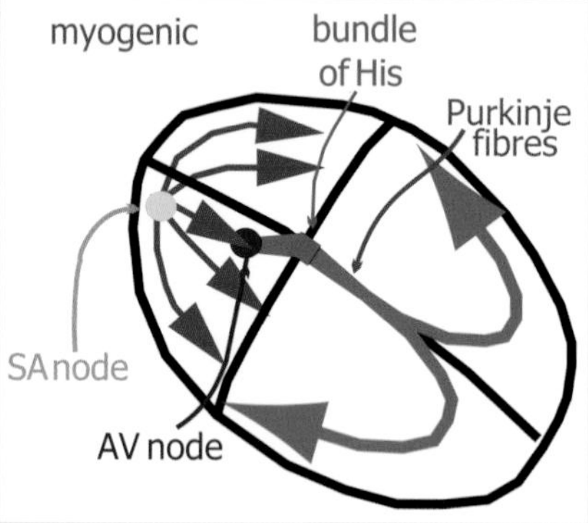

6) Figure 2.15 shows a diagrammatic picture of the cardiac impulse. Using the information in this diagram, describe the flow of blood during the specific stages of the cardiac cycle in relation to the cardiac impulse. In your answer explain how the heart valves help control the direction of blood flow.   8 marks

7) $\dot{Q}$ = SV x HR. Explain the meaning of this equation and give typical resting values that you would expect in an endurance-based athlete.   6 marks

8) A fit 18 year old female student performs a 400m time trial in one minute.
   a)   Sketch and label a graph to show a typical heart rate response from a point 5 minutes before the start of the run, during the time trial, and over the 20 minute recovery period.   4 marks

   b)   Explain why heart rate takes some time to return to its resting value following the exercise period.   2 marks

   c)   Identify a hormone that is responsible for heart rate increases prior to and during an exercise period.   1 mark

   d)   Heart rate is regulated by neural, hormonal and intrinsic factors. How does the nervous system detect and respond to changes in heart rate during an exercise period?   4 marks

Practice questions

9) Table 2.3 shows the rate of blood flow (in cm³ per minute) to different parts of the body in a trained male athlete, at rest and while exercising at maximum effort on a cycle ergometer.

Table 2.3 – **estimated blood flow at rest and during maximum effort**

organ or system	estimated blood flow in cm³ min⁻¹	
	at rest	during max effort
skeletal muscle	1000	26400
coronary vessels	250	1200
skin	500	750
kidneys	1000	300
liver & gut	1250	375
other organs	1000	975

Study the data carefully before answering the following questions.

a) The rate of blood flow to the 'entire body' increases significantly during exercise. Explain briefly how the heart achieves this. 2 marks

b) What percentage of the total blood flow is directed to the skeletal muscle at rest and during maximum effort? Show your calculations. 3 marks

c) How is blood flow to various regions of the body controlled? 4 marks

10) a) What is meant by the concept 'venous return mechanism'? 2 marks

b) Describe how it is aided during physical activity when a person is exercising in an upright position. 3 marks

c) Explain the importance of the skeletal muscle pump mechanism during an active cool-down. 2 marks

d) What effect does enhanced venous return have upon cardiac output and stroke volume? 3 marks

11) A simple equation for the calculation of blood pressure can be written as:
Blood Pressure = Cardiac Output x Resistance to blood flow
Identify one factor that affects resistance to the flow of blood within systemic blood vessels. 1 mark

12) Table 2.4 identifies differences in total blood volume, plasma volume, and blood cell volume between untrained and highly trained endurance males (same age, height and body mass). Comment on the data that is presented in table 2.4 and suggest how the trained athlete would benefit from these increased volumes. 4 marks

Table 2.4 – **blood volumes in trained and untrained males**

subjects	total blood volume (dm³)	plasma volume (dm³)	blood cell volume (dm³)
trained male	7	4.2	2.8
untrained male	5.6	3.2	2.4

Answers link: http://www.jroscoe.co.uk/downloads/as_a1_revise_pe_ocr/OCRAS_A1_ch2_answers.pdf

CHAPTER 3: The respiratory system

Respiratory anatomy and dynamics

STUDENT NOTE Prior knowledge of the structure and function of the respiratory system is assumed, but your syllabus requires understanding of the respiratory structures.

From figure 3.1 you will see that the **air pathway** as the air is breathed in follows the route: **nasal cavity** to **pharynx** to **larynx** to **trachea** to **bronchi** to **bronchioles** to **respiratory bronchioles** (the smaller tubes which branch out from the bronchioles) to **alveolar ducts** (the tubes connecting the respiratory bronchioles to the alveoli) to **alveoli**.

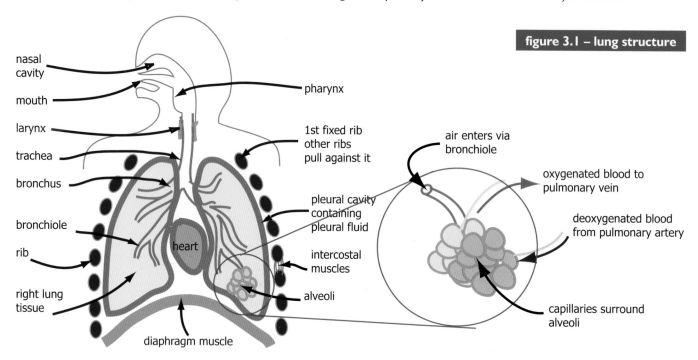

figure 3.1 – lung structure

The **trachea** consists of an incomplete ring of cartilage that keeps the airway open and allows swallowing. The nasal cavity, pharynx, larynx, trachea and bronchi have ciliated linings and **mucous glands** to provide a cleaning and filtering mechanism for incoming air.

Lung structure

The **pulmonary pleura** is a self-enclosed serous membrane covering the lungs. It lines the thoracic cavity, middle wall of the thorax and diaphragm. This membrane secretes pleural fluid into the pleural cavity thereby reducing friction between lung tissue and ribs, aiding inspiration as pleural pressure reduces, and expiration as pleural pressure increases.

Alveoli (see figure 3.1) are elastic, moist, and permeable (as single layered epithelium cells) and are surrounded by a network of capillaries. These are adapted for gaseous exchange, as oxygen travels through the capillary walls **from** the lung space **into** the blood within the capillaries, and carbon dioxide travels in the opposite direction through the capillary walls.

Functions of the respiratory system

The primary organs of the respiratory system are lungs, as described above, which function to take in oxygen and expel carbon dioxide as we breathe. **Pulmonary ventilation** is '**the process by which we move air into and out of the lungs**', involving the mechanisms of inspiration and expiration.

The respiratory system at rest

Lung volumes and capacities

Interpretations from spirometer readings

A **spirometer** is a device that is used to measure pulmonary volumes. Figure 3.2 presents a typical lung volume trace resulting from a person breathing into a calibrated spirometer, at rest and during exercise. Note that during the exercise period tidal volume increases because of the encroachment on inspiratory reserve volume (IRV) and expiratory reserve volume (ERV), but more noticeably on the IRV.

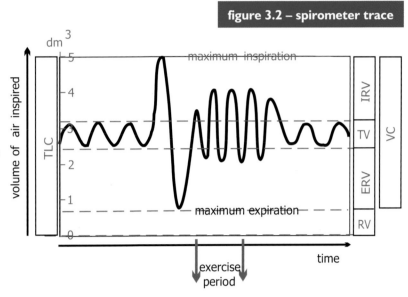

figure 3.2 – spirometer trace

Definitions for pulmonary volumes

Average values for male and females are shown in table 3.1. Lung **volumes** vary with age, gender, body size and stature, and are defined and explained in table 3.1.

Table 3.1 – **lung volumes and definitions**

lung volumes		definitions	average values (ml)		change during exercise
			male	female	
TLC	total lung capacity	total volume of air in the lungs following maximum inspiration.	6000	4200	slight decrease
VC	vital capacity	maximum volume of air that can be forcibly expired following maximum inspiration.	4800	3200	slight decrease
TV	tidal volume	volume of air inspired **or** expired per breath.	600	500	increase
IRV	inspiratory reserve volume	volume of air that can be forcibly inspired above resting tidal volume.	3000	1900	decrease
ERV	expiratory reserve volume	volume of air that can be forcibly expired above resting tidal volume.	1200	800	decrease
RV	residual volume	volume of air remaining in the lungs after maximal expiration.	1200	1000	stays same
$\dot{V}E=TV \times f$	minute ventilation	volume of air inspired **or** expired in one minute.	7200	6000	dramatic increase

Lung **capacities** are made up of combinations of lung volumes.
The following list uses as examples the average **male** values from table 3.1 above.

Inspiratory capacity (IC)	= TV + IRV	(3600 ml)
Expiratory capacity (EC)	= TV + ERV	(1800 ml)
Vital capacity (VC)	= TV + IRV + ERV	(4800 ml)
Functional residual capacity (FRC)	= RV + ERV	(2400 ml)
Total lung capacity (TLC)	= VC + RV	(6000 ml)

Minute ventilation

Minute ventilation ($\dot{V}E$) is defined as '**the volume of air that is inspired or expired in one minute**'. Minute ventilation can be calculated by multiplying tidal volume (**TV**) by the number of breaths (**f**) taken in one minute (see the last row of table 3.1 page 49. Below are examples of minute ventilation values you would expect at rest and during differing intensities of exercise. A normal male resting breathing frequency is about 12 breaths per minute, and this is the value of **f** in the first row of the list below. This would increase to about 25 (breaths per minute) for submaximal exercise, and rapid breathing of about 55 breaths per minute during maximal exercise.

(dm³)	$\dot{V}E$	=	TV	x	f		
at rest	7.2	= 0.6	x	12	= 7.2	litres per minute or 7200 ml per minute – since 1 dm³ is 1 litre or 1000 ml.
sub-max	60	= 2.4	x	25	= 60	litres per minute or 60000 ml per minute.
max	121	= 2.2	x	55	= 121	litres per minute or 121000 ml per minute.

Hence from sub-maximal to maximal exercise breathing rate or respiratory frequency doubles. This dramatic increase often corresponds with the onset of anaerobic metabolism or the onset of blood lactate accumulation or **OBLA** at the expense of a decreasing tidal volume.

What is actually happening is a regulation of minute ventilation in response to **increased carbon dioxide** production and the need to get rid of carbon dioxide during expiration. The tidal volume decreases slightly because it is not physically possible to inspire the maximum possible volume of air during maximal exercise at a high breathing rate. This regulatory response is discussed further on page 55. Figure 3.10 on page 54, compares the changes in minute ventilation with time during low intensity and high intensity exercise.

Mechanics of breathing, the physiology of the respiratory system

The actual mechanism of breathing is brought about by changes in air pressure (**intrapulmonary pressure**) in the lungs relative to atmospheric pressure, and as a result of the muscular actions of the 11 pairs of intercostal muscles and the diaphragm.

Mechanics of breathing

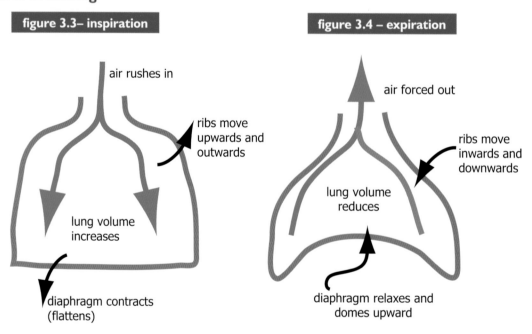

figure 3.3– inspiration	figure 3.4 – expiration
air rushes in	air forced out
ribs move upwards and outwards	ribs move inwards and downwards
lung volume increases	lung volume reduces
diaphragm contracts (flattens)	diaphragm relaxes and domes upward

STUDENT NOTE For a summary view of the mechanics of breathing, see figure 3.3 for inspiration, 3.4 for expiration, and table 3.2 on page 51.

Table 3.2 – **inspiration and expiration at rest and during exercise** (see figures 3.3 and 3.4 on page 50)

inspiration	expiration
at rest	**at rest**
external intercostal muscles contract.	external intercostal muscles relax - a passive process.
diaphragm contracts – becomes flatter.	diaphragm relaxes – domes upward into chest cavity – a passive process.
internal intercostal muscles relax.	
ribs and sternum move upwards and outwards.	ribs and sternum move downwards and inwards.
increase in chest cavity volume.	decrease in chest cavity volume.
pressure between pleural membranes is reduced.	pressure between pleural membranes is increased.
allows elastic pulmonary tissue to expand.	compresses elastic pulmonary tissue.
lung volume increases.	lung volume decreases.
pulmonary air pressure falls below atmospheric pressure (outside the body).	pulmonary air pressure is driven above atmospheric pressure (outside the body).
hence atmospheric air is forced into the lungs.	hence atmospheric air is forced out of the lungs via the respiratory passages.
until lung pressure equals the pressure outside again.	until lung pressure equals the pressure outside again.
during exercise	**during exercise**
additional muscles in the chest and torso contract. (scalenes, sternocleidomastoid, pectoralis major / minor)	internal intercostal muscles and abdominal muscles contract powerfully, acting on ribs and body cavity.
chest cavity volume further increased.	chest cavity volume is further reduced.
more air forced into the lungs.	more pulmonary air is forced out of the lungs.

The process of transport of respiratory gases

Several factors affect the rate at which the gases taking part in the respiration process are exchanged (figure 3.5).

Diffusion

The exchange of gases between lungs and blood and their movement at tissue level takes place passively by **diffusion.**

This is the movement of molecules through space by random collision with other molecules. This process would eventually result in random mixing of all the molecules present in a space. Molecules move using this process through gases and liquids, and can migrate through membranes (like tissue boundaries such as cell walls).

A diffusion gradient is a situation where the concentration of molecules of a particular substance (say oxygen for example) is greater on one side of a space than on the other side of the same space. Hence a diffusion gradient will cause molecules to move across a space (or membrane) **by random** mixing or random molecular collision with membrane walls. Steep **diffusion gradients** are maintained by the factors shown in figure 3.5, and help move substances from higher concentrations to lower concentrations where they take part in the respiration process.

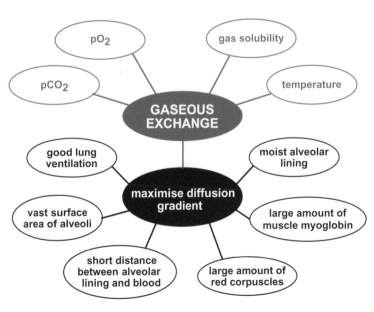

figure 3.5 – factors affecting gaseous exchange

pO$_2$ · gas solubility · pCO$_2$ · temperature · **GASEOUS EXCHANGE** · good lung ventilation · moist alveolar lining · **maximise diffusion gradient** · vast surface area of alveoli · large amount of muscle myoglobin · short distance between alveolar lining and blood · large amount of red corpuscles

Diffusion gradient

Gases diffuse from high to low pressure, and so the rate of exchange (either at lungs or tissue site) depends on the **partial pressure** of each gas (in blood or tissue site or alveolar air), **gas solubility** (in blood or tissue cell fluids), and **temperature.**

Partial pressure

Partial pressure (**p**) is defined as '**the pressure a gas exerts within a mixture of gases**', so pO_2 and pCO_2 are the partial pressures exerted by oxygen and carbon dioxide respectively within a mixture of these and other gases (for example nitrogen) present in the air or the tissues. The partial pressure of a gas is directly related to the concentration (number of molecules per cubic metre) of gas molecules in a space. At a given temperature, the bigger the **p**, the more molecules of gas are present.

Gaseous exchange

Gaseous exchange is the process whereby oxygen from the air **in the lungs** is transferred by diffusion to the blood flowing through the alveoli (see figure 3.6). At the same time, carbon dioxide is transferred from the blood arriving at the lungs, into the air in the lungs, which is subsequently breathed out. The gases travel **through** the capillary and alveolar walls, with oxygen diffusing into the blood, and carbon dioxide diffusing **out** of the blood.

figure 3.6 – oxygenation of haemoglobin

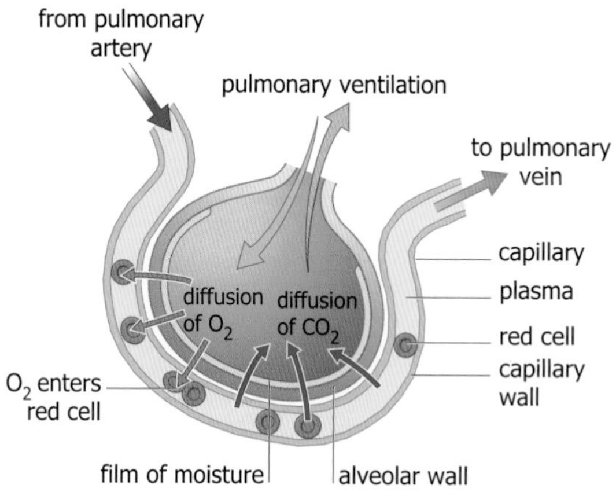

from pulmonary artery

pulmonary ventilation

to pulmonary vein

diffusion of O_2 diffusion of CO_2

capillary
plasma
red cell
capillary wall

O_2 enters red cell

film of moisture   alveolar wall

figure 3.7 – tissue respiration

diffusion of CO_2

capillary

plasma

tissue fluid

diffusion of O_2

diffusion of O_2

tissue cell

The reverse process happens at the **tissue site** (for example, active muscle tissue – see figure 3.7). Here, oxygen is carried by blood into the tissues and there it diffuses into tissue cells. At the same time, carbon dioxide diffuses **out of** tissue cells into the blood (which then flows back through the venous system and the heart and back to the lungs).

How gaseous exchange is achieved in the alveoli

The first step in oxygen transport involves the diffusion of oxygen **from** the **alveoli** into the blood.

In venous blood (arriving at the lungs from tissues) the partial pressure of oxygen (pO_2) = 5.3 kPa. The partial pressure of oxygen in alveolar air is 13.3 kPa, so the oxygen travels through the alveolar and capillary walls from the lung space **into** the blood where it combines with haemoglobin to form **oxyhaemoglobin ($Hb(O_2)_4$)** as follows:

$$Hb + 4O_2 \rightarrow Hb(O_2)_4$$

One of the **short-term effects** of physical activity is to cause a **small increase** in **pulmonary blood pressure**, which distorts red blood corpuscles within the alveolar capillary system, and this enables **10 times as much oxygen** to be picked up as at rest.

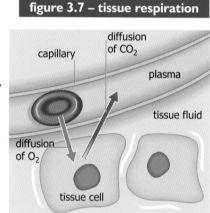

figure 3.8 – oxyhaemoglobin dissociation curve

% saturation of haemoglobin with oxygen (y-axis: 0 to 100)

oxygen partial pressure / kPa (x-axis: 0 to 14)

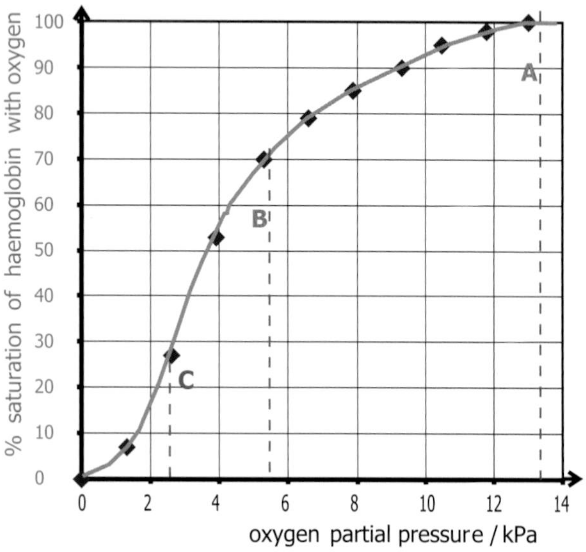

The oxyhaemoglobin dissociation curve (see figure 3.8) describes the percentage of haemoglobin saturated with oxygen at a given pO_2. At 13.3 kPa pressure, oxygen will combine with Hb at 98% of the maximum possible (see the red vertical line labelled **A** on figure 3.8, this is at 13.3kPa and intersects the graph line at almost 100%). This means that Hb leaving the lungs is almost completely saturated with O_2. (Note that 3% of oxygen dissolves in blood plasma). Blood carrying this O_2 then travels out of the lungs to the heart via the pulmonary vein, then out to the body through the aorta.

How gaseous exchange is achieved in the alveoli

At altitude, the pO_2 is less, which means that haemoglobin cannot carry as much oxygen as at sea level, therefore reducing the ability to perform physical work. This is called **hypoxia** (lowered pO_2).

At the same time, carbon dioxide is transferred in the opposite direction, from the blood into the alveolar air. The concentration of CO_2 in atmospheric air is about 0.049% (very small), and therefore pCO_2 in venous blood arriving (via the heart) from the body tissues is higher than in the alveoli air (breathed into the lungs). Therefore CO_2 diffuses through the alveolar membrane (from blood to air in lung) and is expired. Between 3% and 6% of air breathed out is CO_2 (see table 3.3).

Table 3.3 – **differences between inhaled and exhaled air**

	differences between inhaled and exhaled air		
	inhaled(%)	exhaled air at rest (%)	exhaled air during exercise (%)
O_2	21	17	15
CO_2	0.049	3	6

How gaseous exchange is achieved at the tissue cell site

The second step in oxygen transport involves the transfer of oxygen from the blood into tissue cells.

The role of myoglobin

Myoglobin is a substance somewhat similar to haemoglobin in that it attracts and binds to molecular oxygen. Myoglobin has a greater affinity for oxygen than haemoglobin and is located within cells, where its role is to enable oxygen to be carried across a cell to the **mitochondria** where the oxygen is consumed and energy transfer takes place (which, for example, enables muscle tissue to contract). Arriving (arterial) blood has an oxygen partial pressure ($pO_2 = 13.3$ kPa). This is greater than tissue pO_2 since the oxygen is being used up in the cells during the energy creating process. Because **myoglobin** in the tissue cells has a greater affinity for oxygen than does haemoglobin, oxygen diffuses **through** the capillary and cell walls **from** the blood **into** the tissue cells. Myoglobin then facilitates oxygen transfer to the mitochondria, notably at the start of exercise and during intense exercise when cellular pO_2 decreases considerably.

Oxygen transfer at rest

At a pO_2 of 5.5 kPa, which is the normal pO_2 in resting tissue capillaries, haemoglobin is about 70% saturated (this corresponds to red vertical line **B** in figure 3.8 page 52). This means that approximately 30% of the oxygen bound to haemoglobin is released into the blood and can diffuse into the tissue spaces.

Oxygen transfer during vigorous exercise

During **vigorous exercise** the pO_2 in tissue spaces may decline to levels as low as 2.5 kPa. Therefore, looking at line **C** in figure 3.8, only about 25% of the haemoglobin remains saturated, and 75% of the oxygen bound to haemoglobin is released into the blood and can diffuse through the capillary walls into the active tissue spaces. The absorption and utilisation of oxygen from the blood leads to a difference in the oxygen content of arterial and venous blood. This difference is known as the **arterio-venous oxygen difference** or a-$\overline{v}O_{2diff}$.

The effect of pH, pCO_2 and temperature on oxygen release

Other factors influence the degree to which oxygen binds to haemoglobin. **During exercise**, tissue cell and blood temperature increases, pCO_2 increases due to the greater need for energy, and pH decreases due to the greater presence of H^+ ions from lactic acid or creation of H^+ from dissociating carbonic acid by the released CO_2. All these conditions cause reduction in the affinity of haemoglobin for oxygen. This means that more O_2 is released (than would be the case if no exercise were being taken), and hence more O_2 is then available to active tissue sites which are working harder. **So the harder the tissue is working, the more O_2 is released**.

The effect of increases in acidity, pCO_2 and temperature is to cause the oxyhaemoglobin dissociation curve to shift downward and to the right (enhanced unloading). This phenomenon is called the '**Böhr effect**'.

Carbon dioxide transport (figure 3.9)

CO_2 is produced in the cells as an end product of tissue cell respiration (production of energy from combination of fuel with oxygen). Hence, the fluid within muscle tissue cells has a higher pCO_2 than in the blood. Therefore CO_2 diffuses back through cell and capillary walls in the **opposite** direction (from tissue to departing blood). CO_2 is transported in venous blood as:

- **Carbonic acid** mostly dissociated into H^+ and HCO_3^- (70%).
- **Carbaminohaemoglobin** (23%).
- **CO_2 dissolved in blood plasma** (7%).

In the lung capillaries carbon dioxide is released, then it diffuses from the blood into the alveoli and is expired out of the lungs.

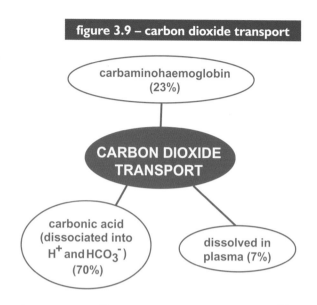

figure 3.9 – carbon dioxide transport

Ventilation during exercise and recovery

STUDENT NOTE	You will be required to sketch and interpret these patterns in your exam.

During the short period before exercise begins, during the exercise period, and during the recovery period immediately after exercise (see graph in figure 3.10) the following describes the reasons for the changes in rate of ventilation or minute ventilation.

- **Anticipatory rise** in $\dot{V}E$ is due to the hormonal action of **adrenaline** and **noradrenaline** on the respiratory centre in the brain. This rise is caused by the excitement in anticipation of exercise beginning.

- **Rapid rise** of $\dot{V}E$ on exercise beginning is due to **proprioceptor** sensory **stimulation**, and also due to continued release of hormones. During this period, exercise is anaerobic in nature and does not require oxygen from the respiratory system. However, an oxygen debt is building up, and this will need to be dealt with later.

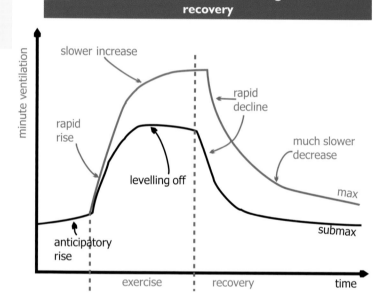

figure 3.10 – minute ventilation during exercise and recovery

- During **sub-maximal** exercise, a **levelling off** of $\dot{V}E$ occurs as a **steady state** is developed between oxygen required and provided by the respiratory system. Some recovery of O_2 debt (aerobic) occurs.

- During **maximal** workloads there is a continued **slower increase** in $\dot{V}E$ as anaerobic systems continue to be stressed. This produces lactic acid + CO_2 + K^+, which stimulate **chemoreceptors** at maximal level. The main stimulant for increased rates of ventilation is the presence of carbon dioxide in the blood flowing past chemoreceptors. See paragraph and figure 3.11 on page 55 for details of the location and function of these receptors which stimulate the respiratory centre in the brain.

- As exercise ends, there is a **rapid decline** in $\dot{V}E$ due to cessation of proprioceptive stimuli and the withdrawal of hormones, then a levelling out to pre-exercise values.

- Later, after maximal work, there is a **much slower decrease** in $\dot{V}E$ due to the clearance of metabolites such as **lactic acid** and **carbon dioxide** as systems return to normal resting values.

- An **active recovery** maintains $\dot{V}E$ at a higher level to ensure that there is a continual supply of oxygen (compared with resting values) that can be used to clear metabolites such as lactic acid and carbon dioxide.

Neural regulation of pulmonary ventlation

The **respiratory control centre** (**RCC**, see figure 3.11) is located within the medulla oblongata of the brain and regulates pulmonary ventilation. Rate of breathing (also called the **frequency** of breathing (**f**) and defined as **'the number of breaths taken in one minute'**) and **depth of breathing** (known as **tidal volume** (**TV**) and defined as **'the volume of air inspired or expired in one breath'**) are controlled by neurones within the medulla. Although the medullary neurones establish a basic rhythm of breathing, their activities can be influenced by input from other parts of the brain and by input from peripherally located receptors discussed in figure 3.12 page 56.

The RCC consists of two parts: the **inspiratory** and **expiratory** centres:

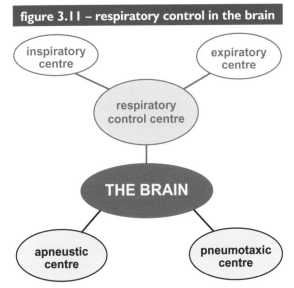

figure 3.11 – respiratory control in the brain

- The **inspiratory centre** is responsible for the basic rhythm of ventilation. At rest impulses are sent via the phrenic and intercostal nerves to the external intercostal muscles and diaphragm causing these muscles to contract to bring about inspiration. When stimulation ceases these muscles relax causing expiration.
- The **expiratory centre** is inactive during quiet breathing. However, during forceful breathing such as during exercise, the expiratory centre actively sends impulses to stimulate the muscles of expiration (sternocleidomastoid, scalenes, pectoralis major and minor) to increase the **rate of breathing** (refer to table 3.2 on page 51 to remind yourself of the mechanics of breathing).

Neural control of breathing (figure 3.12 page 56)

Two additional **brain centres** aid the control of breathing:

- The **apneustic centre** controls the intensity of breathing. It does this by prolonging the firing of the inspiratory neurones, thereby increasing **TV**.
- The **pneumotaxic centre** antagonises the apneustic centre, resulting in the fine-tuning of the breathing rate (**f**). The body exquisitely regulates the rate and depth of breathing in response to metabolic needs. Figure 3.12 page 56, lists the primary factors involved in ventilatory control. This is another example of **negative feedback control**, where, for example, an increase of carbon dioxide in venous blood tends to increase breathing rate which helps extract the carbon dioxide from pulmonary blood and reduce carbon dioxide in blood arriving back at the heart from the lungs.

Chemical control

The **chemical** state of the blood largely regulates pulmonary ventilation at rest.

- **Central chemoreceptors** (located in the medulla) are major regulators, and **respond to increased concentration of carbon dioxide in the blood**. The partial pressure of CO_2 is termed pCO_2, and this regulation process tries to keep pCO_2 to below 5.3 kPa as well as controlling increased acidity (or decreased pH due to H^+ ions from carbonic acid formed in the blood plasma).
- **Peripheral chemoreceptors** (in the aortic and carotid bodies) provide an early warning system as they sense the constituents of blood as it passes them.
- Both central and peripheral chemoreceptors respond to **increased** pCO_2 and **decreased** pH and pO_2 (oxygen concentration in the blood).

These receptors send messages to the inspiratory centre which then stimulates respiratory muscles to increase **rate** (**f**) and **depth of breathing** (**TV**) as described above. For example, lack of oxygen at high altitude stimulates respiration which has nothing to do with exercise, but indicates how these receptors work. This chemical control, via the pneumotaxic and apneustic centres of the brain, adjusts ventilation to maintain arterial blood chemistry within narrow limits. This means that these brain centres attempt to keep blood oxygen to a maximum, and blood carbon dioxide to a minimum by causing the person to adjust breathing rate and depth.

Proprioceptors in joints and muscles

Proprioceptors (such as working muscle spindles) send signals to the RCC about the tension within and state of contraction of a muscle, and hence when a muscle is being used intensely. During physical activity increased stimulation will increase rate and depth of breathing via the inspiratory centre as described above.

Lung stretch receptors

A type of **proprioceptor,** these lung receptors are located within the walls of bronchi and bronchioles. When stimulated these receptors relay information, via the vagus nerves, to the RCC to inhibit the inspiratory centre, resulting in expiration via the expiratory centre. As expiration proceeds, the stretch receptors are no longer stimulated and the decreased inhibitory effect on the inhibitory centre allows the inspiratory centre to become active again, known as the **Hering-Breuer Reflex**. Its overriding effect is to prevent over-inflation of the lungs.

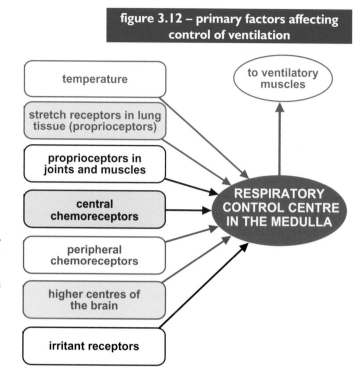

figure 3.12 – primary factors affecting control of ventilation

Temperature

Thermoreceptors (located in the hypothalamus region of the brain) respond to increases in body and blood temperatures. These receptors directly excite the neurones of the RCC and help control ventilation during prolonged exercise.

Irritant receptors

The activation of touch, thermal and pain receptors can also stimulate the RCC.

Higher centres of the brain

Through the **cerebral cortex** it is possible consciously to increase or decrease rate and depth of breathing. Swimmers and sports divers **hyperventilate** and **breath-hold** to improve physical performance. At the start of a swimming race athletes hyperventilate on the starting blocks to prolong breath-hold time during the swim. In short course racing, the breath-hold time can be the whole of the racing time. Snorkel divers hyperventilate to extend breath-hold time. During breath-hold time the pO_2 content of the blood can fall to critically low values before arterial pCO_2 increases to stimulate breathing.

Emotions acting through the limbic system can also affect the RCC.

Practice questions

1) When the inspiratory muscles contract, which one of the following statements is true?
   a. the size of the thoracic cavity increases in diameter.
   b. the size of the thoracic cavity increases in length.
   c. the volume of the thoracic cavity decreases.
   d. the size of the thoracic cavity increases in both length and diameter.

2) Which one of the following determines the direction of gas movement?
   a. solubility in water.
   b. partial pressure gradient.
   c. temperature.
   d. pH.

Practice questions

3) Which one of the following has the greatest stimulating effect on the respiratory centres in the brain?
   a. oxygen.
   b. carbon dioxide.
   c. calcium.
   d. willpower.

4) The maximum amount if air that can be expired after a maximum inspiration is called the:
   a. tidal volume (TV).
   b. expiratory reserve volume (ERV).
   c. vital capacity.
   d. minute ventilation.

5) During exercise, which one of the following statements is true?
   a. the arterial percent oxyhaemoglobin saturation is decreased.
   b. the venous percent oxyhaemoglobin saturation is decreased.
   c. the arterial pCO_2 is measurably increased.
   d. the arterial pH is measurably decreased.

6) Describe the structures involved in gaseous exchange in the lungs and explain how gaseous exchange occurs within this tissue.   6 marks

7) a) The diagram in figure 3.13 represents the lung volume changes based on a number of spirometer readings during various breathing actions. With reference to the trace, briefly explain resting tidal volume (TV), expiratory reserve volume (ERV), vital capacity (VC), and residual volume (RV).   4 marks

   b) Using the information in the spirometer trace, state what happens to the following volumes during the exercise period: residual volume, inspiratory volume (IRV), and expiratory volume (ERV).
                                  3 marks

   c) Why does tidal volume change by only a small amount during the exercise period?   3 marks

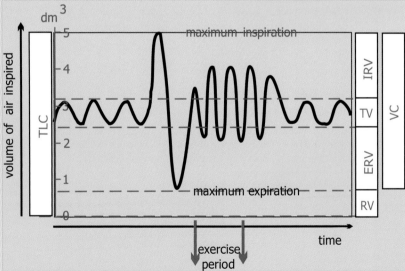

figure 3.13 – spirometer trace

Practice questions

8) A student measured the volume of air that he or she ventilated at rest and during submaximal exercise. The results are shown in table 3.4.

Table 3.4 – **ventilation at rest and during submaximal exercise**

activity level	inhalation volume	breathing rate	minute ventilation
	(TV)	**(f)**	**volume ($\dot{V}E$)**
at rest	500 ml	one every 6 seconds	**A**
submaximal exercise	800 ml	one every 2 seconds	**B**

Define what is meant by the term 'minute ventilation volume' and calculate the values for A and B, clearly showing the method used.

4 marks

9) The binding of oxygen to haemoglobin depends on pO_2 in the blood and the affinity of haemoglobin with oxygen. The curves in figure 3.14 show how different concentrations of carbon dioxide affect the saturation of haemoglobin at varying partial pressures of oxygen.

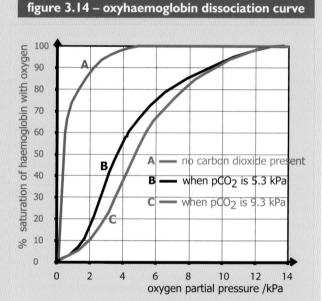

figure 3.14 – oxyhaemoglobin dissociation curve

a) Explain what is meant by partial pressure of oxygen (pO_2).

1 mark

b) What are the values of percentage saturation of haemoglobin on the three curves when the partial pressure of oxygen is 5.0 kPa?

3 marks

c) What are the implications of the carbon dioxide values for curves B and C for an athlete?

2 marks

d) Why is the partial pressure of oxygen (pO_2) important to the process of gaseous exchange?

3 marks

10) A hockey player has a match in one hour's time.
Describe how inspiration occurs during this resting period.
During the hockey match, the player must increase the volume of gas exchanged in the lungs and muscles. Explain the changes in the mechanics of breathing (inspiration and expiration) which facilitate this increase.

8 marks

11) A level. Describe the effect of exercise on pO_2, pCO_2 and pH and explain how ventilation might be increased during exercise.

20 marks

Answers link: http://www.jroscoe.co.uk/downloads/as_a1_revise_pe_ocr/OCRAS_A1_ch3_answers.pdf

EXERCISE PHYSIOLOGY

CHAPTER 4: Diet and Nutrition

A **balanced diet** is (figures 4.1 and 4.2) the combination and proportions of carbohydrates (CHO), fats, proteins, roughage, water and essential minerals and vitamins which best provide for a sportsperson's nutritional requirements. Table 4.1 gives the details of each food type and its contribution to life.

figure 4.1 – a balanced diet

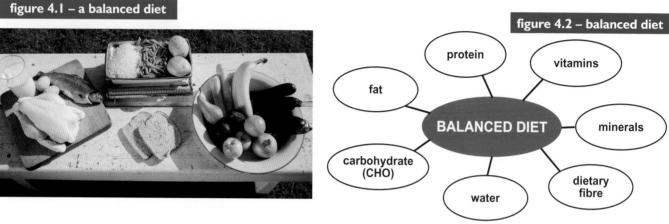

figure 4.2 – balanced diet

protein · vitamins · fat · BALANCED DIET · minerals · carbohydrate (CHO) · water · dietary fibre

Table 4.1 – **summary of dietary content**

type of food / sources	function as a food fuel - how it is used	energy content (kJ g⁻¹)	percentage in a balanced diet
carbohydrate (**CHO**) sugars, rice, potatoes, pasta	**main energy supply**, absorbed as glucose in small intestine, transported around body as blood glucose. available for immediate energy. excess stored as muscle and liver glycogen and as fat.	17	60 %
fats butter, oil, pastry, fried food	**secondary energy supply**, absorbed as fatty acids and glycerol in the small intestine, stored as triglycerides in adipose tissue. **triglycerides** conveyed to the liver via the circulatory system. in the liver they are converted to **glucose**, available as delayed (20 minutes delay) energy source for long duration low intensity **aerobic** exercise.	39	20-25 %
proteins meat, eggs, milk, cheese, nuts	absorbed as **amino acids** in the small intestine, used for growth and repair by all tissues. used as an energy source when body is depleted of CHO and fat. excess protein not needed for tissue repair is broken down and used as an energy supply.		10-15 %
vitamins	organic substances needed for crucial functions in almost all bodily functions. regulate metabolism and facilitate energy release. have important functions in bone formation and tissue synthesis.		small amounts essential.
minerals	**calcium** provides structure in bones and teeth. **iron** is needed for red blood cell production. **other minerals** assist in synthesising glycogen, fat and protein.		small amounts essential.
dietary fibre wholegrain cereals, vegetables	non-starch, structural polysaccharide including cellulose, only available from plant sources. gives **bulk** to food residues in the intestines. aids **gastrointestinal** functioning.		large amounts necessary 20 to 40 grams per day.
water	constitutes 72% of **muscle weight** and around 50% of adipose tissue, provides the body's transport and reactive medium. **transports** nutrients and leaves the body in urine and faeces. **lubricates** joints, keeping bony surfaces from grinding against each other. provides **structure** and form to the body, some sports drinks are designed to meet both energy and fluid needs of athletes.		large amounts necessary. up to 5 litres per day

Energy intake and expenditure

Energy balance in physical activity and performance.

Energy

In scientific terms, **energy** and **work** mean the same thing and so are interchangeable concepts. Energy is **the capacity or ability of a system to do work**, measured in **joules** or calories, where one calorie equates to 4.18 joules.

Metabolism involves all the chemical reactions of biomolecules within the human body that encompass synthesis (anabolism) and breakdown (catabolism).
Metabolic rate is the rate at which metabolism occurs.

Metabolic rates, energy expenditure

Resting metabolic rate (RMR) and Basal metabolic rate (BMR)

The **BMR** is the **least rate of energy usage** needed to carry out **basic body functions**, and would be measured while lying down after 8 hours sleep or 12 hours fasting.

Typical values for men and women at 20 years of age are:

* BMR_{male} = 100 kJ kg^{-1} per day BMR_{female} = 90 kJ kg^{-1} per day
* BMR_{male} = 0.069 kJ kg^{-1} min^{-1} BMR_{female} = 0.063 kJ kg^{-1} min^{-1}

Instead of BMR, most researchers now use the term **resting metabolic rate** (RMR) because most measurements follow the same conditions required for measuring BMR. Hence BMR and RMR values are essentially the same. RMR values are measured 3 to 4 hours following a light meal.

Establishing basal values provides the important energy baseline for constructing a sound programme of weight control by use of diet, exercise or the effective combination of both.

The **total daily energy expenditure (TDEE)** is determined by three major components:

*   **Resting metabolic rate** (RMR) - accounting for 60 - 75% of TDEE.
*   The **thermic effect of feeding** (TEF) - accounting for 10% of TDEE .
*   The **thermic effect of activity** (TEA).

The energy expended during and in recovery from physical activity above the resting state and accounts for between 15-30% of a person's TDEE.
World class athletes nearly double their TDEE with 3 or 4 hours of intense training.
Most people can sustain a metabolic rate 10 times their resting value during continuous 'big muscle' exercise such as fast walking, running, cycling and swimming.
Important factors that affect TDEE include physical activity, age, gender, climate, lifestyle, size and metabolic rate.
For example, cold environments increase energy metabolism during rest and exercise.

Therefore:
a person's **total daily energy expenditure (TDEE) = all energy requirements for activity + RMR + TEF**

Note that **all energy requirements for activity** includes the **TEA** as part of the **activity** and accounts for 15 - 30% of TDEE.

Table 4.2 – **metabolic rate contribution by different activities**

activity	energy expenditure (kJ kg^{-1} min^{-1}) over RMR
sitting at rest	0.10
walking	0.26
jogging and swimming (moderate)	0.6
cycling (moderate)	0.46
vigorous exercise	1.09

A typical TDEE example for a female athlete of mass 56 kg is set out in table 4.3.

Table 4.3 – **total daily energy calculation**

activity	duration of activity (minutes)	energy expenditure (kJ kg^{-1} min^{-1}) over RMR	total energy (kJ) for body mass
sitting at rest	480	0.10	2688
walking	230	0.26	3349
swimming	30	0.6	1008

+RMR	5080
+TEF	1213
total TDEE	13338

Metabolic equivalent task (MET) system

Exercise intensity can also be measured on the basis of the **MET system** in which it is assumed that the amount of oxygen the body consumes is directly proportional to the energy expended per kilogramme per minute.

The resting metabolic rate (as in sitting at rest) is referred as 1.0 MET. So an activity that is rated as a 2 MET activity (such as slow walking) would require double the resting metabolic rate or 7 millilitres of oxygen per kilogramme per minute (7 ml O$_2$ kg^{-1} min^{-1}). Moderate jogging or swimming requires 15 METs, and very vigorous exercise could be as much as 30 METs. Hence activity intensities can be classified by their oxygen requirements as multiples of the resting metabolic rate.

Although the MET system is a useful guideline for training, it fails to account for changes in environmental conditions or changes in physical conditioning.

The need for a balanced diet

The food pyramid shown in figure 4.3 illustrates the approximate proportions of the different food groups which should be consumed in a balanced diet.

The foods in the lower part of the pyramid should form the main part of a balanced diet, while those at the top should be eaten in smaller quantities.

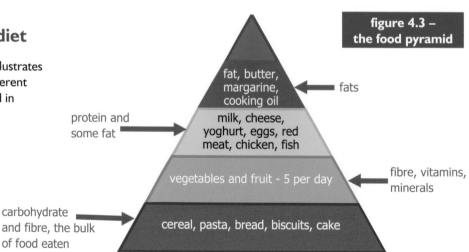

figure 4.3 – the food pyramid

fat, butter, margarine, cooking oil — fats

protein and some fat → milk, cheese, yoghurt, eggs, red meat, chicken, fish

vegetables and fruit - 5 per day — fibre, vitamins, minerals

carbohydrate and fibre, the bulk of food eaten → cereal, pasta, bread, biscuits, cake

Energy balance

When energy intake is equal to energy expenditure a **neutral energy balance** is achieved, as a result of which a person's weight remains constant. This concept can be expressed as:

ENERGY INTAKE = ENERGY EXPENDITURE

This means that there would be no tendency for this person to add adipose tissue to his or her body structure.

Positive energy balance

This definition of obesity highlights the major cause of obesity, namely an obese person would have energy intake far greater than energy expenditure, which would be the result of inactivity and too much dietary fat intake.

This relationship is expressed as:

ENERGY INTAKE > ENERGY EXPENDITURE

to create a **positive energy balance**, which means that more energy is eaten as food than energy is used via exercise.

Excess carbohydrate (CHO) from food is stored as glycogen. When glycogen stores are filled, CHO together with excess fat intake are converted to fatty acids and glycerol, and then are stored as triglycerides or **fat** in adipose tissue. This is situated around major organs such as the heart and stomach, underneath the skin, and in skeletal muscle. Upper body obesity poses the most significant risk to disease.

Excessive weight gain is associated with certain health conditions such as **coronary heart disease** and **hypertension** (high blood pressure) with an increased risk of mortality and morbidity.

Controlling obesity

The only method of controlling obesity is to shift the energy relationship so that energy output exceeds energy intake – known as a **negative energy balance** and expressed as:

ENERGY INTAKE < ENERGY EXPENDITURE

This means that more energy is used via exercise than is eaten as food.

Achieving optimal weight for activities

The following table 4.4 shows how the body fat content for people of various age groups depends on whether they are fit or not. The data takes us up to 40 years of age.

Table 4.4 – **example data of relative body fat values for untrained and trained males and females**

| | relative body fat (%) | | | |
| | untrained | | trained | |
age group	females	males	females	males
15-19	20-24	13-16	12-20	7-13
20-29	22-25	15-20	10-18	6-12
30-39	24-30	18-26	12-20	8-14

The achievement of optimal body mass will require manipulation of the **energy balance**. When energy input and output are balanced (**energy intake = energy expenditure**), an athlete's body mass will be stable, with no tendency to add to or subtract from stored adipose tissue.

Dietary requirements for exercise

Table 4.5 – **a comparison of daily energy intake for athletes**

activity	daily energy intake kJ – females	daily energy intake kJ – males
Tour de France		25000
triathlon	10000	20000
rowing	12600	14700
swimming	8400	15500
hockey	9200	13400
soccer	9600	14700
running	9200	13000
gymnastics	6000	9000
body building	5900	14500

figure 4.4 – endurance cyclists consume huge amounts of energy

Within rather broad bands, a balanced diet from a regular food intake provides the nutrient requirements for active individuals (as observed in the Food Pyramid figure 4.3 page 62). However, dietary requirements depend on the **intensity** and **duration** of the exercise period. This means developing a diet that is tailor-made to suit the needs of the individual.

Carbohydrate requirements

Glycogen is the most important and most valuable fuel stored in the body for any type of exercise. Physically active individuals should obtain between 60% and 70% of daily energy intake from carbohydrates – particularly unrefined, low glycemic foods such as fresh acidic fruits (apples, pears, oranges) and most vegetables.
The longer the duration of the activity, the greater the % of CHO intake.

In activity lasting longer than 90 minutes, as in the case of marathon running, dietary manipulation techniques, such as **carbo-loading**, will increase muscle glycogen stores to above normal levels. Carbo-loading is a process where extra carbohydrate is taken in after a short period of carbohydrate starvation.

For rapid carbohydrate **replenishment** after exercise, carbohydrate foods with a high **glycemic index** are recommended, for example, foods such as bananas, brown rice, pasta, raisins or wholemeal bread. Food should be eaten within two hours of completing the physical activity. This is because eating these foods will be more efficient in increasing blood glucose concentrations and hence stimulating the greater insulin release needed to convert glucose to glycogen.
Optimal glycogen replenishment will benefit individuals involved in regular intense physical activity, such as playing in tournaments that span over a period of days.

Protein requirements

Physically active individuals need more protein than inactive people do (between 1.2-1.4 grams per kg body mass per day). Additional protein intake is needed to compensate for increased muscle breakdown that occurs during and after intense exercise. Protein is also needed to build new muscle cells (known as muscle hypertrophy).

In strength and power-based activities, additional protein intake is recommended (between 1.4-1.8 grams per kg body mass per day).

Fat requirements

Fat intake should be restricted, unless additional body mass is required, for example, extreme performers such as sumo wrestlers. Unsaturated fats are preferable to saturated fats.

Vitamin and mineral requirements

Getting the right balance of vitamins and minerals can be sourced from the daily-recommended intake of fresh fruit and vegetables.

Table 4.6 – **summary of vitamins, food sources, major bodily and exercise related functions**

vitamin or mineral	food sources	major bodily functions	exercise related functions
vitamin C (ascorbic acid)	citrus fruits, tomatoes, green peppers, salad greens.	aids the formation of: hormones, bone tissue, collagen.	produces more bone mass, strengthens: cartilage, tendons, ligaments (collagen).
vitamin D	fatty fish, eggs, dairy produce, liver.	increases absorption of: calcium, phosphorous.	produces more bone mass to support body during physical activity.
vitamin B1 (thiamine) **vitamin B2 (riboflavin)** **vitamin B6 (pyridoxine)** **vitamin B12 (cobalamin)**	pork, organ meats, legumes, greens. avocados, yoghurt, eggs, meat, legumes. nuts, beans, fish, rice, liver. muscle meat, fish, eggs, dairy produce.	**all B complex group:** essential for the working of certain enzymes in the body. these vitamins play co-enzymes roles used in the breakdown of nutrients by binding the substrate with its specific enzyme.	protects immune system (stressed during exercise). assists carboloading for long duration aerobic activity. assists carboloading for long duration aerobic activity. assists carboloading for long duration aerobic activity. assists in aerobic and anaerobic exercise and recovery (EPOC).
sodium	common salt.	controls blood pressure and blood volume needed to enable muscles and nerves to work properly.	body water balance, acid-base balance, nerve function.
iron	liver, red meats, dark green vegetables.	constituent of haemoglobin and enzymes involved in energy metabolism. helps transfer oxygen in red blood cells.	important for anaerobic and aerobic (VO_{2max}) during exercise and recovery.
calcium	cheese, milk, dark green vegetables.	builds and maintains teeth and bones. important for active growing children, and important for elderly people.	weight bearing exercises. resistance exercises. reduce risk of osteoporosis.

Hydration and electrolyte balance

Fluid intake has almost become an obsession with modern sportsmen and women. Modern athletes frequently use **isotonic sports drinks**, such as Isostar and Red Bull, just prior to competition to maintain rehydration and alertness respectively.

Exercise is thirsty work. Fluid loss during exercise depends on the intensity and duration of the exercise, temperature and humidity, body size and fitness levels. The longer and more intense the exercise period, for example in a long distance race, the more the need to drink before, during and after the event.

Bearing in mind that water comprises 60% of total body mass, it is important that **water balance** is maintained during exercise. **At rest**, water loss occurs via evaporation from the skin (sweat) and excretion with the majority lost as urine. Water intake will depend on climate and body mass. The modern fashion of carrying water bottles for ready consumption reflects modern concerns about water balance.

Hydration during exercise

During exercise, more water is produced during tissue respiration along with heat energy as a by-product of the metabolic process. In order to prevent the body from heating up too much, water is transported to the skin where **sweating** occurs. The loss of water from the skin by **evaporation** causes the skin to fall in temperature, and hence reduces the effect of heat production in muscle. But far more water is lost as sweat than is produced by tissue respiration, the amount of sweat being determined by external temperature, body mass and metabolic rate. There is increased water loss via expired air due to increased breathing, but the kidneys decrease urine flow in an attempt to decrease dehydration. The total effect is that the body loses more water than is produced or retained, and this must be replaced if exercise is to continue at a maximal rate.

figure 4.5 – Paula Radcliffe could be taking in water throughout a marathon

Loss of water

- Also, the loss of water raises the osmotic pressure in body fluids because the electrolytes become more concentrated in these body fluids.
- The thirst mechanism does not exactly match the body's hydration state, so more fluid should be consumed than thirst dictates.
- Only by **replenishing water** content can the electrolytes return to normal concentrations.

In extreme exercise situations (for example during a marathon, figure 4.5) 6-10% of body water content is lost, hence the need for water intake during exercise. This means that during 1 hour's exercise an average person could expect to lose around 1 litre of fluid, and even more in hot conditions. This could represent as much as 2 litres an hour in warm or humid conditions.

Dehydration and loss of performance

Excessive loss of fluid impairs performance as blood plasmavolume decreases and body temperature rises. The graph in figure 4.6 shows how heart rate is affected by fluid intake during prolonged exercise.

Heart rate rise without fluid intake is explained earlier, but the graph also shows how heart rate is kept constant - if suitable water is taken during the exercise.

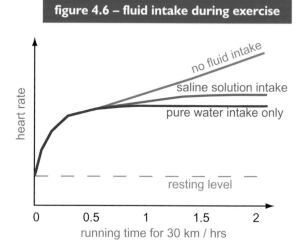

figure 4.6 – fluid intake during exercise

The potential benefits of sports drinks

Sports drinks are designed to supplement energy, fluid and protein needs of the athlete.

Hypotonic sports drinks are designed to quickly replace fluids lost through sweating as they are low in carbohydrates at around 4% glucose.

They are very popular with athletes who need fluid without the boost of carbohydrate.

Isotonic sport drinks contain concentrations of salt and glucose (between 5-7%) that match the same levels of concentration as in the blood.

Both hypotonic and isotonic sports drinks are an important source of energy during exercise as they reduce the risk of dehydration.

During recovery, hypertonic drinks contain much higher levels of glucose - up to 20%. This highly concentrated drink is used to replenish depleted glycogen stores and should be drunk as soon as the exercise period has been completed.

Ergogenic aids

An **ergogenic aid** is a performance enhancer, anything that gives a mental or physical edge whilst exercising or competing.

Figure 4.7 summarises the categories of illegal ergogenic aids used by sportspeople, as identified in the syllabus.

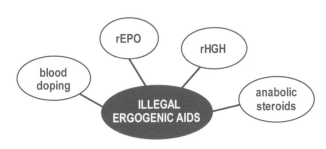

figure 4.7 – illegal ergogenic aids

WADA

The **World Anti-Doping Agency** (**WADA**) is the world body set up in 1998 tasked with enforcing the international regulations on doping or drug taking. WADA aims to bring together governments, the IOC, International Governing Bodies and National Governing Bodies (NGBs) to sort out the difficulties posed by athletes performing on the international stage.

This issue was brought to a head at the Athens Olympics in 2004, when two of the host nation's best athletes went missing just before the games and a compulsory drug test. These athletes faked a road accident and sought hospitalisation falsely in order to avoid taking the test. The same athletes had a record of going missing from international training venues just before the IAAF drug testers arrived - and even being found registered under false names in hotels so that their **whereabouts** could not be definitely fixed.

WADA has introduced the '**Athlete passport**' which contains an on-going collection of an individual's urine and blood profiles which have so far been collected and tested during the international athlete's performance lifespan. Samples are stored and then made available for retro-testing when appropriate. It is projected that future profile collection could include endocrine information.

Eight Russian athletes at London 2012 tested positive following retests in 2016. Many of these athletes were medal winners and so should be stripped of their medals. These athletes can appeal against bans through Human Rights Courts, and so disputes take a long time to resolve.

In the meantime **clean athletes** are waiting for medal upgrades and relevant prize money, and have lost out on opportunities of gaining commercial sponsorship as well as not experiencing the glory of a medal ceremony. They may even struggle to motivate themselves to continue to train and compete within the cheating global arena.

The impact of drug scandals on society is to question whether the performances of so many great athletes are cheat free.

Modern developments

The most insidious attempt by the cheaters is to use **gene doping** to enhance performance. Gene doping is defined by WADA as '**the non-therapeutic use of cells, genes, genetic elements, or of the modulation of gene expression, having the capacity to improve athletic performance**'.

For example, **Insulin-like growth factor 1** (IGF-1) is a protein that is important in promoting the growth of skeletal muscle. Injected into an athlete, a harmless virus, such as IGF-1, could carry a performance-enhancing gene and splice it into a muscle cell to increase muscle mass and achieve increased muscle hypertrophy.

Protein chemicals may be indistinguishable from their natural counterparts. In such cases, nothing unusual would enter the bloodstream so officials would detect nothing in a blood or urine test.

Almost all modern sportspeople use sports supplements (figure 4.15 page 72) as part of their diet. Such supplements are aimed at filling the gaps in diet caused by inappropriate dietary content, or at enhancing features of food or drink taken which would be required to enhance sporting requirements for such a diet.

Illegal ergogenic aids - doping

The following table 4.7 shows the ergogenic effects (benefits?) and risks associated with the different methods of doping.

Table 4.7– **the categories of illegal pharmacological and physiological substances used in top level sport today**

type of substance	known ergogenic effects	known health risks
rHGH (pharmacological aid) recombinant human growth hormone cloned through genetic engineering.	mimics body's naturally occurring hormone HGH produced by the pituitary gland which increases protein synthesis and lean muscle mass. stimulates bone growth. increases blood glucose levels. enhances healing after musculo-skeletal injuries. used by power athletes such as sprinters, weight lifters, American football players.	muscle joint weaknesses. acromegaly (giantism) causes bone thickening of hands, feet and jaws. causes glucose intolerance, diabetes, hypertension and heart disease. enlargement of internal organs.
anabolic steroids (pharmacological aid) related to naturally occurring hormone testosterone. example: THG. tetrahydrogestrinone stanazolol.	increases synthesis of protein within cells. increases fat free mass, strength and power for aggressive sports such as American football or wrestling. reduces recovery time between sessions. increases muscle strength and bulk, promotes aggressiveness.	excessive aggressive behaviour outside the activity. testicular atrophy in men. masculinisation in women. liver damage. cardiovascular diseases. causes acne. causes pituitary failure.
blood doping (physiological aid) refers to **any means** by which a person's total volume of red blood cells can be increased. often achieved by transfusion of red blood cells previously withdrawn from the recipient. **rEPO** (pharmacological aid) recombinant erythropoietin cloned through genetic engineering **is a form of blood doping.**	blood doping temporarily increases red blood cell count (polycythemia) and hence O_2 carriers, hence increases $\dot{V}O_{2max}$ and energy delivery to enhance aerobic performance. rEPO mimics body's naturally occurring hormone EPO that stimulates red blood cell production to increase oxygen transport and therefore increases aerobic capacity, hence aids recovery in endurance based activities such as long distance cycling (Tour-de-France) and marathon running.	problem of mismatching can lead to transfusion reaction or allergic reaction. also runs the risk of hepatitis or HIV pathogen. major risk of thrombosis (blood clot) and heart failure due to increase in blood viscosity. reduces resting heart rate to dangerously low level during sleep. taking rEPO reduces production of naturally occurring hormone EPO.

Legal ergogenic aids - intermittent hypoxic training - IHT

Hypoxic training is the practice of limiting oxygen availability while training.

Intermittent Hypoxic Training (IHT) is achieved by using aerobic and/or anaerobic interval training methods alternating between low oxygen air during the exercise period and normal air during rest relief. This is achieved by either using a mask attached to an altitude generator that adjusts to the required oxygen concentrations or training in an hypobaric chamber.

Although substantially different than sleeping and training at altitude, the goal of IHT is the same: improving athletic performance and/or acclimatization to high altitude.

Recent studies, typically limited to treadmill running or stationary cycling, indicate that intermittent hypoxic training at lactate threshold intensity and medium duration (30-40min) is an effective training means for improving aerobic capacity and endurance performance at sea level.
IHT training methods are used by distance runners, triathletes and endurance cyclists.

Living high, training low – hypobaric houses/tent/sleep masks

An athlete will live and sleep in a hypobaric house situated at sea level, and will train and exercise outside the chamber (at normal oxygen levels, and in his or her normal training environment). This has the effect of elevating EPO, red blood cell levels (hence haemoglobin), myoglobin, mitochondria and oxidative enzymes in a similar way to altitude training.

A more recent development is the **hypoxic tent** (figure 4.8) or the **hypoxic sleep mask**. This is a less expensive system in which a tent or sleep mask is infused with low oxygen air (extra nitrogen infused) but at normal sea-level pressures. Hence a sportsperson can sleep in a tent and gain hypoxic adaptations while asleep.

figure 4.8 – a hypoxic tent - sleep high, train low!

Legal ergogenic aids - cooling aids

Cold therapies (**cryotherapy**) are popular ergogenic aids for cooling core body temperatures. They reduce the effect of delayed onset of muscle soreness (DOMS) and are well established in the treatment of acute sports injuries.

The value of **cold therapy** lies in its ability to decrease cellular metabolism, reduce inflammation, swelling and pain, and promote vasoconstriction. Cold packs do this by absorbing heat from the injury. The more heat absorbed, the faster the pain relief and healing. Cooling aids are very cheap to buy and easy to use, and do make a big difference to sports performances in terms of preventing overheating, dehydration, cramp and early fatigue. There are a variety of cooling aids available ranging from ice jackets, wet ice packs, ice gels and chemical packs.

figure 4.9 – use of ice jackets in a competitive situation

Ice or cooling jackets

Cooling jackets (packed with ice or chemical coolants) are used to attempt to reduce the core temperatures of sports participants in very hot conditions. For example, the Australian rowing eight in the Atlanta Olympic Games 1996 as shown in figure 4.9.

Wet-ice packs

Water is a much better conductor of heat energy than air or plastic. By being wet, the wet-ice pack allows for greater heat energy transfer out of the body compared to gel or chemical packs. For example, tennis players use wet-ice packed towels during match intervals in long hot matches.

figure 4.10 – are ice baths fun?

Ice baths

Ice baths (figure 4.10) use the fact that **chilling** the affected area can **reduce local inflammation**. The ice bath is thought to constrict blood vessels, flush waste products such as lactic acid and reduce swelling and tissue breakdown.

Athletes use total immersion ice baths or cryogenic chambers to implement this therapy. The use of ice baths is very popular during the recovery phase of a training session as it assists in the removal of lactic acid (DOMS) and aids the healing process of damaged tissue.

Precautions should be taken because prolonged application (immersion) at very low temperatures could initiate frostbite!

Ice therapy and injury

The use of **cold therapy** in acute sports injuries as well as in rehabilitation of the injured athlete and injury prevention has become a generally accepted treatment method. Various cooling methods that are adjustable and compress the injured area are recommended.

Research has shown that the impact of injury is substantially reduced by the use of cold therapies. The sooner the cold therapy is used following injury, the more effective the therapy. The use of ice packs, ice towels, ice massage, frozen gel packs and ice baths are just a few examples of cold therapies that are used in acute sports injury treatments.

Nutritional aids

When and what should you eat before an exercise period?

* Food should be eaten between 3-4 hours prior to the competition so that it is well digested and absorbed into the bloodstream.
* The meal needs to be high in carbohydrates, low in fat and moderate in fibre to aid the digestive process.
* An example meal could be pasta bake with spinach, a banana and a still flavoured drink.

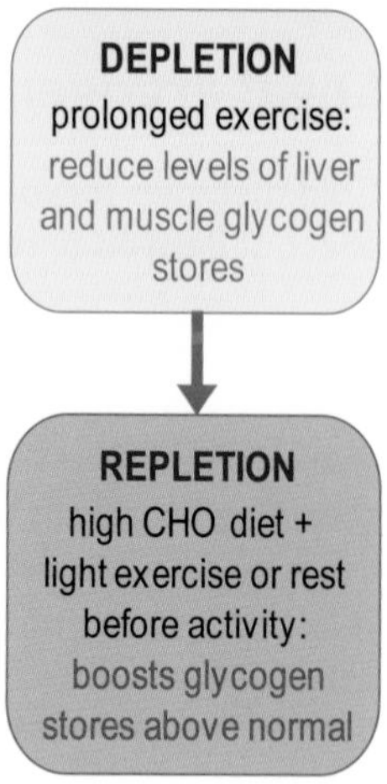

Glycogen - carbohydrate loading (known as carbo-loading)

Carbo-loading aims to raise muscle glycogen stores above their normal resting levels prior to endurance competitions with over 90 minutes continuous activity. This process is suitable for activities with low anaerobic and high aerobic components.

Figure 4.11 outlines the **depletion-repletion** model upon which carbo-loading is based. It is suitable for any activities lasting longer than 15-20 minutes. Note that a two-day high CHO diet beforehand provides the best CHO boost for an endurance event.

> **figure 4.11 –**
> **carboloading**
>
> **DEPLETION**
> prolonged exercise:
> reduce levels of liver
> and muscle glycogen
> stores
>
> ↓
>
> **REPLETION**
> high CHO diet +
> light exercise or rest
> before activity:
> boosts glycogen
> stores above normal

Carbo-loading - glycogen supercompensation

The graph in figure 4.12 shows how the muscle glycogen level returns to above normal values when the **depletion-repletion** process is undertaken as outlined in the previous paragraph. In effect the body reacts to a loss of glycogen by vigorously replacing it to a level above normal. This is a normal reaction to **biological stress**.

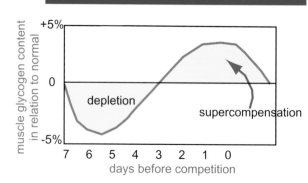

figure 4.12 – glycogen supercompensation

Composition and timing of meals

Pre-competition nutrition

Should consist of:
* Fluids for hydration.
* Light complex CHO such as pasta or wholemeal bread at least 3 hours before activity.
* Fruit (banana) contains complex CHO.
* Small amounts of glucose.

The effect is to provide the slow release of blood glucose and reduce hunger sensations.

Post-competition or training nutrition

Should consist of:
* **Hypertonic** sports drink immediately after exercise has finished.
* This begins **replenishment of blood glucose** and **glycogen** stores.
* A **high CHO** meal within 15 minutes of exercise ending (or as soon as possible) continues glycogen replenishment.

Caffeine

- Consuming caffeine before prolonged exercise increases fat metabolism thus sparing precious glycogen reserves for later.
- Caffeine produces a state of **nervousness**, and can disrupt normal sleeping patterns therefore contributing to fatigue.
- Abrupt ceasing of caffeine intake can lead to severe headaches.

Bicarbonate use

- **Bicarbonate loading** is a process whereby a performer ingests bicarbonate prior to a competition.
- An athlete can increase plasma bicarbonate levels that provide additional alkaline content in the body mass, thus allowing higher concentrations of lactic acid in the blood.
- Theoretically, this could delay the onset of fatigue in all-out anaerobic activity such as a 400 metre race.
- Bicarbonate loading can cause cramping, vomiting, bloating and diarrhoea.

Potassium nitrate as a supplement

This substance is a natural constituent of beet (beet juice), and has been linked to improvement in endurance athlete' performance.

This applies to runners running further than 5k, to long distance cyclists and to triathlon athletes.

Results of trials are mixed, very little effect is found in elite athletes – probably because they already have the effects produced by extensive training linked to nitrate in a diet - but in medium athletes nitrates have a positive effect on performance.

figure 4.16 – whey protein

Protein supplementation

Many athletes regularly consume sports drinks that are designed to supplement the energy, fluid and protein needs of the athlete. Protein supplements, such as **whey protein** (figure 4.16), are used to increase total protein content of an athletic diet. Sportspeople need more protein than the untrained person to enable muscle hypertrophy and muscle repair following hard training. This particularly applies to sports requiring large muscle mass, as in weight lifting and gymnastics.

Within the section on the Athlete's diet on page 72, a protein shake is recommended as an important protein supplement for a female 800m athlete, particularly following a high intensity training session.

- A controversial area of research is whether there is need for protein supplementation. This is particularly if the athlete is already consuming a balanced diet that meets all his or her nutritional requirements. If this is the case, protein supplementation becomes a very expensive form of energy food.
- Most protein supplements are legal, but can cause liver and kidney damage if taken in excess.
- **Glutamine** is an **amino acid** forming part of **skeletal muscle** and **immune cells**. Supplementation after exercise therefore reinforces the immune system and **reduces the risk of infection** and therefore enhances the process of glycogen synthesis in recovering muscles. Glutamine supplementation is widely used by athletes.

Practice questions

1) Complex carbohydrates do not include:
   a. lipids.
   b. triglycerides.
   c. cholesterol.
   d. haemoglobin.

2) A measure of the energy value in food is:
   a. the resting metabolic rate (RMR).
   b. a joule.
   c. the recommended daily allowance (RDA).
   d. a vitamin.

3) Which one of the following statements is false with respect to the functions of water within the human body?
   a. lubricates joints, keeping body surfaces from grinding against each other.
   b. constitutes 70 percent of muscle weight.
   c. fluid loss during exercise depends on the intensity and duration of the exercise, temperature and humidity, body size and fitness levels.
   d. the major water loss during moderate exercise is as vapour via the respiratory system.

4) For endurance trained athletes, the best carbohydrate strategy for a competition in a marathon or endurance triathlon appears to be:
   a. to consume carbohydrate 3-4 hours prior to the event.
   b. to consume carbohydrate within an hour of the event.
   c. to consume carbohydrate during the event.
   d. all of the above.

5) An expected side effect of creatine supplementation is:
   a. cramping and gain in body mass.
   b. reduction in power output.
   c. muscle weakness.
   d. all of these.

6) Figure 4.17 shows the daily energy intake (kjoules) of elite male and female endurance, strength and team sport athletes.

   a) Account for the differences in the daily intake for males and females.   2 marks

   b) Give reasons why cyclists competing in the Tour de France require a daily intake of up to 25000 kjoules.   3 marks

   c) Why do female body builders have the lowest daily energy intake compared with other female sportspeople?   2 marks

   d) How can a negative energy balance ultimately compromise an athlete's potential to train and compete?   3 marks

7) The ideal precompetition meal should maximise muscle and liver glycogen storage and provide glucose for intestinal absorption during exercise. How can these goals be achieved?   4 marks

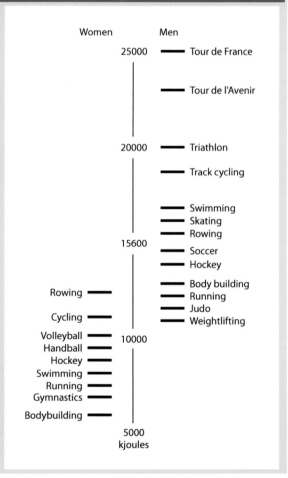

figure 4.17 – daily energy intake for elite athletes

Practice questions

8) An athlete is competing in a decathlon (consisting of 10 track and field events) over a period of two days.

    a) What nutritional advice would you give this athlete during and between the events in order to achieve an optimal performance.   **6 marks**

    b) At the end of day one, how could this athlete replenish his glycogen reserves?   **4 marks**

9) Different classification systems rate the strenuousness of physical activities. How are multiples of resting metabolism, known as metabolic equivalent task (MET) system used to assess energy expenditure associated with differing physical activities intensities?   **3 marks**

10) Identify some of the benefits of taking commercially prepared liquid meals.   **3 marks**

11) Table 4.9 provides information on exercise intensity and duration. Information on the appropriate fuel foods for action has been omitted.

Table 4.9 – **fuel and exercise**

exercise intensity	exercise duration	fuel used
maximal sprint	**short**	
low to moderate	**moderate - up to 2 hours, eg jogging**	
severe	**prolonged - eg cycling**	

    a) Complete the third column to show which fuel foods supply the glycogen needed as exercise intensity and duration change.   **3 marks**

    b) Why is carbohydrate a much faster fuel (energy) source when compared with fat utilisation?   **2 marks**

    c) Although fat reserves have value as a source of energy, in other ways they can be detrimental to sport performance. Discuss.   **6 marks**

12) What are the benefits of adding a small amount of sodium to a rehydration beverage?   **2 marks**

13) Why is water considered an important nutrient to the human body, and why might a person who is exercising need extra amounts of it?   **4 marks**

14) a) Discuss how a balanced diet could be manipulated to increase an athlete's glucose reserves prior to a marathon race.   **6 marks**

    b) Carbohydrates are used as an energy source during both aerobic and anaerobic conditions. It is therefore beneficial that an elite athlete's stores of carbohydrate are at a maximum before competition day. Discuss the advantages and disadvantages of glycogen loading.   **4 marks**

    c) How can an athlete's diet aid the recovery process?   **2 marks**

15) Give a brief outline and comment upon the following techniques, which may be employed in the belief that they will enhance sport performance:

    a)   Whey protein.
    b)   Potassium nitrate.
    c)   Bicarbonate loading.
    d)   Caffeine.   **12 marks**

Practice questions

16) What is an ergogenic aid? Discuss the role which nutritional supplements play in improving performance.   10 marks

17) The dietary requirements of a power athlete and an endurance-based athlete have similarities and differences. Discuss.   8 marks

18) How can an elite athlete assess whether his or her diet meets the demands of their training and competitive programmes?   4 marks

19) Critically evaluate the effects of legal physiological ergogenic aids that an elite performer could benefit from using.   10 marks

20) Cryotherapy methods are used as aids to recovery and rehabilitation for the elite performer. Briefly describe how an ice bath can assist this process.   3 marks

21) Briefly describe an illegal ergogenic aid that would be of benefit to an a endurance athlete. How would the use of this aid help performance? What are the health risks and how is this aid detected?   10 marks

Answers link: http://www.jroscoe.co.uk/downloads/as_a1_revise_pe_ocr/OCRAS_A1_ch4_answers.pdf

CHAPTER 5: *Training methods and aerobic training*

Training methods

As listed in figure 5.1 there are several different types of training that can be used to improve fitness levels. Each type is summarised in table 5.1 on page 79, with examples of sessions and advantages and disadvantages of the different methods.

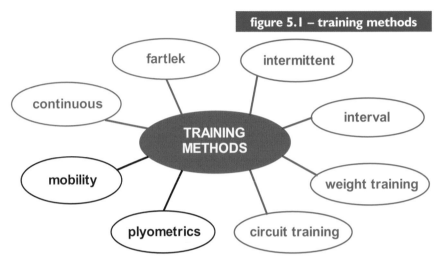

figure 5.1 – training methods

Continuous training

Involves continuous activity in which there is **no rest or break** and is normally associated with developing **aerobic capacity** ($\dot{V}O_{2max}$).

The **duration** of the training session should be at least 20 minutes and upwards. Adjusting the pace or effort of the activity can vary the exercise **intensity** (recommended between 60-75% of maximum heart rate) from long, slow distance training to high-intensity endurance training. **Frequency** of sessions should be at least 3 times per week to benefit from aerobic adaptations.

Fartlek

Fartlek or speed play is a form of continuous training during which the **speed or intensity of the activity is varied** so that both aerobic and anaerobic energy systems and recovery can be stressed.

Intermittent or interval training

This type of training is characterised by periods of **alternating exercise** and **rest**, providing a very versatile training method that enables the individual to perform considerably more work and with greater physiological benefits.

Variables include:
- **Duration** of the exercise period.
- **Intensity** of the exercise period.
- Number of **repetitions** within a set.
- Number of **sets** within a session.
- Duration of the rest intervals (rest relief) or **recovery**.

The exercise **type** and **loading**, number of **repetitions** and **sets**, and length of **rest relief** govern the **adaptive response** produced, thus enabling the individual to select the required intensity of work to stress the relevant energy system:
- **ATP-PC intervals** are characterised by high intensity effort (80-100% of maximum effort) lasting between 3-10 seconds and no more than 2 minutes recovery. Increases ATP-PC stores.
- **Lactic acid intervals** are characterised by medium to high intensity effort (60-80% of maximum effort) lasting between 15-90 seconds with variable recovery depending on exercise duration. Increases blood buffering capacity or increased lactate tolerance.
- **Aerobic intervals** are characterised by low intensity effort (below 50% of maximum effort) lasting beyond 20 minutes with short recovery. Increases aerobic capacity or $\dot{V}O_{2max}$.

High intensity interval training (HIIT)

This type of interval training involves repeated bouts of high intensity training followed by a varied **recovery** time. **Duration** of work periods may range from 5 seconds to 8 minutes long and are performed at an **intensity** of between **80% to 95% of HRmax**.

Repetitions and **sets** are created depending on the intensity and duration of the exercise period. **Recovery** periods are performed at an intensity of between **40% to 50% of HRmax**.

Exercise continues with alternating work and a **1:1 rest relief ratio**.
HIIT benefits both aerobic and anaerobic fitness, blood pressure, cholesterol profiles and body fat whilst increasing muscle mass. The completion of Physical Activity Readiness Questionnaire (**PAR-Q**) is a sensible first step for participants who are planning to increase their levels of physical activity.

Weight training

Weight training is a form of interval training and can be used to develop or stress several components of fitness such as strength and strength endurance depending on the resistance, number of repetitions, sets and rest relief. (see table 5.1 page 79).

Exercises are normally classed in four groups:
- **Shoulders and arms**: bench press, pull downs, curls.
- **Trunk and back**: back hyperextensions, sit ups.
- **Legs**: squats, leg press, calf raises.
- **All-body exercises**: power clean, snatch, dead lift.

Circuit training

A type of interval training that provides all-round body fitness, characterised by a number of exercises or stations performed in succession so that different body parts are exercised successively. The training is normally organised to work for a set time period at each station.

Plyometric training

A type of power training **involving eccentric-to-concentric actions at 100% effort** designed to improve elastic strength and power.
Plyometric leg training occurs when, on landing, the muscle performs an eccentric contraction (lengthens under tension) performed quickly so that the loaded agonist muscle stretches slightly prior to concentric action. This stimulates adaptation within the neuromuscular system as muscle spindles cause a **stretch reflex** to produce a more powerful concentric muscle contraction. The throwing and catching of medicine balls is a way of developing elastic shoulder strength.

In figure 5.2, two athletes are throwing a medicine ball back and forth. The catch phase of this movement is eccentric for the trunk musculature and the shoulders, with the throw movement being concentric in the same muscle groups. Normally this exercise is done too slowly to activate the stretch reflex, but a rapid rebound movement could have the desired effect.

figure 5.2 – catch and throw as eccentric then concentric exercise – similar to plyometrics

Table 5.1 – **training methods examples, advantages and disadvantages**

training method	examples	advantages	disadvantages
continuous training	alternative activities: 30 km bike ride. 3 km run. 30 minute swim.	trains cardiovascular and muscular endurance, needs no specialist equipment, highly suitable for fat burning metabolism / weight loss, time efficient. can be sport-specific, can be assessed using methods such as the Borg scale and exercising heart rate, less chance of injury because of lower intensity workloads.	can lead to tedium. may not be sport-specific, for example usefulness for fencers?
fartlek	continuous activity: 10 minutes jogging. 6 x 20 seconds fast striding with 60 seconds walk recovery. 5 minutes jogging. 2 uphill runs, jog down recovery. 5 minutes jogging.	beneficial to games players where the demands of the game are constantly changing. develops both aerobic and anaerobic capacities.	
intermittent / interval training	endurance interval training for a 5000m runner: session 1: 4 x 1500m @ 80% pace with 5 min rest relief (recovery period). session 2: 20 x 400m in 65 seconds (s) with 20 s rest relief. session 3: 3 x (8 x 200m) with 30 s rest relief between reps and 5 min rest relief between sets.	versatile training method since it can be used in almost any activity (sport specific). effective in establishing levels of required fitness for both anaerobic and aerobic activities. individual able to perform more work during session due to rest periods or intervals between sets.	can lead to over-training and chronic injury (chronic repetitive trauma), because of the repetitive nature and higher training intensity. takes more time to complete session because of rest periods.
weight training	example: athlete selects 2 exercises from each group, (shoulders & arms / trunk & back / legs / all body) working at 85% of 1RM. 4 sets of 5 repetitions 2 minutes recovery / rest relief between sets. this session stresses the ATP-PC energy system & so will enhance the ATP muscle stores and create **muscle hypertrophy**.	can be sport-specific. trains cardiovascular, muscular strength and strength endurance. easy to measure improvements from previous sessions.	needs access to equipment. issues of safety using equipment. can cause chronic injuries through repetitive impact.
circuit training	8 station circuit: each circuit performed 3 times: star jumps, rope climb, v-sit-ups, alternate dumbbell press, shuttle runs, chinnies, step ups, bench dips. performer works for 60 seconds at each station on 1st circuit, 30 seconds at each station on 2nd circuit and 15 seconds at each station on final circuit.	can be sport specific. trains cardiovascular, muscular strength and strength endurance. enables a large number of participants to train together. easy to measure improvements from previous sessions – for example counting the number of repetitions achieved in the time period. time efficient.	needs access to equipment. can cause chronic injuries through repetitive impact.
plyometrics	jumping example: depth jumping from a box and rebounding quickly from impact point, 2 foot bounds over a flight of hurdles, bounding exercises. 3-5 sets of 3-10 repetitions with medium recovery (1-3 minutes).	maximises muscular development by improving power / elastic strength. can be very sport specific, for example in explosive take-off as when jumping and bounding in events such as triple jumping.	because of the repetitive nature, can cause chronic repetitive trauma injuries such as achilles tendinosis, patellar tendinosis and shin splints. because of vigorous nature of exercise, can cause acute injuries such as sudden ruptures of muscle, tendons and ligaments particularly to vulnerable knee and ankle joints (such as a sprained ankle).
mobility or flexibility training	dedicated session after intense specific training session: choose 10 exercises covering all joints / body areas. 4 sets of 10 seconds hold at each exercise.	helps prevent potential injury. sport specific mobility training can improve performance, for example extreme spinal flexibility is needed by elite high jumpers when performing the flight phase of the fosbury flop, or elite gymnasts performing floor or beam moves.	can lead to hyper-flexibility and reduce effectiveness of muscle strength. extreme range of motion isn't necessary in many sports activities – how flexible must long distance runners be? since they don't raise their knees very high or extend their hips very far!

Plyometric training

In figure 5.3, the athlete is performing two-footed jumping (bunny jumps), which would have to be performed quickly to activate the stretch reflex in time with the concentric phase of the jump.

figure 5.3 – bounding and jumping can be plyometric

Flexibility training

Flexibility or mobility training is discussed in detail under the heading of flexibility and stretching on page 97 onwards.

The aim of this type of training is to improve (or maintain) the range of motion over which muscles can act and joints can operate (figure 5.4). This works on the **stress-overload principle** by forcing the contractile tissues such as muscle tissue to operate at full stretch. Mobility work is best done at the end of an anaerobic training session, during cool-down. This is because the muscular system is usually more relaxed at this time, with muscle temperatures slightly higher than during the warm-up.

figure 5.4 – mobility training is essential

Principles of training

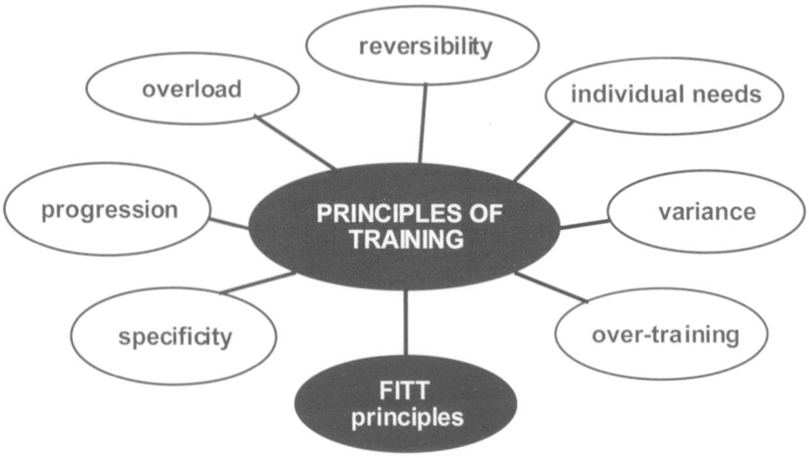

The aims and objectives of training are to improve performance, skill, game ability and motor and physical fitness. Repeated days of training can be considered as positive stress because training improves one's capacity for energy production, tolerance of physical stress and exercise performance. A well-designed training programme follows a set of guidelines called '**principles of training**' (figure 5.5).

figure 5.5 – principles of training

reversibility

overload

individual needs

progression

PRINCIPLES OF TRAINING

variance

specificity

over-training

FITT principles

Specificity

Specificity is defined as '**the relevance of the choice of exercise to the activity to be improved**'.

Choices to be made involve energy demands, strength, power, endurance and skill. This notion is thought to be very important for high performance in a chosen sport. For example, the shot put event requires speed and power developed by stressing the ATP-PC anaerobic energy system. So, in order to put the shot successfully, the shot putter needs to work on explosive muscular power in training. Hence the training programme must **stress** the **physiological systems** that are critical for optimal performance in the given sport in order to achieve the required specific training adaptations. Similarly, the marathon runner requires endurance which must be obtained by stressing the aerobic energy system. Hence his or her training programme must be largely based on lengthy endurance-based runs.

Overload

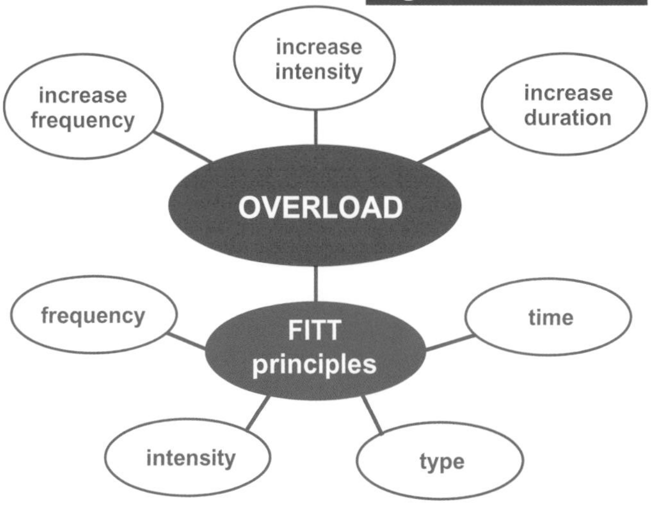

Overload is defined as '**training activities that are harder, more intense and or lengthier than the normal physical activity undertaken by an individual**'.

Overload can be achieved (figure 5.6) by increasing the frequency, intensity or duration of the activity. These terms are also referred to using the acronym '**FITT principles**' described below. Overload places physiological systems under **stress** and the human body responds by becoming more capable of coping with this stress (figures 5.7 and 5.8). This training principle applies to muscular endurance as well as to strength and power training.

The major variables used for increasing or decreasing intensity are:

- Sets.
- Repetitions
- Resistance.
- Rest relief or recovery period.

For example, an athlete performs bench press: 5 sets of 6 repetitions at 85% of 1RM (one repetition maximum as described above on page 79), and 2 minutes recovery between sets. This exercise would stress the anaerobic fast twitch fibres type IIb of the muscles: anterior deltoid, pectoralis major and triceps brachii.

figure 5.6 – overload

increase intensity

increase frequency

increase duration

OVERLOAD

frequency

time

FITT principles

intensity

type

figure 5.7 – athlete wins a marathon

FITT principles of training

F (frequency) = how often do we train? How often we train will determine the physiological adaptations achieved. For example, the elite professional sportsperson may be required to train twice a day and thereby achieve optimal physiological adaptations and improvements in performance. On the other hand, a person who just wants to stay fit by attending three aerobic classes a week at their local leisure centre, may notice minor physiological changes such as easier breathing and less tendency to be out of breath when digging the garden.

I (intensity) = how hard do we train? For the elite athlete, training intensity will vary depending on the training emphasis in relation to the periodised year. **Periodisation** is a concept centred around a cyclical load design principle. In this case the training intensity is increased and decreased according to a set pattern, the first two weeks of a cycle may be easy, and the last two weeks very hard. As a general rule, the closer to the competitive phase the harder the workouts. The person who just wants to keep fit for everyday living may be content with 3 exercise bouts (walking, swimming or cycling) per week for about 30 minutes each at a level at which he or she can hold a conversation with a training partner.

T (type) = what type of training do we do? Type of training relates to the principle of specificity above. Types of training include:
- Continuous.
- Intermittent.
- Circuit.
- Weights.
- Plyometrics.
- Mobility.

(see page 77 and onwards for explanations of these and other types of training)

figure 5.8 – recreational cyclist on a 40 min ride

T (time) = how long do we train for or what is the duration of the activity? The intensity of training and exercise type often determines the duration of the activity. For example an aerobic, bodyweight reducing training programme should last for a minimum 30 minutes because of the time it takes for fat burning metabolism to commence. A plyometric workout may only last for 10 minutes before fatigue sets in, whereas an ultra distance runner may be unlimited by time during a long-distance run.

Progression

Progression is defined as '**a state of moving onwards, which implies an increase in training load as time goes on**'.

The principle of progression involves the gradual application of the overload principle. It should be noted that progression could occur without overload, but that if overload does not happen, then the necessary adaptations to body systems such as the muscular system cannot be made. Such adaptations would normally cause improvement in (for example) endurance or strength.

The key point about progression is that the sportsperson should be performing at a higher level after the training period than before. In figure 5.9, progression is steady and over a period of eight months, training intensity increases, and hopefully overload is sufficient to provide long-term adaptations which would lead to improved performance. In figure 5.10, training intensity progresses much steeper than in figure 5.9 for a month before dropping down to a level above the previous starting point.

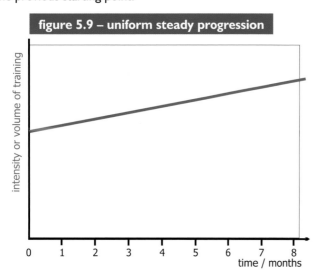

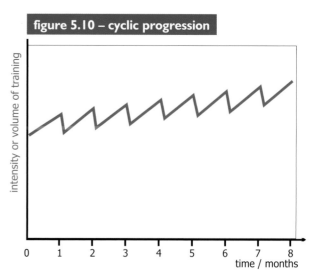

Then training intensity progresses again for another month and so on. The outcome is a cyclic progression with a bigger overload (than steady slow progression) at the end of each cycle.

Over-training

Over-training is explained as '**when the intensity of training and or volume of training are increased to extreme levels, and there is a lack of recovery within or between training sessions leading to an associated decline in physiological function**'. This situation can lead to extreme **muscle fatigue** and **loss of performance**.

Successful training programmes will include **moderation**, which implies that note is taken of the sportsperson's state of physical health, and when signs of deteriorating performance are detected, training loads will be reduced and recovery times increased until feelings of tiredness are reduced.

Individual needs

Every athlete is different and so each of the elements shown in figure 5.5 (page 80) needs to be tailor-made to meet his or her individual needs. This is linked to the specific nature of choice of sport (whether or not the sport demands anaerobic or aerobic activity), the age and gender of the performer and so-on.

Reversibility

Reversibility is also known as **regression** and is defined as '**when training loads are reduced or removed completely, the state of fitness or performance returns to a normal untrained state**'. This is often summed up as '**use it or lose it**'.

Reversibility

This principle explains why performance deteriorates when training stops or intensity of training is reduced. With reversibility, physiological systems revert or **regress** to their normal untrained state eventually. This will not happen immediately, but research has shown that the process begins within 5 days of ceasing training. Interestingly, it is found that adaptations established by longer periods of training remain for longer after training stops, than those produced by a short period of training. In figure 5.11, training and performance are improving up to the fourth month of the period shown. At this point, a minor injury occurs, and the sportsperson cannot train for the following four months. During this second four month period, performance falls as fitness and strength falls.

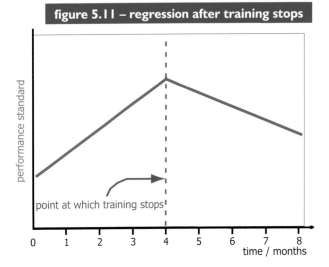

figure 5.11 – regression after training stops

point at which training stops

Variance

Training exercises, drills, or games which are **the same** (with the same outcomes and feelings) week in and week out, will eventually result in a lowering of motivation as the feelings of mastery of the activity are reduced. In other words, the person becomes used to the outcomes of the activity and his or her drive to continue with the same activity reduces.

Tedium is defined as '**training that lacks variety and causes boredom**'. This can be overcome by setting goals for sessions which **vary** (even though the activity itself may be the same), or by completely changing the activity while retaining the same goals (for example goals to improve strength or endurance).

Changing activities in training with the specific aim of reducing tedium is called **variance**, and is a crucial feature of a successful training programme.

Aerobic training

Aerobic capacity is the **ability of the body to inspire, transport and utilise oxygen to perform sustained periods of aerobic activity**. This component is also known as **cardio-respiratory** or **cardiovascular endurance** or **stamina**,

- Aerobic endurance involves the ability of the cardiovascular and respiratory systems to take in and transport oxygen to large muscle groups working dynamically.
- Aerobic endurance (figure 5.12) enables moderate to high intensity exercise to be undertaken for prolonged periods of time as in the case of marathon running.

figure 5.12 – an endurance athlete keeps going for a long time

Oxygen uptake - $\dot{V}O_2$

Oxygen uptake is the amount of oxygen consumed per unit of time (usually 1 minute), it is expressed as $\dot{V}O_2$, and its mean value of $\dot{V}O_2$ at rest = 0.2 to 0.3 litres min^{-1}.

- $\dot{V}O_2$ increases proportionally to work intensity, figure 5.13 (page 84) up to a maximum value - called $\dot{V}O_{2max}$.
- $\dot{V}O_{2max}$ represents the maximum amount of oxygen that can be taken in, transported and consumed by working muscle per minute. Aerobic capacity, aerobic power and maximal oxygen uptake are all terms used interchangeably with $\dot{V}O_{2max}$.
- Because individuals' energy requirements vary with body size, $\dot{V}O_{2max}$ is generally expressed relative to body mass in millilitres of oxygen per kilogram of body weight (ml kg^{-1}min^{-1}). This allows a more accurate comparison of different sized individuals.
- You can see from figure 5.13 (page 84) that $\dot{V}O_{2max}$ is bigger for trained athletes. This is an adaptation produced by aerobic training, which means that the athlete can work harder for longer.
- $\dot{V}O_{2max}$ is therefore a key component of aerobic endurance and is called **aerobic capacity (or aerobic power or maximum oxygen uptake)**, and so represents an accurate indicator of an athlete's fitness.

Values for oxygen uptake - $\dot{V}O_2$

$\dot{V}O_{2max}$ mean values are:

males (20 yo)	= 3.5 litres min⁻¹	
	= 40 ml kg⁻¹ min⁻¹ (for average male body mass 87.5 kg)	
females (20 yo)	= 2.3 litres min⁻¹	
	= 35 ml kg⁻¹ min⁻¹ (for mean female body mass 66 kg)	
endurance athletes	= 4 to 6 litres min⁻¹	
	= 60 to 90 ml kg⁻¹ min⁻¹ (for mean body mass 66 kg).	

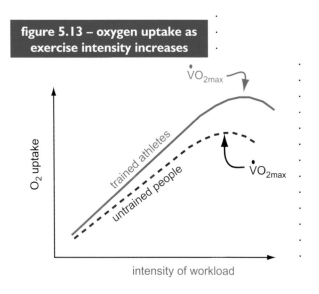

figure 5.13 – oxygen uptake as exercise intensity increases

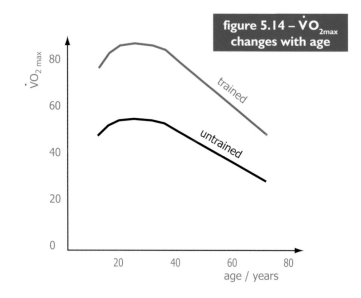

figure 5.14 – $\dot{V}O_{2max}$ changes with age

Table 5.2 – **factors affecting $\dot{V}O_{2max}$**

factor	effect
genetics	accounts for 25% to 50% of the variance in $\dot{V}O_{2max}$ values, for example, the proportions of muscle fibre types are genetically determined, and this could account for specialisms of individuals such as whether a person becomes good at marathon running or weight lifting.
physiology	the limitations of the cardiovascular and pulmonary systems vary, for example, the percentage of slow twitch muscle fibres, heart and lung size, number of red blood cells and mitochondria and the ability of muscle cells to extract oxygen are all physiological factors that will enhance or limit $\dot{V}O_{2max}$.
gender	$\dot{V}O_{2max}$ values decrease in females from late teens onwards, probably because of the tradition of less physical activity for women - highly conditioned female endurance athletes have $\dot{V}O_{2max}$ values around 10% lower than those of highly conditioned male endurance athletes.
age	$\dot{V}O_{2max}$ reduces at about 10% per decade during ageing for sedentary people - and $\dot{V}O_{2max}$ reduces less for active sportspeople as they age (figure 5.14).
training	aerobic training can cause $\dot{V}O_{2max}$ values to be improved by 10-20% (figure 5.13), for example, in an untrained population $\dot{V}O_{2max}$ values peak between 10-19 years. whereas for athletes $\dot{V}O_{2max}$ values peak between 18-32 years, the differences in $\dot{V}O_{2max}$ mean values in trained athletes is due to the specificity of training.
lifestyle	habits such as smoking and a poor diet adversely affect $\dot{V}O_{2max}$ values.
body composition	$\dot{V}O_{2max}$ decreases as the percentage of body fat decreases.
altitude	$\dot{V}O_{2max}$ decreases in proportion to the decrease in atmospheric pressure.

$\dot{V}O_{2max}$ tests as a measure of aerobic endurance

- A $\dot{V}O_{2max}$ test assesses the maximum amount of oxygen that a person can consume per minute during a progressive exercise test to exhaustion.
- $\dot{V}O_{2max}$ is assessed directly when using closed-circuit spirometry (refer to figure 5.15 and table 5.3).
- Simple **predicted** $\dot{V}O_{2max}$ tests are used as indicators of aerobic fitness or stamina, and include the Physical work capacity test (PWC170), the Cooper run/walk test, the Multi-stage shuttle run test, and the Queen's College step test (table 5.3).
- Elite marathon athletes run at optimal percentages of their $\dot{V}O_{2max}$ in order to achieve world class performances.

figure 5.15 – a gas analyser worn during a lab test

Sport Development Centre, Loughbrough University

Table 5.3 – **examples of** $\dot{V}O_{2max}$ **tests**

test/fitness component	description	advantages	disadvantages
Cooper's 12 min run-walk test	participants run or walk for 12 minutes, total distance travelled is measured.	large groups can take part at any one time. everyone can run, cheap equipment.	dependent on type of running shoe. running surface and weather.
Queen's College step test / predicted $\dot{V}O_{2max}$	3 minutes of stepping at a set cadence, $\dot{V}O_{2max}$ predicted from HR recovery.	easy to administer. cheap equipment.	length of leg levers affects results, depends on stepping technique and rhythm, only produces a predicted $\dot{V}O_{2max}$
Closed circuit spirometry / actual $\dot{V}O_{2max}$ (figure 5.15)	a progressive test to exhaustion (treadmill, rowing machine or bike) lasting between 8 and 10 minutes. using a gas analyser O_2 uptake is calculated from measures of oxygen and carbon dioxide in the expired air. $\dot{V}O_{2max}$ value is determined at or near test completion.	high reliability and validity. offers different modes of exercise.	performer has to work to a state of exhaustion. needs specialist testing laboratory equipment. therefore inaccessible to non-elite performers.
NCF multi-stage fitness test	this is the bleep test in which running between two lines 10 m apart increases in tempo until exhaustion. **predicted $\dot{V}O_{2max}$** depends on stage reached.	large groups can take part at any one time. everyone can run, cheap equipment.	need for measured runs between bleeps and slick turns. relies on subject's motivation. test may favour runners.

The importance of aerobic capacity to endurance performers is that it is useful as an indicator showing athletes' maximal physiological capacity. Repeated tests would show the effects of endurance training on $\dot{V}O_{2max}$.

What type of training should be performed?

Improvements in aerobic capacity can be brought about by continuous training and fartlek training (see pages 77 and 79) in which variation in training intensity and exercise choice can be made.

Also intermittent training (pages 77 and 79) can be used to improve aerobic capacity, This method will use long slow runs separated by intervals of time of varying length depending on the intensity of the run. As described on page 78, **high intensity interval training** (HIIT) includes flat out running (high intensity) bouts of long duration with recovery periods allied to the runner's heart rate or time in between bouts. The famous Czech runner Emil Zatopek of the 1952 Olympics apparently did a session of 14 times one mile with 30 second recovery periods between each mile. The variables for changing intensity are sets, repetitions, resistance (or loading), rest relief, and duration of activity.

The use of target heart rates as an intensity guide

A **target heart rate** is a specific heart rate (HR) to be achieved and maintained during exercise. If aerobic adaptations are to occur, training must take place at a HR above the aerobic threshold. This theory is based on the fact that $\dot{V}O_2$ is proportional to heart rate.

Aerobic training zone

This is shown on the graph in figure 5.16.
It shows a range of HR values at which aerobic training should occur.
This will enable adaptations to occur which improve VO_{2max}.

Table 5.4 – **classification of exercise intensity based on 20 to 60 minutes of endurance activity, comparing heart rate maximum, Karvonen's maximum heart rate reserve**

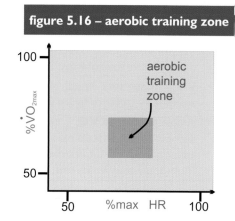

figure 5.16 – aerobic training zone

classification of intensity	relative intensity by HR_{max}	relative intensity by VO_{2max} or HR_{max} reserve - the Karvonen method
very light	<35%	<30%
light	35 - 59%	30 - 49%
moderate	60 - 79%	50 - 74%
heavy	80 - 89%	75 - 84%
very heavy	>89%	>84%

(From Table 19.3 Wilmore, Costill, Kenney 'Physiology of Exercise 4e', 2008, Human Kinetics)

Heart rate maximum (HR_{max}) method

If it is required to operate at 60% of maximum heart rate then the following example shows how to work out the heart rate at which training should occur:

$$\begin{aligned}
\text{Maximum HR } (HR_{max}) &= 220 - \text{age} \\
\text{age} &= 20 \\
\text{Therefore, } HR_{max} &= 220 - 20 \quad \textbf{= 200 bpm} \\[4pt]
\textbf{aerobic threshold HR} &= \textbf{0.6 x } HR_{max} \\
\textbf{Therefore aerobic threshold HR} &= 0.6 \times 200 \quad \textbf{= 120 bpm}
\end{aligned}$$

Target heart rate (HR estimation) Karvonen method

The difference between this method and the HR maximum method is that in the **Karvonen method**, the target HR will depend on the fitness of the athlete.

The following calculation shows the maximum HR at which aerobic exercise can be undertaken if it is required to operate at 60% maximum - according to Karvonen, called the **aerobic threshold heart rate**.

Aerobic threshold (Karvonen) HR $= HR_{rest} + 0.6(HR_{max} - HR_{rest})$

The following example shows how this is used:

$$\begin{aligned}
\text{Again, maximum HR } (HR_{max}) &= 220 - \text{age} \\
\text{age} &= 20 \\
\text{Therefore, } HR_{max} &= 220 - 20 \quad \textbf{= 200 bpm}
\end{aligned}$$

The heart rate at rest is measured at:

$$HR_{rest} = 70 \text{ bpm}$$

$$\begin{aligned}
\textbf{So the aerobic threshold HR} &= 70 + 0.6(200 - 70) \\
&= 70 + 0.6 \times 130 = 70 + 78 \quad \textbf{= 148 bpm}
\end{aligned}$$

Physiological adaptations produced by aerobic training

The **aims of training** are to improve performance, skill, game ability, and motor and physical fitness. **Adaptation** refers to **long-term changes** (figure 5.17) produced in the human body which are caused by training overload.

Cardiovascular systems

The cardiovascular system becomes more efficient as the heart becomes bigger and stronger and pumps more blood per pulse. More **haemoglobin** is available in blood for oxygen transport, and the capillary system in a trained muscle bed is utilised better and developed more.

Cardiac response to aerobic exercise

- The heart becomes bigger and stronger (mainly the left ventricle) as a result of prolonged aerobic exercise (figure 5.18), creating **increased ventricular muscle mass** and **stronger elastic recoil** of the myocardium. This is **cardiac hypertrophy**.
- The increased strength of the cardiac muscle causes a more forceful contraction during ventricular systole.
- Therefore stroke volume increases and HR decreases (this is called **bradycardia**), which provides more oxygen per pulse.
- Blood volume increases with training which in turn increases the size of the left ventricular chamber. This means that more blood volume enters the left ventricle per beat (increased **pre-load**) increasing the stretch of the ventricular walls by the Frank-Starling mechanism.

- Reduced systemic vascular resistance (**decreased afterload**) also contributes to the increase in volume of blood pumped from the left ventricle per beat.
- The net effect is up to 20% bigger stroke volume and greater oxygen delivery to muscles.
- Heart rate during recovery decreases more rapidly after training.
- Cardiac output at maximal levels of exercise increases considerably and is in a response to an increase in $\dot{V}O_{2max}$. This is because the two components of the cardiac output, namely stroke volume and heart rate, balance each other out and there is an increase in $a\text{-}\bar{v}O_{2diff}$ reflecting greater oxygen extraction by the active tissues.
- Cardiac output at rest (or at submaximal exercise) remains unchanged or decreases slightly after endurance training. Hence there is a **decrease in resting heart rate** (HR) and an **increase in HR during maximal workloads**.
- **Blood vessels in the heart evolve** to reduce the blood flow to the heart because the heart muscle itself is more efficient.

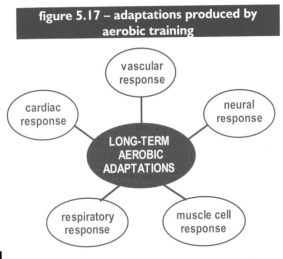

figure 5.17 – adaptations produced by aerobic training

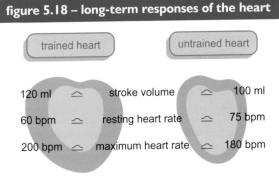

figure 5.18 – long-term responses of the heart

Vascular response to aerobic exercise

The increase in blood flow to muscle is one of the most important factors supporting increased aerobic endurance capacity and performance. This increase is attributable to:

- An **improved capillary system**, there is better dilation of existing capillaries due to increase in blood volume, and there is increased capillarisation of trained muscle.
- **Diversion of a larger portion of cardiac output** to the active muscle, known as an enhanced vascular shunt. Hence increased vasodilation of blood vessels (such as arterioles) and precapillary sphincters to working muscle.
- **Increase in blood volume** is attributed to an increase in plasma volume and number of red blood cells. The increase in plasma volume would result in a reduction in fluid friction drag as the blood flows through blood vessels, which would improve circulation and oxygen availability.
- **Increased elasticity and thickness of smooth muscle** of arterial walls result from extended aerobic exercise which makes arterial walls tougher and therefore less likely to stretch under pressure.
- Hence blood pressure is maintained (which therefore continues to force blood through the capillary network).

Vascular response to aerobic exercise

- Systolic and diastolic **blood pressure decreases** during rest and submaximal exercise. This is because there is a training-induced reduction in sympathetic nervous system hormones. This response decreases peripheral vascular resistance to blood flow, causing blood pressure to drop.

The **net effect** is for the body to develop a more effective blood distribution system both at rest and during exercise.

Respiratory adaptations to aerobic exercise

The respiratory system undergoes the following adaptations to endurance training to maximise its efficiency:
- Pulmonary systems become more efficient, because the musculature of the torso **becomes stronger** and more efficient.
- **Lung volumes increase slightly**, hence greater volumes of air can be breathed per breath (known as tidal volume or TV), and per minute (known as minute ventilation or $\dot{V}E$), hence increased gaseous exchange and $\dot{V}O_{2max}$.
- There is an **increase in vital capacity** at the expense of residual volume, hence a decrease in breathing rate at submaximal workloads.
- **Maximal pulmonary ventilation** is substantially increased following a period of endurance-based training – compare 100 to 120 dm^3min^{-1} for untrained sedentary subjects with in excess of 200 dm^3min^{-1} for highly trained endurance athletes.
- Two factors can account for an increase in maximal pulmonary ventilation. These are **increased tidal volume** (TV) and **increased respiratory frequency** (f) during maximal exercise.
- There is **increased capillarisation of alveoli**, and more alveoli are utilised, hence increased gaseous exchange and $\dot{V}O_{2max}$.
- There is an increase in **pulmonary blood flow** (due to increase in stroke volume) and **plasma volume**. This increase in pulmonary driving pressure causes a bigger distortion in red blood cells as they pass through the alveolar capillaries. Hence greater O_2 transfer.

Muscle cell metabolic adaptations to aerobic exercise

Table 5.5 – **summary of adaptations produced by aerobic exercise**

adaptations to muscle cells produced by aerobic training
body fat proportion is reduced by between 4% and 12%.
more **myoglobin** is created in muscle cells.
more and bigger **mitochondria** are created in muscle cells.
muscle cells have increased **oxidative enzymes** which increases aerobic cell activity (such as pyruvate dehydrogenase) produced within muscle cell mitochondria. Hence there will be increased activity of Kreb's cycle and the electron transport chain to restore ATP in muscle cells.
increase in utilisation of **fat** in adipose tissue as an energy source.
increase in stores of **glycogen** in muscle which enables more fuel to be available for aerobic work.
conversion of type IIb to type IIa fibres, so increasing the proportion of aerobically active muscle cells.
better **recruitment** of **slow twitch** fibre (type I) motor units making muscle usage more efficient.
reduction of **delayed onset muscle soreness** (**DOMS**).
glycogen sparing is a muscle cell response within the specific muscle cells of the person who has undertaken sustained aerobic training.
fats are used earlier on in exercise inside the muscle cells being trained, thus **conserving glycogen stores** (respiratory factors indicate greater use of fats).
increase in a-$\bar{v}O_{2diff}$. This is due to a more effective distribution of arterial blood away from inactive tissue to active tissue and an increased ability of active muscle to extract more oxygen.
lower mixed venous oxygen content contributes towards the increase in $\dot{V}O_{2max}$ in trained athletes.

Metabolic physiological adaptations to aerobic exercise

Endurance exercise training induces a number of metabolic adaptations in skeletal muscle.

Mitochondria

- Mitochondria are the '**power houses**' of tissue respiration, in which the biochemical processes of respiration and energy production occur.
- Aerobic training is responsible for increases in the mitochondrial content and **respiratory capacity** of muscle fibres.
- **Mitochondrial density** is the most important of these with an associated increase in respiratory capacity.
- An increase in both size and number of mitochondria are responsible for the increase in mitochondrial content of muscle tissue.
- These adaptations are limited to the muscle fibres that are recruited to contract.
- For example, in runners and cyclists the increase in mitochondria is limited to the muscles of the lower leg.
- Research indicates that the mitochondrial content of **type II fibres** increase to a greater extent in response to very strenuous endurance training than that of type I fibres.
- This is because type II fibres are generally recruited during intense strenuous exercise and interval training appears to be necessary to induce a large increase in mitochondrial content.

Myoglobin

- More myoglobin is created **in muscle cells** and so there is increased capacity to **transfer oxygen** from haemoglobin to active muscle tissue cells.

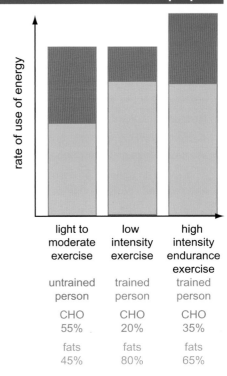

figure 5.19 – contribution of CHO and fats for trained and untrained people

Glycolytic enzymes

- Endurance training appears to result in minor changes in glycolytic enzyme activation in skeletal muscle, which increases aerobic cell activity (such as pyruvate dehydrogenase) produced within the muscle cell mitochondria.
- Hence there will be increased activity of **Kreb's cycle** and the **electron transport chain** to **restore ATP** in muscle cells.

Glycogen sparing

- Increases in muscle and liver glycogen stores enable more fuel to be available for aerobic work.
- Long-term aerobic training results in increased **utilisation of fat,** with a proportional **decrease in carbohydrate utilisation** during submaximal exercise.
- Depletion of muscle and liver glycogen stores are less rapid and there is an increase and earlier oxidation of fat oxidation (reflected by a lower respiratory exchange ratio) thus conserving glycogen stores, known as '**glycogen sparing**'.
- This training adaptation enables the trained athlete to **not use glycogen up immediately**, but save it for later on in an exercise effort, or when the intensity of the exercise increases as is illustrated in figure 5.19.

$\dot{V}O_{2max}$

- A greater capacity of the cardiovascular system to deliver oxygen to active muscle is due an increase in the number of capillaries surrounding each fibre and improved the oxygen exchange between capillary and fibre due to an increase in **a-vO$_{2diff}$** (arterio-venous oxygen difference) as active muscle tissue extracts more oxygen from surrounding capillary beds, which in turn are supplied by a more effective distribution of arterial blood away from inactive tissue to active tissue.
- Increases in maximum aerobic power ($\dot{V}O_{2max}$) is induced by strenuous prolonged endurance training as is illustrated on page 84, (figure 5.13).

Delayed onset of muscle soreness (DOMS)

- The muscle's **respiratory capacity** is of primary importance in determining the work rate at which blood lactate accumulation begins.

- Research suggests that the proportion of **slow-twitch fibres** may play an important role in determining the relative lactate threshold due to their aerobic characteristics such as mitochondrial and myoglobin density.

- The net training effect is that the same work rate requires a smaller percentage of the muscles' maximum respiratory capacity.

- Figure 5.20 compares the OBLA in untrained and trained athletes.

- Note that in **untrained** people blood lactate increases sharply at about 50% of $\dot{V}O_{2max}$, whereas **trained** athletes can exercise up to 70% of $\dot{V}O_{2max}$ before lactate concentration in the blood increases markedly.

- Hence **trained** athletes begin OBLA at **higher work intensities**, especially since trained athletes have higher values of $\dot{V}O_{2max}$ in the first place.

- All this means is that the **lactic-aerobic threshold** moves to higher values of $\dot{V}O_{2max}$.

- It is the metabolic consequences of these adaptations in muscle that are responsible for an increase in endurance and the ability to exercise at a higher percent of $\dot{V}O_{2max}$ in the trained state, by slowing down glycogen depletion and reducing lactate production, thereby delaying onset of muscle soreness.

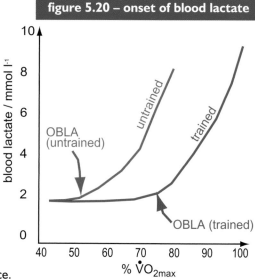

figure 5.20 – onset of blood lactate

Musculo skeletal adaptations

- **Selective hypertrophy** occurs in different muscle fibre types since highly trained endurance athletes have larger slow twitch than fast twitch fibres.

- Hence increased potential for aerobic energy production, decreased energy cost and delay in OBLA.

- **Conversion of type IIb muscle fibres to type IIa fibres**, so increasing the proportion of aerobically active muscle cells.

- **Better recruitment** of slow twitch fibre type I motor units making motor units more efficient.

- Aerobic exercise adaptations on bone tissue show greater **bone mineral densities**, such as increased calcium absorption.

- Therefore an athlete can train harder and longer supported by **increased bone strength** and reduced risk from injuries such as fractures.

Increased thickening of articular cartilage

- McCutchen's **weeping theory of lubrication** proposes that when a joint is exercised, synovial fluid is squeezed in and out of the articular cartilage at the points of contact, providing the articular surfaces with nutrients and oxygen and long term thickening. Thus increasing **joint nourishment and strength** and reducing risk of injury.

- Increased **strength of connective tissues**, such as tendons and ligaments, increase joint stability and again reduce the risk of injury.

How to plan an aerobic training programme

- **Assess** aerobic fitness level, for example do the NCF multistage fitness test to assess predicted $\dot{V}O_{2max}$.
- Determine aerobic **fitness goals**, such as improving cardiovascular performance or sport performance.
- Consider **time constraints** - time of day/days available/times per day.
- Look at **exercise preference** - could be general or sport specific.
- Consider the **type of training** (continuous or interval) needed.
- Consider what **facilities** are available such as a gym, track, pool in town, or paths, lanes in the country.
- Apply relevant **training principles** such as progression, overload, duration, frequency, intensity and variance.
- Place **basic elements** within a session such as warm-up, work-out and cool-down.
- An example of a training programme for an elite 800m runner is illustrated in table 5.6 (page 91).

Table 5.6 – **example training programme for an elite male 800m runner**

day	time of day	training
day 1	am evening	30 min medium paced run continuous. 30 min medium paced run continuous.
day 2	am pm	30 min easy paced run continuous. 3 sets of (2 x 400m (55s) 2 x 200m (26s)) interval 20 min recovery between sets.
day 3	am	45 min medium paced run continuous.
day 4	am pm	30 min easy paced run continuous. 2 x 30m, 40m, 50m, 60m walk back recovery interval session 2 sets of 3 x 200m (25s) 5min recovery. 15 min recovery between sets.
day 5	rest	
day 6	pm	competition.
day 7	am	long medium paced run, 60 min continuous.

Practice questions

1) Mary is a 20 year old college student. What is her theoretical maximum heart rate?
   a.   195.
   b.   100.
   c.   205.
   d.   200.

2) Which of the following cannot be considered as a metabolic adaptation to endurance training?
   a.   increased maximal oxygen uptake.
   b.   increased maximal rate of fat oxidation.
   c.   increased adrenaline response to exercise.
   d.   lower respiratory exchange ratio (RER) during submaximal exercise.

3) The overload principle applied to the development of:
   a.   cardiovascular endurance.
   b.   flexibility.
   c.   strength.
   d.   all of these.

4) Immediately following high intensity interval training HIIT) the performer should:
   a.   sit down and rest.
   b.   take a shower.
   c.   continue to do low intensity exercise.
   d.   breathe deeply for five minutes.

5) Cardiovascular activity can result in the following benefit to the heart
   a.   increase in cardiac output.
   b.   increase in resting heart rate.
   c.   increase in blood pressure.
   d.   decrease in heart size.

6) a)   Define the term $\dot{V}O_{2max}$ and describe two main factors which limit $\dot{V}O_{2max}$.   3 marks

   b)   Describe a field test used to estimate a person's $\dot{V}O_{2max}$.   3 marks

Practice questions

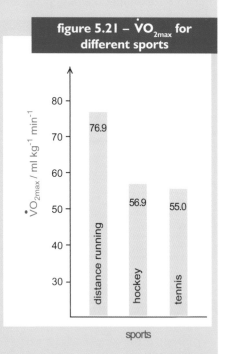

figure 5.21 – $\dot{V}O_{2max}$ for different sports

7) a)   Figure 5.21 shows variation in $\dot{V}O_{2max}$ between three different sports. Suggest reasons for variations in $\dot{V}O_{2max}$ between these three sports.

3 marks

b)   Explain the potential physiological advantages for endurance athletes having a high $\dot{V}O_{2max}$.

2 marks

c)   What other factors contribute to an individual's $\dot{V}O_{2max}$?

3 marks

8) $\dot{V}O_{2max}$ is the best indicator of cardiovascular endurance capacity and increases substantially in response to long-term endurance training. Define the term $\dot{V}O_{2max}$ and identify its units of measurement. Through what mechanisms does this improvement occur?

8 marks

9) a)   Identify two valid and reliable submaximal tests that measure endurance or stamina. Why are submaximal tests often favoured over maximal tests?

4 marks

b)   Explain why fitness testing is necessary for both the coach and the athlete?

3 marks

10) Using practical examples from the cardiovascular systems explain the difference between a short-term response and a long-term adaptation to exercise.

4 marks

11) Identify the long-term adaptations an elite performer would expect to occur to the structure and the functioning of the cardiovascular system, as a result of an intense aerobic training programme.

10 marks

12) Jodie Swallow is a top class female British Triathlete, and has a resting heart rate of 36 beats per minute. Give reasons why such an athlete might have a low resting heart rate.

4 marks

13)   Describe and account for some of the long-term effects of regular aerobic training methods on respiratory volumes.

6 marks

14) Describe four changes that occur in muscle cells as a result of an endurance-based training programme.

4 marks

15) A Level. Your PE group has been asked to devise a running training schedule for an elite 1500m runner. Using your knowledge of both intermittent and continuous training methods show how you could use this information to produce both aerobic and anaerobic adaptations. Justify the content of your training programme for an elite 1500m runner, with regard to the expected respiratory adaptations.

20 marks

16) Describe a method of monitoring exercise intensity and give an advantage and disadvantage for the method you have selected.

5 marks

17) A group of students wish to create an aerobic weight training programme. Suggest how they could calculate working intensities that would give them optimal strength endurance gains. Illustrate your answer with examples.

8 marks

18) Continuous training is one of the least used methods of training by top performers. Identify the main characteristics of continuous training and suggest how this can benefit a performer.

4 marks

19) Fartlek training is a type of training that is used to develop aerobic capacity. What does the term Fartlek mean? Answer by outlining the training principles used to create a typical Fartlek training session.

3 marks

20) What is meant by the term high intensity interval training (HIIT)? How can this type of training be of benefit to an untrained sedentary individual?

6 marks

Answers link: http://www.jroscoe.co.uk/downloads/as_a1_revise_pe_ocr/OCRAS_A1_ch5_answers.pdf

CHAPTER 6: *Strength, flexibility and periodisation training and the impact of training on lifestyle diseases*

Strength training

Strength

Strength is defined as '**the maximum force exerted by a specific muscle or muscle group during a single maximal muscle contraction – or one repetition maximum (1RM)**'.

figure 6.1 – dynamic strength requires maximum strength

- **Static strength** is exerted without change of muscle length, for example holding a weight at arms length, or pushing hard in a stationary rugby scrum thus creating an isometric muscle contraction.

- **Dynamic** or **explosive strength** is the maximal strength exerted during a movement or exercise in which muscle length changes. Most sports use this type of maximal strength. This is the sort of strength weight lifters use in competition when performing an Olympic lift (figure 6.1), the most usual in sports situations, such as throwing and sprinting. Most sports activities require flat out movements such as sprinting and therefore require dynamic strength.

- A sub-category of dynamic strength is **elastic or plyometric strength** or the ability to apply as large a force as possible using an eccentric muscle contraction (in which the active muscles get longer) followed by a concentric muscle contraction (in which the active muscles get shorter). Examples of plyometric movements include rebound jumping and high jump take-off (illustrated on page 80).

- Strength can be assessed with the use of **dynamometers**.

- Strength exercises stress **fast twitch muscle fibres type IIb** which are able to generate high forces rapidly. Long-term, this type of exercise results in **muscle hypertrophy** (enlargement of individual muscle fibres).

Strength endurance (sometimes called muscular endurance) can be defined as '**the ability of a muscle or muscle group to sustain repeated contractions over time sufficient enough to cause muscular fatigue**'.

- Strength endurance relies on the ability of the body to produce energy under aerobic and anaerobic conditions.

- This type of exercise stresses slow twitch muscle fibres and fast twitch muscle fibres type IIa – both muscle fibre types are fatigue resistant.

- Simple tests that evaluate local strength endurance include the Multi-stage abdominal test and maximum chin test i.e. the total number of chin-ups completed to exhaustion or within one minute.

Factors affecting strength

- Strength exercises stress **fast twitch fibres type IIb** which are able to generate high forces rapidly. Long-term, this type of exercise results in **muscle hypertrophy** (enlargement of individual muscle fibres).

- **Muscle fibre type** is inherited, and strength is affected by fibre type distribution. For example, sprinters tend to have a majority of fast twitch type II, and endurance athletes tend to have a majority of slow twitch type I.

- **Type of muscle contraction**, because **eccentric** work exceeds the isometric maximum by about 30%. This is due to the ability of the neuromuscular system to mobilise a greater number of motor units when under the greater stress of an eccentric movement under tension. During this type of contraction, a large force acts to brake and control the movement.

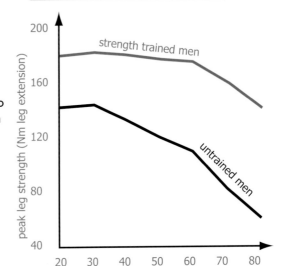

figure 6.2 – strength changes with age

y-axis: peak leg strength (Nm leg extension) — 40, 80, 120, 160, 200

x-axis: age / yrs — 20, 30, 40, 50, 60, 70, 80

strength trained men

untrained men

Factors affecting strength

- **Muscle cross sectional area**, in which people with larger muscles tend to be stronger! **Females** in general have muscles with smaller cross section than males, hence a smaller muscle mass. Peak power is less for females by about 20%.
- **Muscle mass differences** between individuals is a large factor, as is the effects of age (figure 6.2 page 93).
- **Regression** or **detraining** is a factor which will affect strength in as little as 5 days after training stops. The amount and rate of regression depends on the length of time training has occurred.

Table 6.1 – **types of muscle contraction as a factor affecting strength**

type of contraction	strength gain over range of motion	least possibility of muscle soreness	skill improvement
isokinetic	excellent	excellent	excellent
isometric	poor	good	poor
isotonic	good	poor	good

Examples of strength fitness tests

Table 6.2 – **examples of standardised maximal tests**

test	fitness component	description / protocol	advantages	disadvantages
grip strength dynamometer	**strength**	a grip dynamometer is squeezed as tightly as possible with one hand.	easily performed.	motivation can affect result. there is a technique to this exercise.
Sergeant jump	**power**	two-foot standing take-off. measure between standing two armed reach and highest single hand jumped reach.	easy to administer. high correlation with peak anaerobic power.	skill factor. height differences between performers.
NCF sit-up test	**strength endurance**	sit-ups are performed in time to a bleep regime. a score is given at the point of exhaustion.	easy to administer.	depends on motivation.
1RM	**strength**	choose an exercise perform single lifts until failure, last successful lift is the 1RM.	exercises are standard.	most weight lifting exercises are very technical, this can affect results.

Different methods of strength training

This section considers several strength training methods used by sports performers as summarised in figure 6.3.

Intermittent or interval training

This type of training is characterised by periods of **alternating exercise** and **rest**, providing a very versatile training method that enables the individual to perform considerably more work and with greater physiological benefits.

Variables include:
- **Duration** of the exercise period.
- **Intensity** of the exercise period.
- Number of **repetitions** within a set.
- Number of **sets** within a session.
- Duration of the rest intervals (rest relief) or **recovery**.

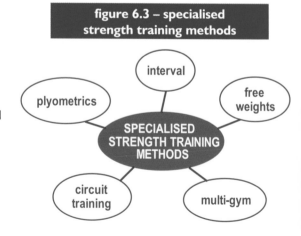

figure 6.3 – specialised strength training methods

Intermittent or interval training

The exercise **type** and **loading**, number of **repetitions** and **sets**, and length of **rest relief** govern the **adaptive response** produced, thus enabling the individual to select the required intensity of work to stress the relevant energy system:

- **ATP-PC intervals** are characterised by high intensity effort (80-100% of maximum effort) lasting between 3-10 seconds and no more than 2 minutes recovery. Increases ATP-PC stores.
- **Lactic acid intervals** are characterised by medium to high intensity effort (60-80% of maximum effort) lasting between 15-90 seconds with variable recovery depending on exercise duration. Increases blood buffering capacity or increased lactate tolerance
- **Aerobic intervals** are characterised by low intensity effort (below 50% of maximum effort) lasting beyond 20 minutes with short recovery. Increases aerobic capacity or VO_{2max}.
- See table 5.1 on page 79 for examples of interval training.

Weight training

Weight training is a form of interval training and can be used to develop or stress several components of fitness such as strength and strength endurance depending on the resistance, number of repetitions, sets and rest relief. This is discussed on page 78 and an example on page 79.

Circuit training

A type of interval training that provides all-round body fitness, characterised by a number of exercises or stations performed in succession so that different body parts are exercised successively. The training is normally organised to work for a set time period at each station. See table 5.1 on page 79 for details of how to include these exercises in a session.

Plyometric training

Plyometrics, also known as **stretch-shortening cycle** exercise, is a form of **resistance** training involving **eccentric-to-concentric** actions at 100% intensity, performed quickly so that the muscle stretches prior to the concentric contraction. The details of plyometric training are covered on page 78 with an example on page 79.

Physiological adaptations produced by anaerobic training (figure 6.4)

- The **adaptations** produced by these types of training are almost exclusively **anaerobic**, with muscle elastic strength and hypertrophy as the primary aim.
- Plyometrics additionally involve neuro-muscular adaptations such as the **recruitment** of additional **fast twitch** motor units and **improved coordination** of fast twitch motor units as the eccentric effect is utilised.

- For the training to be **most effective**, the greatest force is applied when the **concentric phase** of a movement **coincides** with the **stretch reflex response** occurring at the limit of eccentric stretch.

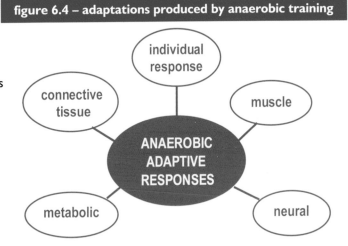

figure 6.4 – adaptations produced by anaerobic training

Connective tissue response

In response to anaerobic training there will be:
- Increase in thickness and strength of **tendons**.
- Increased flexibility of **ligaments**.
- Thickening and improved **elasticity of cartilage**.
- Improved capability of cartilaginous tissue to absorb and expel synovial fluid (McCutchen's weeping lubrication theory), hence improved **cushioning** against impact within a joint.
- Strengthening of **bone tissue** due to increased depositing of calcium, therefore reduced risk of injury.

Individual response

Adaptive response to anaerobic training depends on the individual:
*   Fitness.
*   Genetic differences.
*   Gender.
*   Psychological factors.
*   Maturation.

Muscle cell adaptations

Table 6.3 – **adaptations produced by anaerobic exercise**

adaptations to muscle cells produced by anaerobic exercise
fast twitch muscle **hypertrophy** - increase in size by increased cross sectional area of a muscle.
increase in the number of **myofibrils** within each muscle cell.
increase in the **sarcoplasmic** volume within each cell.
increase in the size and strength of the contractile proteins, **actin and myosin**, leading to increase in the mass of fast twitch fibres, increases in **maximum possible peak power**, and the ability to maintain maximal power output for longer.
increase in the number of fast twitch muscle fibres (**hyperplasia**), which means that the proportion of type II muscle fibre increases and the proportion of type I decreases.
toughening of **proprioceptors** so that more force is required to stimulate inhibitory signals, an improved agonist / antagonist response.

Metabolic adaptations

Table 6.4 – **adaptations produced by anaerobic exercise**

metabolic adaptations to muscle cells produced by anaerobic exercise
increase in muscle **cell stores** of substances such as ATP, PC, and glycogen, and increase in anaerobic enzymes such as creatine kinase (CK), PFK, GPP, and LDH, which makes the muscle stronger and more powerful.
these processes enable an improved capacity of alactic (ATP-PC) and lactic acid systems to resynthesise ATP, and hence to deliver energy more rapidly.
improved toleration of **lactate** in fast twitch fibres, and improved ability to remove lactate from muscle cell into blood - which enhances lactate thresholds and **reduces OBLA.**
reduction of **delayed onset muscle soreness** (**DOMS**), particularly following eccentric training.

Neural adaptations

Table 6.5 – **adaptations produced by anaerobic exercise**

neural adaptations to muscle cells produced by anaerobic exercise
increased rate of response of **CNS** (Central Nervous System), **recruitment** of additional **fast twitch** fibre motor units. improved coordination of fast twitch fibre motor units.
reciprocal innervation, in which **antagonist action is reduced** without conscious effort as a sportsperson performs a powerful movement (using agonists as prime movers). this leads to a small **increase in strength** of the performer in learned and **specific** movements.
adaptations in which more muscle fibres are recruited within an activity will better utilise fast twitch muscle fibres at their existing level before hypertrophy occurs. Initial measured strength gains are almost exclusively via this process.
improved motor unit **synchronicity** and increased firing rates.
lowering of neural inhibitory **reflexes**.
net result is **activation** of prime movers in a specific action to affect **maximal force capacity**.

Sports for which strength is required

Most sports will require strength in some form or other, and in different body parts depending on the sport.

Weight lifting, throwing events in athletics, sprinting, srummaging in rugby, wrestling, martial arts are all sports in which strength is required, with most requiring strength endurance in addition.

Flexibility training

figure 6.5 – flexibility/stretching

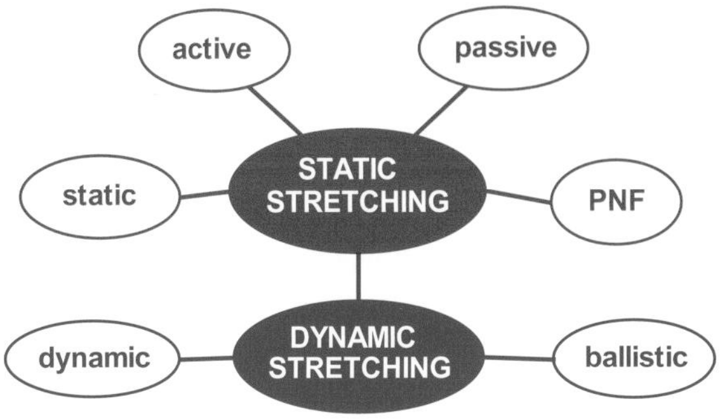

Flexibility

Flexibility is defined as '**the ability to move a joint through its complete range of movement**'.

- Flexibility concerns the **stretching** of muscles and tissues such as ligaments and tendons around skeletal joints.
- The degree of movement is determined by the joint type.
- A gymnast needs great flexibility to achieve desired movement patterns.

STATIC STRETCHING — active, passive, static, PNF

DYNAMIC STRETCHING — dynamic, ballistic

Factors affecting flexibility

- The **aim** of flexibility training is to improve (or maintain) the **range of motion** over which muscles can act and joints can operate. In simple language this can be expressed as how far you can reach, bend and turn.
- **Joint flexibility** depends on the joint type, the distensibility of the joint capsule, adequate warm-up, muscle viscosity and the compliance of ligaments and tendons.
- The greater the **length** and **elasticity** of **ligaments**, **tendons** and **muscle tissue**, the greater the range of motion.
- **Gender**, **ageing** and **body composition** affect flexibility, females are generally more flexible, older people are less flexible, and obese people tend to be less flexible (mostly because the extra mass gets in the way).
- Flexibility is improved by stressing all these components. The effect produced is based on the **stress-overload** principle by forcing the contractile tissues such as muscle tissue to operate at full stretch.
- Mobility work is best done at the end of an anaerobic training session, during cool-down. This is because the muscular system is usually more relaxed at this time, with muscle temperatures slightly higher than during the warm-up.

Types of stretching and flexibility exercises

There are **two** main types of stretching (figure 6.5):
- **Static**.
- **Dynamic**.

figure 6.6 – hold this static stretch

Static stretching

Static stretching refers to stretching exercises that are performed **without movement**. In other words, the individual gets into a stretch position and **holds** the stretch for a specific amount of time.

Static stretching is performed by placing the body in a position **whereby the muscle to be stretched is under tension**. At this point the position is held to allow the muscle to lengthen. This is a very safe and effective form of stretching with a limited threat of injury. See figure 6.6 as an example of a static stretch.

Isometric stretching is a type of static stretching (meaning it does not use motion) which involves the resistance of muscle groups through tensing of the stretched muscles. A chair, wall, the floor or a partner can act as the resistance to bring about a static contraction and isometric stretch. Aside from increasing range of motion, a second purpose of isometric stretching is to develop **strength in stretched positions**.

Active stretching

Active stretching is **slow stretching** in which flexibility is achieved **without assistance**. This form of stretching involves using only the strength of the opposing muscles (antagonist) to generate a held stretch (held for 10-15 seconds) within the agonist. The contraction of the opposing muscles helps to relax the stretched muscles. See figure 6.7 as an example of an active stretch. Active stretching is a very effective form of conditioning.

figure 6.7 – active stretch

Passive stretching

Passive stretching is similar to static stretching, however a **partner** or **apparatus** can be used to help further stretch the muscles or joints. Figure 6.8 is an example of a passive stretch in which the floor is assisting the position.

figure 6.8 – passive stretch

Dynamic stretching

Dynamic stretching refers to stretching exercises that are performed with **movement** and are classified depending on the vigorousness of the bounce. Dynamic stretching uses a **controlled**, **soft bounce** or **swinging movement**, that moves a particular body part to the limit of its range of movement and is a preferred method over ballistic stretching.

Ballistic stretching

- **Ballistic stretching** involves **aggressive**, **dynamic** or **rapid**, **bouncing** or **swinging** movements during which the contraction of the agonist forces the antagonist to relax.

- Ballistic stretching fails to allow the stretched muscle time to adapt to the stretched position and instead may cause the muscle to tighten up by repeatedly triggering the stretch reflex.

figure 6.9 – ballistic stretch

- Ballistic stretching should be **used towards the end of a warm-up** because the muscle temperatures are slightly higher than at the start of the warm-up phase.

- Ballistic stretching is considered to be an outdated form of stretching because of its vigorous nature and risk of muscle tear injury.

- Activities such as trampolining rely on ballistic stretching during routine work such as a ten-bounce routine. Figure 6.9 shows a side-to-side swinging movement aimed at stretching the lower trunk muscles.

STUDENT NOTE

Note that the **aim** of stretching training is to initiate anaerobic adaptive changes which involve the neuromuscular system, particularly reciprocal innervation (in which the antagonist action at a joint is inhibited), and **toughening of proprioceptors** so that more force is required to stimulate inhibitory signals. **Sensory organs**, such as Golgi tendons and muscle spindles (within the muscle belly), will become **less sensitive** which would allow **large muscle forces** to develop in a given muscle as a joint is stretched to its limit, which in an untrained person could cause injury.

Proprioceptive Neuromuscular Facilitation (PNF)

figure 6.10 – PNF

PNF is a progression on passive stretching, whereby after a stretch is held, the muscle is contracted **isometrically** for **between 6-10 seconds**. It then **relaxes** and is **contracted** again, usually going further the second time. This is known as the **CRAC** method (Contract-Relax-Antagonist-Contract).

This method is best described in **three** stages:

Stage 1:
• The athlete and partner assume the position for the stretch (figure 6.10 a), then the partner extends the body limb until the muscle is stretched and tension is felt.

Stage 2:
• The athlete then contracts the stretched muscle isometrically for 5-6 seconds and the partner must inhibit all movement (figure 6.10 b).

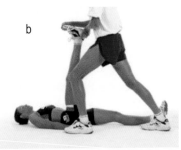

Stage 3:
• The muscle group is relaxed, then immediately and cautiously pushed past its normal range of movement (figure 6.10 c) for about 6 seconds.

Allow 30 seconds recovery before repeating the procedure 2-4 times. The aim of PNF is to **toughen** up or inhibit proprioceptors (such as **muscle spindles and Golgi tendons**) in the relaxation of muscle tissue. This is a **long-term** adaptation.

Evaluating flexibility

To assess the flexibility of an individual, measurements can be made, for example, the red arrow in figure 6.11.

The goniometer

A goniometer is a device containing a 180° protractor for measuring the maximum angle turned through by the bones at a joint, which is then a measure of the flexibility of the joint. The centre of a goniometer is positioned at the axis of rotation of the joint, and the arms of the goniometer (figure 6.11b) are aligned with the long axis of the two bones which articulate at the joint.

figure 6.11 – flexibility measurements

a   sit and reach test

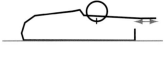

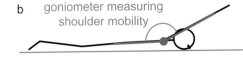

b   goniometer measuring shoulder mobility

Physiological adaptations caused by flexibility training

• Limited stretching of soft tissues such as **ligaments** and **tendons** will cause an increase in resting or residual length.
• Stretching of **skeletal muscle tissue** causes an **inhibition** of the stretch reflex within the particular muscle.
• As muscle spindles lengthen, the stretch reflex limits flexibility, therefore this inhibition would improve flexibility.

Training programmes for flexibility

• **Assess** your flexibility using the sit and reach test for example.
• Determine your **flexibility goals**, such as hip mobility for a gymnast.
• Consider your **time constraints** - time of day/days available/times per day.
• Look at your **exercise preference** - could be general or sport specific.
• Consider the **type of training** (static, passive, ballistic or active) you need to do.
• Consider what **facilities** are available to you such as a gym, or availability of a carpet at home!
• Apply relevant **training principles** such as progression, overload, duration, frequency, intensity and variance.
• Place basic elements within a session such as warm-up, work-out and cool-down.
• An example of a flexibility training program for a novice athlete is illustrated in table 6.6 (page 100).

Training programmes for flexibility

Table 6.6 – **flexibility training programme for a novice athlete**

sessions	programme
day 1	during cool-down, static stretching (6 exercises), 6 repetitions at each exercise, hold end point for 6 seconds, 15 second rest between repetitions.
day 3	during warm-up, ballistic stretching (6 exercises) 6 sets of 20 performed in a circuit.
day 5	separate session, active stretching or PNF (10 exercises), 6 repetitions at each exercise, hold end point for 6 seconds, 15 second rest between repetitions. for PNF, hold end point for 6 seconds, relax, then force past end point for a further 3 seconds.

Sports and activities for which flexibility is important

Gymnastics (figure 6.12), trampolining, diving, dance all require extreme flexibility. But most sports require athletes to acquire flexibility as part of routine training so that they may not be exposed to extremes of position which could lead to injury.

figure 6.12 – a gymnast is flexible

Periodisation

Periodisation is a method of training which varies training intensity cyclically, organised in periods and cycles of training. Such cycles of training take place long-term, over time spans of months and years.

Each period within a training plan will have a specific aim or objective within the overall training plan, for example:

- **Period 1** may be aimed at basic conditioning.
- **Period 2** may be aimed at strength development.
- **Period 3** may be aimed at speed development.

figure 6.13 – a single periodised year

months	nov	dec	jan	feb	mar	apr	may	jun	jul	aug	sep	oct
phases		1			2			3	4		5	6
periods	preparation						competition					recovery/transition

The time intervals within this training method can be defined as follows:

- A **period** is a basic year subdivision between 1 and 6 months.
- A **macrocycle** is a phase lasting between 4 and 26 weeks.
- A **mesocycle** is a phase lasting 2 to 4 weeks which would be part of a macrocycle.
- A **microcycle** is a phase lasting 1 week or less, and is the basic repetitive cycle of activities.
- Sometimes **daily cycles** of up to 3 sessions may be required for elite performers.

Figure 6.13 shows how periods and cycles can be laid out for a whole year. Note that an elite athlete may need a four or five year periodised programme to peak for an Olympic Games.

Planning a periodised training programme

- You will need to utilise the principles of training, decide on general activities, and then decide on specific activities.
- You will need to break down activities into relevance to different energy systems and ensure that this fits the energy system profile for your sport.
- You will next decide on time allocations (**duration**), and decide on the volume of work in a session (**intensity**).
- Figure 6.14 is an example breakdown of training intensity over the days of a microcycle (in this case 7 days, one week).

figure 6.14 – variation in training intensity during a microcycle

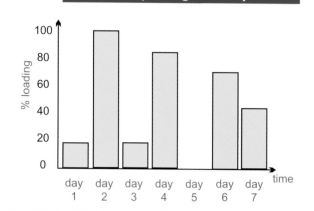

Planning a periodised training programme

- Note that elite athletes who don't need to plan round the working week (most people would have to fit in with school, college or work), often use 5, 6 or 8 day micro cycles to fit in with the time needed to recover from intense training.

- Decide on how many times to train in the microcycle (**frequency**).
- Set out sets and repetitions within an activity (**repetition**).
- Ensure that **warm-up** and **cool-down** are included.
- Make notes on **progression** for future microcycles.
- Ensure that appropriate rest and **rest relief** is indicated.

Planning mesocycles

- Establish **maximum training intensity** using fitness tests - this is the initial **100%** training intensity.
- Then decide on a **starting point** below this (for example, 80%).
- Plan a **progressive intensity** mesocycle rising to 100% in say 4 weeks (figure 6.15).
- Plan the subsequent **4-week cycle** taking the load up to 110%.
- Subsequent 4-week cycles progress to planned goal for the year.

figure 6.15 – training intensity by mesocycle

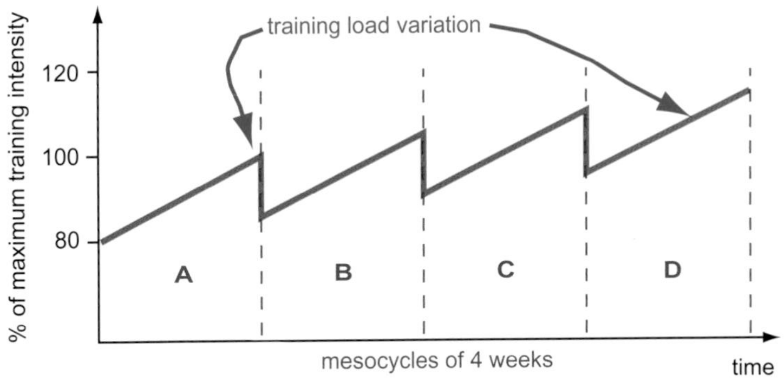

Alternative methods of periodisation

- The example in figure 6.13 (page 100) is a single periodised year (just one competitive period). The same sort of arrangements can be made for two competitive periods - called a **double periodised year**.

- Figure 6.16 shows the possible layout for a **double periodised** year, the blue vertical line shows the end of the first competitive period.

- At this point the second half of the year (period) begins and the process of structure towards the second competitive period starts. Research has shown that this sort of programme can initiate greater progress in various indicators of fitness (strength, speed, endurance).

figure 6.16 – a double periodised year

months	nov	dec	jan	feb	mar	apr	may	jun	jul	aug	sep	oct
phases	1	2		3	4	5		6		7	8	9
periods	preparation			trans	comp	preparation				trans	comp	

trans = transition   comp = competition   recovery

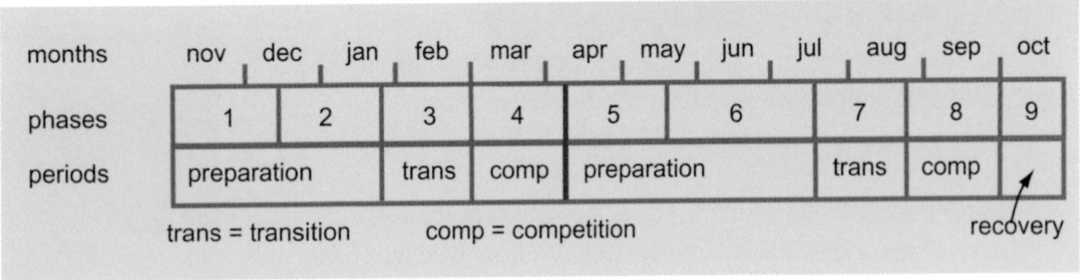

Tapering and peaking

- The periodisation method of training enables the coach to vary training intensity and quantity, so that a performer can **peak** for a major games such as the Olympics.
- This peaking usually involves **tapering**, which means that training intensity gradually reduces over a period of up to 14 days beforehand, which enables the athlete to be fresh and full of energy for the big event.

Peaking is partly psychological. How a performer feels about him or herself, and how confidence is flowing, are often as important as the state of fitness or strength.

See page 79 for details of various training programmes.

The effect of training on lifestyle diseases

The long-term effect of aerobic exercise on the cardiovascular and cardio-respiratory systems is outlined on page 87. The body cells within those headings are actually modified by aerobic exercise to enable them to be more efficient - particularly in respect of delivering energy to the muscular system so that the person taking the exercise can perform well or 'better' in a sporting situation.

The neuromuscular system is similarly detailed on page 88 onwards in respect of aerobic exercise, and page 96 in respect of anaerobic or high intensity exercise. The effects will be to strengthen the muscular system which will affect posture and joints (restricting the development of arthritis for example).

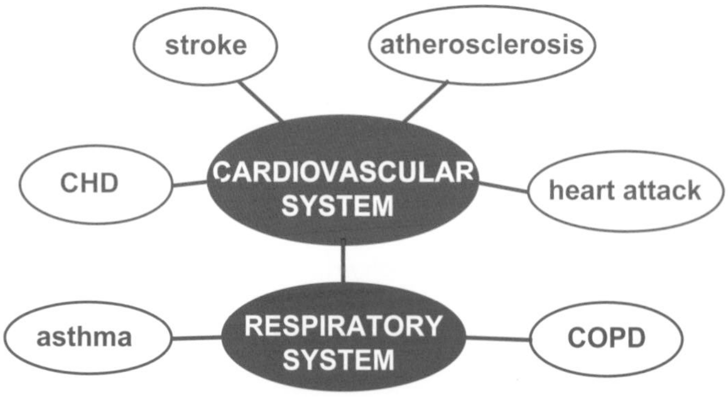

Health and the cardiovascular system

Cardiovascular diseases include diseases of the heart and blood vessels (see figure 6.17). The majority of patients suffering from cardiovascular diseases have **hypertension** (high blood pressure).

figure 6.17 – lifestyle diseases

- **Hypertension** is a condition that occurs when a person's blood pressure is continually high, equal to or greater than 140/90 mmHg. High blood pressure is often associated with excess weight and with hardening of the arteries (**arteriosclerosis**). Hypertension is a major contributing factor in **atherosclerosis**, coronary heart disease (CHD), and **strokes**.

- **Arteriosclerosis** is a consequence of **hardening** of the **arteries** usually occurring in older people, and which is a process enhanced by lack of exercise. During hard exercise, the artery walls are stretched as blood flow is increased, and this exercises the muscular layer within the walls. If this process is not done, this muscle will atrophy, and the walls become more rigid. This happens mostly in the lower limbs, and involves a gradual **calcification** of the **tunica media** (the muscular middle wall of an artery).

figure 6.18 – atherosclerosis

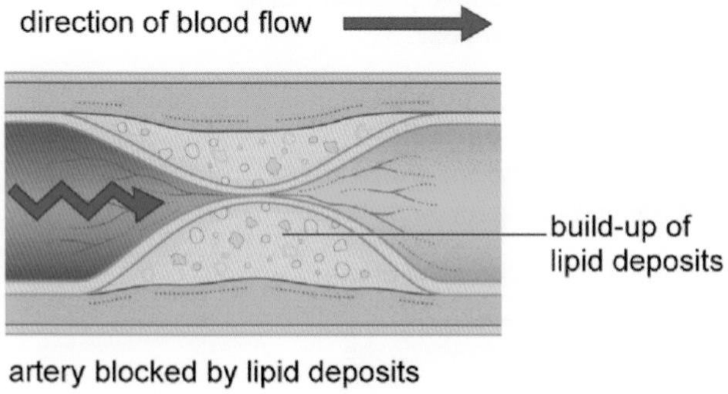

direction of blood flow

build-up of lipid deposits

artery blocked by lipid deposits

- **Atherosclerosis** (figure 6.18) is the most common form of arteriosclerosis and is usually described as **furring up** of the **arteries**. It is caused by lipid (fat) deposits accumulating in the inner lining of arteries, resulting in a narrowing of the arterial lumen, thereby impeding blood flow. When the deposits eventually block one of the coronary arteries, a **coronary heart attack** results.

- **CHD** (coronary heart disease) is one of Britain's greatest killers and encompasses diseases such as **angina** and **heart attacks** or **coronary thrombosis**. Angina begins as a chest pain, which is due to ischemia or lack of blood and hence oxygen to the heart muscle itself. The first symptoms of CHD are usually noticed during physical exertion or excitement and the subsequent increase in heart rate. Heavy, cramp-like pains are experienced across the chest. Angina is normally treated and controlled with drugs and relaxation, but a person suffering from this condition has a higher risk of suffering from a **coronary thrombosis**.

- A **coronary thrombosis** or heart attack is a sudden severe blockage in one of the coronary arteries, completely cutting off the blood supply to part of the myocardial tissue. This blockage is often caused by a **blood clot** formed within slowly moving blood in an already damaged, partially obstructed coronary artery. Heart attacks can be severe or mild, depending on the positioning of the blockage. In a severe blockage the heart may stop beating. This is called a **cardiac arrest**. About half of all cardiac arrest cases die. In 2008, coronary heart disease accounted for 30% of all UK deaths in people aged less than 75 years.

Protection against cardiovascular disease

- There is good evidence that **regular exercise** can have a protective effect on the heart and circulatory system. Stamina-building activities such as jogging, cycling and swimming will improve the efficiency of cardiac tissue and blood circulation.

- Regular exercise **reduces resting heart rate** and **increases stroke volume** because of a bigger, stronger, more efficient heart. This enables a person to have the same resting cardiac output at a lower heart rate and therefore less stress on the heart. Improved blood flow to the coronary muscle itself will reduce myocardial demands as the heart becomes more efficient, and therefore a person is less likely to suffer angina and/or coronary heart disease.

- Amounts of **cholesterol** (a constituent of animal fat in the diet) and **triglycerides** (fat) that reach the fuel transport system of the body are statistically associated with a high incidence of **hypertension** and **atherosclerosis**, and therefore there is an increased probability of heart disease and **coronary thrombosis**. Therefore diets should include less animal fat (saturated fats) to reduce this risk.

figure 6.19 – obesity and inactivity

- With regular exercise, **resting blood pressure is lowered** and the balance of cholesterol (a constituent of animal fat in the diet) and triglycerides (fat) is improved. Being physically active can increase the proportion of high density lipoproteins (**HDL** – the good cholesterol) to low density lipoproteins (**LDL** – the bad cholesterol).

- The function of HDL is to remove and transport fat molecules from cells, including cholesterol. Increasing concentrations of HDL particles are strongly associated with decreasing accumulation of atherosclerosis within the walls of arteries, lowering blood pressure, maintaining a healthy weight by **decreasing body fat**, reducing the risk of getting diabetes and cardiovascular diseases associated with obesity (figure 6.19).

- The exercise process increases elasticity and thickness of the smooth walls of arterial muscle, which makes the walls of the arteries tougher and less likely to stretch under pressure, thereby reducing arteriosclerosis and hypertension.

- Equally, regular exercise will reduce the risk of potential blood clots, thereby reducing the risk of coronary thrombosis.

- Also, with **regular exercise**, there is an increase in blood volume and blood cell count, and hence an increase in $\dot{V}O_{2max}$.

- In addition there is a **decrease in blood viscosity** and resistance to blood flow which again are cardio protective adaptations.

All these aerobic adaptive responses will enable the individual to sustain physical activity for longer and be able to increase work-load intensities.

What exercise?

In addition to the positive physiological effects of exercise on the body, a person will feel and look well. The type of exercise undertaken to protect your body from coronary heart disease will depend on your present physical condition. The major questions to be asked in devising an exercise programme are:

- How often (**frequency**)?
- How much (**intensity**)?
- How long (**duration**)?

Health and the respiratory system

Intense **aerobic** exercise has the effect of forcing the person to breathe more deeply and more often (the **vital capacity** of the lung is fully utilised, and the breathing frequency (**f**) increases). At submaximal workloads there is a slight decrease in the breathing rate. During maximal workloads there is a big increase in breathing rate, hence much bigger values in minute ventilation are achieved.

This has the effect of exercising the **respiratory muscular system** – namely, the diaphragm and intercostal muscles. If exercise is continued at least two to three times per week, these **muscles will get fitter** and more capable of working without cramps and conditions like stitches.

Health and the respiratory system

The efficiency of the respiratory system will depend on the utilisation and capacity of the alveoli to take oxygen from air breathed in and transmit it to blood flowing through the alveolar capillary bed. Long-term physical activity **increases blood flow** to the upper lobes of the lungs to **increase utilisation of lung alveoli**, hence increasing gaseous exchange and therefore $\dot{V}O_{2max}$. At submaximal workloads $\dot{V}O_2$ will be less because of greater efficiency of oxygen uptake.

Increased efficiencies of the respiratory system will improve **recovery** from exercise and reduce **oxygen debt** during exercise.

Asthma

Asthma can also reduce respiratory efficiency by making breathing difficult, particularly during exhalation. Asthma is caused by an increased constriction (tightening or narrowing) of the smooth muscle of bronchioles in response to a variety of stimuli, and/or by increased mucous secretions and swelling of mucous membrane lining the respiratory bronchioles. The stimuli for asthma can be any one of a number of allergy causing substances (which can be breathed in), such as grass pollen, household dust, cat fur, or feathers. During **exercise-induced asthma** (EIA), the bronchioles dilate during exercise (for example during running), and constrict at the end of exercise, making breathing difficult.

The treatment for asthma would be a steroid-based inhaler, which would need to be registered for competitions. An extended warm-up prior to training, competition or match also helps to control asthma of the EIA variety.

Chronic obstructive pulmonary disease (COPD)

COPD is the overall label which applies to such diseases as **emphysema** and **chronic bronchitis**. Emphysema is a permanent enlargement of the alveoli accompanied by the destruction of the alveoli walls leading to loss in elasticity of lung tissue. This opens bronchioles during inspiration which collapse during expiration, trapping huge volumes of air in the alveoli and causing difficulties in breathing due to poor air flow.

Bronchitis has excessive **mucus production** impairing ventilation and gas exchange.

The major cause of these effects is **smoking** – more than 80% of people with COPD have a history of smoking. Another important risk factor for COPD is the **environment** in which people work and live. Dust and fumes are attributed to up to 19 percent of COPD in smokers, and up to 31 percent of COPD in nonsmokers. The cumulative exposure to indoor and outdoor air pollution is also relevant. For example, miners' exposure to coal dust and heating engineers' exposure to asbestos dust, caused major COPD. Genes are being recognized as having an important role in the development of COPD.

The effects of exercise on asthma and obstructive pulmonary disease (COPD)

Exercise is good for chronic obstructive pulmonary disease (COPD) and asthma. Many world class athletes suffer from asthma, including Paula Radcliffe and David Beckham. The key point is to control and reduce the risk of asthmatic symptoms and use reliever inhalers when necessary.

* Regular exercise improves **lung function**, thus increasing stamina and reducing breathlessness as outlined below.
* Some individuals experience their asthma (such as wheezing, chest tightness, and cough) almost exclusively when they exercise and are said to have '**exercise-induced asthma**'.
* These symptoms are controlled with the use of reliever inhalers.
* **Respiratory Muscle Training** (RMT) is a technique that aims to improve respiratory muscle function through specific exercises. RMT is normally aimed at people who suffer from asthma, bronchitis, emphysema and COPD.
* RMT and/or regular aerobic exercise at around 50-60% of HRmax, can increase the **strength** and **endurance** of the **respiratory muscles** and therefore improve respiration.
* These adaptations are due to increased utilisation of lung tissue (particularly the lower lobes where infections such as pneumonia are likely to occur), improved **elasticity of pulmonary alveoli walls**, improved capillary networks surrounding alveoli, resulting in improved gaseous exchange and lung capacities.
* In addition, the need for medication and the **risk of infection** associated with COPD are reduced.
* For example, a six week daily programme of RMT significantly reduces the amount of oxygen these same breathing muscles require during exercise, resulting in more oxygen being available for other muscles.

Practice questions

1) Cardiovascular activity can result in the following benefit to the heart:
   a.   increase in cardiac output.
   b.   increase in resting heart rate.
   c.   increase in blood pressure.
   d.   decrease in heart size.

2) Flexibility is affected by:
   a.   length of ligaments.
   b.   length and elasticity of muscle and tendons.
   c.   bone structure of joint.
   d.   all of these.

3) The ability to exert force against resistance is:
   a.   balance.
   b.   coordination.
   c.   muscular strength.
   d.   muscular endurance.

4) Which one of the following would tell you if an athlete had good muscular endurance?
   a.   how far the athlete could run in 12 minutes.
   b.   how far the athlete could sit and reach.
   c.   how many curl ups the athlete could do.
   d.   how good the athlete's grip strength is.

5) Which one of the following activities does not measure strength?
   a.   press up.
   b.   Cooper 12 minute run.
   c.   long jump take off.
   d.   maximum bench press.

6) a)   Define the fitness components of strength, static strength and strength endurance.
         How does each component relate to athletic performance?   6 marks

   b)   Identify and describe a valid and reliable test that measures either strength or strength endurance.   3 marks

7) Individuals respond to a given training programme in different ways and to different extents.
   Identify some of the factors that affect strength.   6 marks

8) A Level. Discuss the various forms of interval training programmes a sports performer may use within their training
   programme. Identify the advantages and disadvantages of each type of interval
   training that you have selected and indicate the sport or event most likely to
   benefit from each one.   20 marks

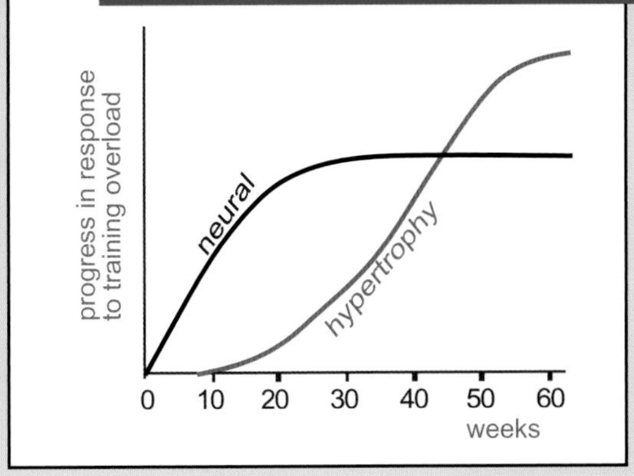

9) a)   The graph in figure 6.20 illustrates neural and hypertrophic
         adaptations that have occurred in skeletal muscle tissue
         following 60 weeks of strength training. Explain why early
         increases in strength are more associated with neural
         adaptations, but later long-term gains are almost solely
         the result of muscle hypertrophy.   6 marks

   b)   What effect would a strength-training programme have on
         anaerobic capacity and muscle fatigue?   4 marks

   c)   How could these strength gains be used in the planning of a
         strength-training schedule for an elite power performer?
                                                          3 marks

figure 6.20 – anaerobic adaptations to high intensity exercise

Practice questions

10) a) Plyometric training is a type of power training, which involves performing exercises with maximum power and speed. Describe the main concepts of plyometric training, illustrating your answer with an example of an exercise. Identify the type of sports performer who would most benefit from this training method.   **6 marks**

b) Discuss the advantages and disadvantages of plyometric training.   **4 marks**

c) Why does muscle soreness (DOMS) often occur following a plyometric training session and how could muscle soreness be reduced?   **4 marks**

11) a) Describe an appropriate interval training session for a specific component of fitness in a named sport.   **3 marks**

b) Discuss the advantages of using interval training in both aerobic and anaerobic training programmes.   **3 marks**

12) a) Figure 6.21 shows a curve that represents the intensity of training over a single periodised year. Draw in a further two curves that represent volume of work and technique.   **2 marks**

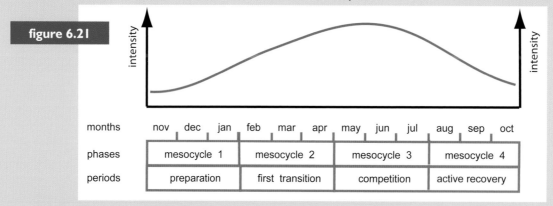

figure 6.21

months	nov	dec	jan	feb	mar	apr	may	jun	jul	aug	sep	oct
phases	mesocycle 1			mesocycle 2			mesocycle 3			mesocycle 4		
periods	preparation			first transition			competition			active recovery		

b) The competitive phase lets the performer peak for competition. Using the intensity curve explain how strength development changes over the periodised year. Gives examples of work volume in terms of sets, repetitions, and percentages of 1RM.   **6 marks**

13) a) Stretching is a key element in any warm-up. Using an example, identify two other elements of a warm-up and explain how they help to prepare an athlete.   **4 marks**

b) Describe three different methods of stretching and state a sport that would benefit most from each type.   **6 marks**

c) Identify two physiological adaptations to skeletal tissue following a three-month flexibility training programme.   **2 marks**

14) a) Give two advantages of using static stretching within a flexibility programme.   **2 marks**

b) Identify two structural limitations to muscle flexibility.   **2 marks**

15) A Level. Discuss the following statement: 'An unhealthy lifestyle has a detrimental effect on the cardiovascular and respiratory systems'. Describe and explain the benefits of regular physical activity on the respiratory system.   **20 marks**

16) A Level. Periodisation is a training concept that explains the variation in training volume and intensity over a specific period of time. Outline the basic structure of a single periodised year and illustrate how a coach is able to use this structure when planning a training programme for an athletics group.   **20 marks**

Answers link: http://www.jroscoe.co.uk/downloads/as_a1_revise_pe_ocr/OCRAS_A1_ch6_answers.pdf

BIOMECHANICS

CHAPTER 7
BIOMECHANICAL PRINCIPLES, LEVERS
AND THE USE OF TECHNOLOGY

CHAPTER 7: *Biomechanical principles, levers and the use of technology*

Newton's laws of motion

Newton's first law

Newton's first law of motion describes what happens when **zero net force** acts, which means that all forces acting must cancel out. In figure 7.1 the forces (green arrows) **cancel out**. The vertical forces are the same size (arrows are the same length) but in opposite directions. The horizontal forces are also of the same size and in opposite directions, hence all forces cancel out.

When there is zero net force acting on an object:
* The object is **stationary**.
* **Or** the object moves at **constant velocity**.

Hence when any object moves at constant velocity, all forces must cancel out, the net force must be zero.

figure 7.1 – a sprinter at constant speed

Inertia

The first law is also known as the law of **inertia**. The concept of inertia is that a massive object will remain at rest and will require a force to shift it, and once moving, will require a force to change its motion (accelerate or decelerate it). Sometimes, the word **inertia** is used to represent the **mass** of a body or object.

Newton's second law

Newton's second law of motion describes what happens when a **net force acts** on a body. **A net force** produces **acceleration** or **deceleration** of the body or changes the direction of the body (swerving). In the motion of a sprinter the acceleration is produced by the net force applied, which must be forwards if the sprinter is accelerating forwards. When the sprinter **decelerates**, there is a net **force backwards**. In figure 7.2, the vertical arrows (representing vertical forces) are the same length but in opposite directions, and hence cancel out. The horizontal forces are both acting backwards, therefore there is a net force acting backwards on her. This means that she is **decelerating** (horizontally!).

* Newton's second law also says that the bigger the **net** force, the greater the **acceleration** of the person.
* Hence a **stronger** sprinter should be able to **accelerate** out of the blocks quicker.
* However, the more mass an object has, the less the acceleration for a given force.
* Hence a heavier (more massive) sprinter will accelerate less than a lighter sprinter.

This is expressed mathematically as:

$$F = m \times a$$
(force = mass × acceleration)

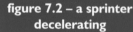

figure 7.2 – a sprinter decelerating

As discussed above, slowing down (**deceleration**) is also caused by force. Hence a bike hitting a barrier encounters a large force, since a large deceleration slows the bike very quickly, possibly wrecking it and hurting the rider. However, if the cyclist had applied the brakes moderately, he or she would have encountered less deceleration, taking longer to stop, but would do so safely.

Newton's third law

Newton's third law of motion describes what happens when **two bodies** (or objects) exert forces on one another. Action and reaction are equal and opposite and always occur in pairs.

Action acts on one of the bodies, and the **reaction** to this action acts on the other body. At a sprint start, the athlete **pushes back** on the blocks as hard as possible (this is the 'action' - see figure 7.4e page 109), and the blocks **push forward** on the athlete (this push forward is the 'reaction force'). The reaction provides forward acceleration on the athlete. In figure 7.4c (page 109), a swimmer pushes backwards on the water with hands and feet (this is the force in **black**, the **action**). At the same time, the water thrusts the swimmer forward (this is the force in **red**, the **reaction force**).

Newton's third law

For **internal forces** within the body, for example in figure 7.3, the origin (**O**) and insertion (**I**) of a muscle pull in opposite directions to change the shape of the body. In this example, the **action** is the pull of the muscle (red arrow) on the origin of the muscle, and the **reaction** is the pull of the muscle (**black arrow**) at its opposite end, on the insertion. The effect is to change the shape of the person, by pulling the origin towards the insertion, and bending the limb in question.

Reaction forces

Reaction forces are forces acting via Newton's third law as explained above. When one object pushes on another, the first object experiences a force equal but opposite in direction to the second (figure 7.4):

- **a**, the jumper pushes down on the ground (black arrow), the ground pushes up on the jumper (red arrow).
- **b**, the weight lifter pulls up on the weight (black arrow), weight pulls down on lifter (red arrow).
- **c**, the swimmer pushes backwards on the water (black arrow), the water pushes forward on the swimmer (red arrow).
- **d**, canoeist pushes backwards on the water (black arrow), reaction force thrusts the canoe forward (red arrow).
- **e**, sprinter pushes back and down on the ground (black arrow), the ground pushes upwards and forwards on the sprinter (red arrow).
- **f**, in cycling, the tyre on the rear wheel pushes backward on the ground (black arrow), the ground pushes forward on the rear wheel (red arrow).

Force

Force is push or pull. The unit of force is the **newton** (10N is approximately the weight of 1 kg). Force changes the state of motion of an object, and causes acceleration or deceleration or change of direction.

One newton of force is the force required to produce an acceleration of 1 ms^{-2} in a mass of 1 kg. This is related to the inertial property of mass - the more force applied, the more acceleration produced (see Newton's second law, page 108).

Force has **direction** and size (**value**), and is therefore a vector. When describing a force it is important to explain where the force acts (the point of action), as well as the direction.

Vectors and scalars

The ideas behind **vectors** and **scalars** are used extensively in maths and physics. A **vector** is a quantity which has **size** (called magnitude) and **direction**. By quantity we mean something like weight, displacement, velocity, acceleration, force, and momentum, all of which are vectors, and therefore have to have a direction connected to them as well as value or size. For example, a force could be 100 newtons downward (the downward specifies the direction), an acceleration could be 10 metres per second squared forwards (the forwards specifies the direction).

figure 7.3 – forces at origin and insertion

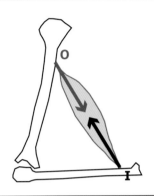

figure 7.4 – examples of reaction forces

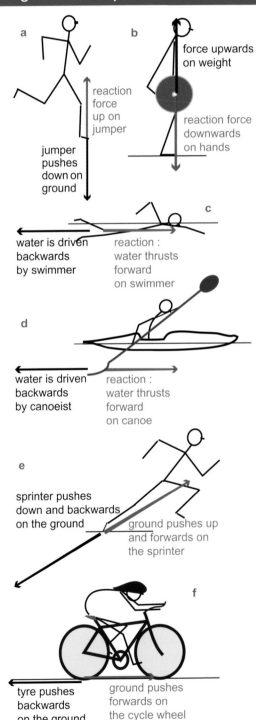

a

reaction force up on jumper

jumper pushes down on ground

b

force upwards on weight

reaction force downwards on hands

c

water is driven backwards by swimmer

reaction : water thrusts forward on swimmer

d

water is driven backwards by canoeist

reaction : water thrusts forward on canoe

e

sprinter pushes down and backwards on the ground

ground pushes up and forwards on the sprinter

f

tyre pushes backwards on the ground

ground pushes forwards on the cycle wheel

Vectors and scalars

Usually in maths, the direction is specified by the angle to the x-axis in a graph of an arrow drawn on the graph, with the size (magnitude) represented by the length of the arrow (figure 7.5).

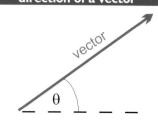

figure 7.5 – direction of a vector

Net Force

The point of this is that when more than one vector has to be taken into account, then they must be added together taking note of the direction of each vector. In figure 7.6 for example, two forces of 500 newtons are acting, the green force acts upwards, and the red force acts downwards. Because they are acting in opposite directions, they add up to nil, in other words they exactly cancel out to give zero net force. Note that this gymnast is also in unstable equilibrium (see page 114).

figure 7.6 – vectors cancel out

- In figure 7.7, the vertical forces acting on the sprinter are the weight (W = force due to gravity) acting downwards, and the ground reaction force (R) acting upwards. These two forces are identical in value but opposite in direction and therefore cancel out exactly to give zero net force vertically.

- The horizontal forces are the friction force (F) acting forwards, and the **air resistance** or drag (A) acting backwards. These two forces are equal in value but opposite in direction, and hence cancel out to give zero net force acting horizontally.

- Hence relatively large forces can act, but they can cancel out because of their direction. Note that zero net force does not mean that the sprinter is stationary, see Newton's first law of motion (page 108).

- Equally, when the forces are added up and there is an unbalanced **resultant** (the forces **do not cancel out**), then there is a **net force** acting. The body on which this force is acting will then accelerate in the **direction** of this net force as specified by Newton's second law (page 108).

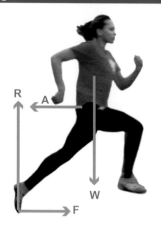

figure 7.7 – forces cancel out

A scalar

A **scalar** is a quantity which has size or value only. Quantities like mass, speed, energy, power, and length have a value only. For example, a person could have a mass of 60 kg, or an amount of 1000 joules of energy are used up when performing an exercise. No directional angle is required when talking about these quantities.

Energy is a scalar which has a value only, and the value of energy consumed daily by a Tour de France cyclist is 6,000 kilocalories - which has no direction.

Speed (measured in metres per second - ms^{-1}, distance and time are scalars which are linked by a simple equation.

$$\text{Speed} = \text{distance travelled per second (ms}^{-1})$$

$$\text{Speed} = \frac{\text{distance travelled in metres (m)}}{\text{time taken to travel in seconds (s)}}$$

Weight and mass

These two ideas are often confused. **Mass** is a scalar and represents the total quantity of matter in an object. **Weight** is the force due to gravity on a mass (with a direction towards the centre of the Earth). Weight will vary slightly over the surface of the Earth depending on the gravitational field strength. The gravitational field strength changes slightly depending on the thickness of the Earth's crust, the longitude, the proximity of large mountains, and the height above sea level. Weight is approximately 10 newtons for each kilogramme of mass, and will act on the centre of mass of a body (the point which represents the averaged position of all the mass of a body), with examples shown in figure 7.8. Hence if the mass of the sprinter in figure 7.7 is 50 kg, then her weight would be 50 x 10 = 500 newtons towards the centre of the Earth.

figure 7.8 – weight of various bodies

sprinter

diver tumbling

Weight is also the predominant force acting on an object projected into flight.

Friction

Friction is a force which acts sideways between two surfaces which tend to slide past one another. This force enables sportspeople to accelerate, slow down, swerve, walk, and run.

The magnitude of friction depends on the **grip of footwear** on floor surface, and the **nature of the surface** itself (rough, smooth, slippy, greasy and so on), for example:

figure 7.9 – friction

- **Studs and spikes** increase friction to enable better swerving and accelerating and decelerating in games or track situations. This applies to soft or wet surfaces.

- For **dry hard surfaces**, solid smooth rubber soles can give better friction as in discus or hammer shoes, rock climbing shoes, or tennis shoes for concrete surfaces.

- In **snow and ice**, long slender footwear (skates or skis) have low forward friction, but high sideways friction.

Note that friction acts forwards on the feet of the accelerating runner (see figure 7.9).

friction acts forward on the foot of the accelerating sprinter

Friction depends on the force pressing the surfaces together, but not on the area of contact. For example:

- The inverted wings on racing cars increase the down force on wheels. This increases cornering friction between the wheels and the ground.
- When riding a mountain bike up a steep hill, you should sit back over the rear wheel to increase downward force on the rear wheel, so that there is more friction between the rear wheel and the ground.
- Friction also enables swerving by games players in rugby, soccer, hockey, and tennis. The friction force then acts sideways to the direction of motion, and changes the direction of motion.
- The direction taken after a bounce by a spinning ball depends on the direction of spin and the friction between the ball and the ground.

Rolling or sliding friction

- **Rolling friction** is the term which describes the force between surfaces which do not move relative to one another, like a wheel rolling over a surface, or a foot driving and pushing without slipping. The friction can be anything from zero up to a maximum just before slipping occurs. As soon as slipping occurs, the friction force falls, and would not be enough to keep a sportsperson upright (so he or she slips over!).

- **Sliding friction** occurs when the two surfaces are moving relative to one another, and is always less then the maximum rolling friction. This is why ABS (**advanced braking systems**) will reduce braking force on wheels if sensors detect the beginning of sliding.

Fluid friction

Fluid friction (or **drag**) is a term applying to objects moving through fluids (gases or liquids). The force acts in the opposite direction to the direction of motion. This term applies to the **air resistance** experienced by objects moving through air.

Fluid friction force depends on the shape and size of the moving object, the speed of the moving object, and the streamlining effect (summarised in figure 7.10).

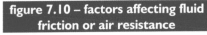

figure 7.10 – factors affecting fluid friction or air resistance

Drag and air resistance

In order to minimise drag, the following developments affect sport:
- The body position and shape for a swimmer.
- The shape of helmets for cyclists.
- The use of lycra clothing.
- The shape of sports vehicles (cars or bikes).

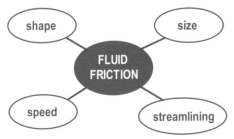

shape   size

FLUID FRICTION

speed   streamlining

Low values of fluid friction

This discussion concerns **low values of drag** compared with other forces. Examples are:

- Any sprinter or game player for whom air resistance is usually much less than friction effects and weight. Therefore streamlining is seen as less important.

- A shot or hammer in flight, in which air resistance would be much less than the weight, and therefore the angle of release should be around 45°.

High values of fluid friction

High values of drag will occur for any sportsperson or vehicle moving through water, and hence fluid friction is the critical factor governing swimming speed.

- Body shape or cross section, and clothing (surface material to assist laminar flow, see below), are adjusted to minimise fluid friction.

A cyclist (figure 7.11) travels much faster than a runner and therefore has high fluid friction:

- He or she crouches low to reduce forward cross section.

- The helmet is designed to minimise turbulent flow.

- Clothing and wheel profiles are designed to assist streamlining.

Cross sectional area is the area of the moving object as viewed from the front. The smaller the better to reduce drag, hence cyclists crouch down, and keep elbows in!

Laminar flow and drag

Fluid friction (or drag) depends on **laminar** flow, the smooth flowing of air or water past an object. Laminar means flowing in layers, and streamlining assists laminar flow. Figure 7.12 shows images of a streamlined helmet, and a non-streamlined helmet. The point of the streamlined shape is that the air moves past it in layers whereas in the case of the non-streamlined helmet, vortices are formed where the fluid does not flow smoothly. When this happens bits of fluid are flung randomly sideways which causes drag. The drag is caused by bits of fluid being dragged along with the moving object (the cycle helmet).

Free body diagrams

Pin men (free body) diagrams are used to represent the human body with forces acting on it when answering exam questions. Free body diagrams are a way of doing this without any anatomical details.

In figure 7.13, a runner is represented by a pin man, with forces depicted by red arrows. The figure shows four forces acting, two forces acting up on the foot and down on the body, and two forces acting backwards on the body and forwards on the foot. Longer arrows mean greater force.

The **point of action** of a force is also important, remembering that drag forces will act over the whole body but are usually represented by a single arrow acting somewhere in the middle of the body. A friction force will act on the foot of the runner, and the weight will act on his or her centre of mass. Reaction forces act at the point of contact between two objects (on the foot of the runner in figure 7.13).

figure 7.11 – a cyclist needs good streamlining

fluid friction (drag) depends on forward cross section and streamlining

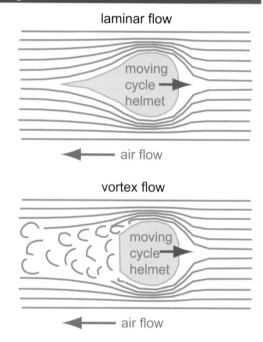

figure 7.12 – laminar flow and vortex flow

laminar flow

moving cycle helmet

← air flow

vortex flow

moving cycle helmet

← air flow

figure 7.13 – pin-man or free-body diagram

Momentum

Momentum is a concept derived from Newton's second law which says:

force = rate of change of momentum

(linear) **momentum = mass** x **velocity**

Note that linear means in a straight line, and that momentum includes both mass and velocity.

- Hence an object which has a lot of momentum requires a lot of force to stop it, which is a good argument for fast heavy rugby players or American footballers.
- Momentum is a **vector** (and therefore has direction).

Distance and displacement

Distance is a scalar - usually measured in metres, **displacement** is a distance (also measured in metres) as the crow flies from start to finish of a movement. **Displacement** therefore has a value and a direction and is a **vector** (pages 109-110 for an explanation of vectors and scalars).

For example, the total distance run in a 10k race will be 10,000 metres - and this is the measure which the runner will be interested in. But the displacement will be zero, since the start and finish of a 10k race are usually in the same place. Start and finish of a marathon race are often not in the same place, so the displacement between start and finish will have a value in metres and a direction. But again, runners will be interested in the distance ran, not the displacement between start and finish.

figure 7.14 – a sprinter at constant speed

Speed and velocity

Speed	= <u>**distance moved**</u> **time taken**	or	$v = \dfrac{s}{t}$	unit ms^{-1}

= **scalar** (no direction)

= distance moved in 1 second

Velocity = speed in a given **direction** = **vector**

figure 7.15 – Jason Robinson sidesteps left then right

The vector property of velocity is important because not only does it add up or cancel out a bit like the force example in figure 7.14, but it can change direction without changing value. Examples of this are a swerving rugby player (figure 7.15), or the head of a hammer which moves in a circular path, both of whose velocity changes in direction.

The swerving rugby play is running forwards but exerts a force **sideways** to the direction of motion. This force is part of the friction between his boots and the ground (players often slip when performing this manoeuvre). His direction of motion will therefore change - hence the swerve.

This means that the player or the hammer head is accelerating towards the centre of the arc (circle) in which it is moving, which means that from Newton's second law (see page 108) a force is required (also towards the centre of the arc in which the object is moving).

Acceleration

Acceleration = <u>**change of velocity**</u>
time taken to change $a = \dfrac{v - u}{t}$ unit ms^{-2}

- **Acceleration** will be in the same direction as net force, and therefore acceleration is a vector (has direction).
- In the case of the swerving rugby player, the direction of acceleration is along the radius of the path of the player. This is a **radial acceleration**.
- **Deceleration** is **negative acceleration** (slowing down).

Stability and the centre of mass

Centre of mass

Centre of mass (CofM) is the single point (on a body) which represents **all the spread out mass** of the body. So, since gravity acts on mass to produce weight, the weight acts at the centre of mass of a body. In figure 7.16, the weight is marked as a green arrow, and it acts downward on the CofM. The CofM can be defined as **'the point of balance of the body'**. As limbs are moved, or the torso changes shape (as when bent over for example), so the position of the centre of mass of the body will move as in figure 7.16. Note that the CofM does not always lie within the body shape, when the torso is bent, it can lie well outside the body mass.

Note that the right hand image in figure 7.16 is that of the layout position for the Fosbury flop high jump technique. The CofM lies underneath the body, and can be below the bar even though the athlete clears the bar.

Balance

The CofM must be **over the base of support** if a person is to be balanced. In figure 7.17, with the leg stuck out sideways, the centre of mass moves to a position to the left of a vertical line through the foot. So, the weight (force) acts downwards through the centre of mass (see the green vertical line in figure 7.17, also known as the centre of gravity projection), and will topple the person to the left. Therefore to maintain balance, the person must lean to the right (as we look at her), and thereby bring the CofM back vertically over the supporting foot.

Toppling

Toppling is caused by the weight acting vertically at the CofM and therefore to **one side** of the near edge of the base of support. This fact can be used by divers or gymnasts to initiate a controlled spinning (twisting) fall. And hence lead into somersaults, cartwheels or twists.

Stability

If an object has its CofM over the base of support, it is said to be in equilibrium. If a slight movement of the object will make it topple, then the object is said to be in unstable equilibrium. An example of this would be a beam gymnast who must carefully control the position of her CofM if she is to remain on the beam (figure 7.18).

The gymnast who lies on the floor would be said to be in neutral or stable equilibrium (figure 7.19). When pushed, he would remain in the same position (or nearly the same) without toppling or falling.

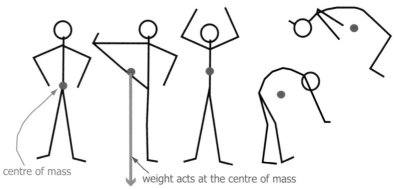

figure 7.16 – centre of mass position changes with body shape

centre of mass

weight acts at the centre of mass

figure 7.17 – a gymnast topples to the left

weight causes toppling to the left

figure 7.18 – unstable equilibrium

figure 7.19 – neutral or stable equilibrium

Components of a lever

The term **internal forces** describes the forces acting (figure 7.20) when a muscle pulls on its **origin O** and **insertion I**. The force on the origin (in red) is equal in size but opposite in direction to the force on the insertion (in black). This changes the **shape** of the person.

figure 7.20 – forces at origin and insertion

Levers

A lever is a **means of applying force at a distance** from the source of the force and has a **fulcrum (pivot)**, **effort** and **load**. In the human body, usually a **joint** and the **attached limbs** or bones act as a lever. **Force** is applied as **effort** by a **muscle** or group of muscles. The **load** is the **force applied** to the **surroundings** by the lever.

Classification of levers

Class 1 lever

This is a see-saw lever with the fulcrum in between the effort and the load. It is found rarely in the body, for example the triceps/elbow/forearm lever (figure 7.21), or the atlas/neck muscles used in the nodding movement.

Sometimes, there will be mechanical advantage and disadvantage depending on the relative distances of the load and effort from the fulcrum. Basically, the further away the load, the less the advantage of the lever.

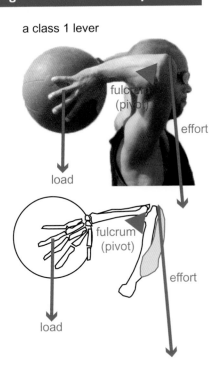

figure 7.21 - elbow/triceps lever

a class 1 lever

Class 2 lever

This is a wheelbarrow lever where the load is bigger than the effort, and the fulcrum is at one end of the lever with the load in between the effort and the fulcrum. This is found rarely in the body, the main example being the Achilles tendon/calf muscles (gastrocnemius and soleus) and ankle joint lever (figure 7.22). This is used in most running or walking movements with the fulcrum underneath the ball of the foot as it drives the body forward. This class of lever always has a **mechanical advantage** - the load is always bigger than the effort.

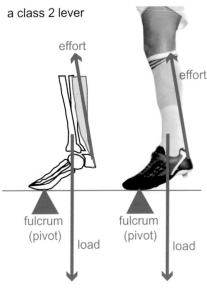

figure 7.22 - ankle/calf lever

a class 2 lever

Class 3 lever

This class of lever again has the fulcrum at one end of the lever arm, with the effort in between the load and the fulcrum. It has a **mechanical disadvantage**, the effort is always bigger than the load and is the most common system found in body. For example the elbow/biceps/forearm lever (figure 7.23), or the knee/quadriceps/tibia/fibula systems (figure 7.24 page 116).

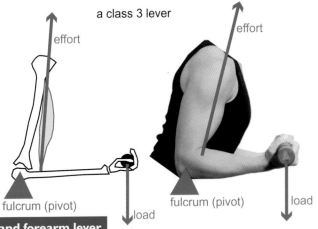

a class 3 lever

figure 7.23 – the elbow and forearm lever

Effects of the length of lever

The **length of the lever** or **resistance arm** of the lever (**d** in figure 7.25) affects the **load** able to be exerted by the lever, and the **speed** at which the hand can move. The longer the lever **d**, the smaller the value of the load for a given biceps strength and value of the **effort arm** (distance between effort and pivot). The longer the lever arm **d**, the faster the load can be applied (as the limb moves through its range - a longer limb - the hand would move further in the same time).

This means that the hand of a thrower with long arms will be moving faster than the hand of a thrower with short arms if each is turning (rotating) at the same speed.

The **shorter** the **effort arm** the less load can be exerted. The shorter the load (resistance) arm of a person the bigger the load can be. This is why successful weightlifters tend to have short arms.

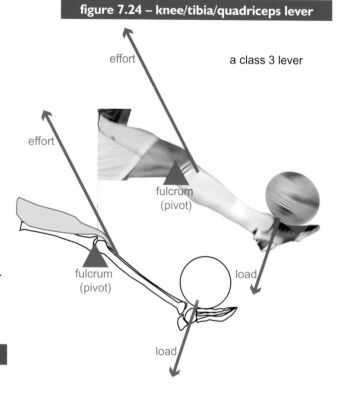

figure 7.24 – knee/tibia/quadriceps lever

a class 3 lever

effort

effort

fulcrum
(pivot)

fulcrum
(pivot)

load

load

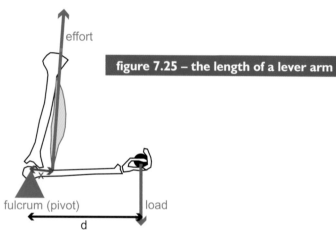

effort

figure 7.25 – the length of a lever arm

fulcrum (pivot)

load

d

Analysis through the use of technology

Modern technology in sport has developed significantly over the past decade. Athletes, coaches, physiotherapists, podiatrists and sports scientists need to understand how to use technology in order to optimise sports performance, especially at the elite level.

Limb kinematics

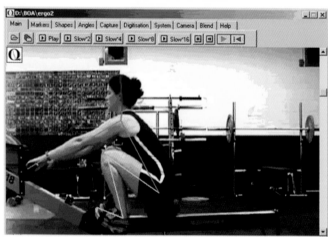

figure 7.26 – video software

Kinematics is the science of motion. In human movement, it is the study of the positions, angles, velocities, and accelerations of body segments and joints during motion. Body segments are rigid bodies such as the thigh, foot and forearm. Joints between adjacent segments include ankle, knee, hip, elbow and shoulder. Position describes the location of a body segment or joint in space.

In limb kinematics **reflective markers** are placed in the appropriate anatomical positions on the performer. High-speed 3D video cameras capture the performance and biomechanical software, such as Quintic and Dartfish, enable a coach to highlight and analyse technical aspects of the performance by using a variety of drawing tools or playback facilities over the actual video footage, as illustrated in figure 7.26. Automatic reports enable the user to analyse a movement which quantifies the key variables. The video clips can be repeated over and over again to reinforce the positive aspects of the performance and/or the ones that need improvement. Over time, the coach and performer can assess if technical improvements have been made.

Force plates

figure 7.27 – force plate output

Force plates are laboratory-based measuring instruments that measure the ground reaction forces generated by a body standing on or moving across them, to quantify balance, gait and other parameters of biomechanics.

- A **force plate** is inserted into the ground at the take off area for a long jump or high jump, or in the space in a track immediately after a sprint start. This enables the patterns of force (figure 7.27) made by a foot striking the plate to be determined.
- This information (combined with video of the same footfall) can tell a coach the precise way in which the foot is active during its strike with the ground, and enables him or her to assess whether **changes in foot posture** are required.

Wind tunnels

figure 7.28 – bike design in the wind tunnel

Wind tunnels are increasingly being used to assess the aerodynamics (improved flow of fluid - air or water - reducing drag or fluid friction) of bikes (figure 7.28), cycle helmets, and cyclist overall profile. This is done by blasting air past the stationary object in a tunnel, and using smoke to illustrate the layers of flow of the air. The task is to avoid vortex generation in the air flow, since smooth (laminar) flow generates less drag.

Factors investigated include:
- Wheel spokes and profiles.
- Width of handlebars.
- Riding posture, and hand position on the bars.
- Type of cloth and design of clothing.
- Forward cross-sectional area of frame and brackets.

Advantages of technology

- Technologies such as limb kinematics, force plates and wind tunnels provide precise, accurate data analysis that measure and improve biomechanical performance, especially at the elite world class level of sport.

Disadvantages of technology

- Many technologies, such as limb kinematics, force plates and wind tunnels are specialised laboratory-based pieces of equipment and have limitations in their sporting applications.
- Such types of equipment is expensive to buy.
- Their complex analysis often requires assistance from research professionals.
- These technologies are mainly located in National Centres for Sport and universities, such as Loughborough University, and so athletes may have to travel to such venues if they wish to use such technologies.

Practice questions

1) For which of the following is the athlete's centre of mass most likely to lie outside of his or her body?
   a. diver performing a tucked dive.
   b. trampolinist in a fully piked position.
   c. gymnast performing a cartwheel.
   d. gymnast performing a layout somersault.

2) In a first class lever, if the resistance arm is 300 mm and the force arm is 30 mm, what force is necessary to balance a weight of 10 N?
   a. 10 N.
   b. 1 N.
   c. 100 N.
   d. none of the above.

3) Which of these is not one of Newton's three laws of motion?
   a. the acceleration of an object is directly proportional to the force causing it and is inversely proportional to the mass of the object.
   b. body moves in a circle about a point called the axis of rotation.
   c. body will continue in a state of rest or of uniform velocity unless acted upon by an external force.
   d. for every action there is an equal and opposite reaction.

4) What is the difference between distance and displacement?
   a. displacement is the distance between the start and end point only, distance is the total distance travelled along the path of motion.
   b. displacement is the total distance travelled along the path of motion, distance is the distance between the start and end point only.
   c. displacement is the distance between the start and end point only, distance is the distance between the start and end point.
   d. displacement is the total distance travelled along the path of motion, distance is the total distance travelled along the path of motion.

5) A rugby prop sprints away from a scrum with an acceleration of 0.2ms-2 for 10s. How far did he travel?
   a. 15 metres.
   b. 10 metres.
   c. 18 metres.
   d. 20 metres.

figure 7.29 – a long jumper in flight

6) a) Explain with diagrams what is meant by the centre of mass of a body.   2 marks

   b) Explain with the aid of pin-man diagrams how the centre of mass of a long jumper changes from the take-off position to the flight phase shown in figure 7.29. 5 marks

7) Figure 7.30 shows a swimmer holding a balance just before the start of a race. Explain how the position of the centre of mass can affect the swimmer's balance. Describe how the swimmer in figure 7.30 can use his knowledge of balance to achieve his most effective block start.   5 marks

figure 7.30 – swimmer starting a race

8) Sketch the lever system which would represent the action of the biceps muscle in flexing the arm. Show on your diagram the resistance arm of the lever.   3 marks

Practice questions

figure 7.31 – long jumper taking off

9) In figure 7.31 of a jumper taking off, name, sketch and label the lever system operating at knee **B** during this action.　3 marks

10) In softball, what order (class) of lever is shown in the hitting action in figure 7.32? State **one** disadvantage and **one** advantage of reducing the bat length for a beginner.　3 marks

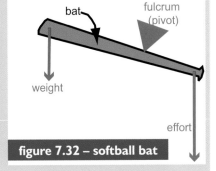

figure 7.32 – softball bat

11) a) Name, sketch and label the lever system which is operating at the ankle of leg **C** when doing the sprint set action illustrated in figure 7.33. 3 marks

   b) This class of lever always has a mechanical advantage. Explain why is this so?　2 marks

figure 7.33 – ankle lever system

12) Table 7.1 shows the speed of a 19 year-old male sprinter during a 200m race.

   a) Plot a graph of speed against time during this race. When does he reach maximum speed and what happens to his speed between 8 and 22 seconds?　7 marks

   b) Acceleration is the change of speed per second. Use the graph to establish his speed at 0.5 seconds and 1.5 seconds and calculate the average acceleration between 0.5 and 1.5 seconds.　3 marks

   c) Successful games players are often able to change their velocity rapidly in the game situation. Explain the biomechanics behind this ability using examples from a game of your choice.　6 marks

13) a) A sprinter uses her calf muscles to push on the blocks at the start of a run. Explain, using Newton's laws, how this enables her to accelerate forwards out of the blocks.　3 marks

   b) If the resultant forward force was 300 newtons and the runner's mass was 60 kg, what would be her acceleration?　2 marks

   c) What would be the speed of the runner after 1.5 seconds, assuming that the acceleration is the same over that period of time?　2 marks

   d) A squash player drives forward into a forehand stroke. Show how Newton's third law of motion explains his ability to do this.　3 marks

speed (ms⁻¹)	time (seconds)
0.0	0
6.0	1
7.5	2
8.2	3
8.4	4
8.5	5
8.5	7
8.4	8
8.3	10
8.2	13
8.1	18
8.0	22

table 7.1

Practice questions

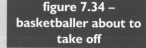

14) a) Use the diagram in figure 7.34 of a basketballer just about to take off into a jump shot, and your knowledge of Newton's Laws of motion to explain why the basketball jumper takes off.   **3 marks**

 b) If the vertical upward ground reaction force on the jumper is 2000N, and the weight of the jumper is 800N, estimate the net upward force acting on him.   **1 mark**

 c) The mass of the jumper is 80 kg, calculate his upward acceleration during this part of the jump.   **2 marks**

figure 7.34 – basketballer about to take off

basketballer

15) a) The graph in figure 7.35 shows the start of a 100m sprint swim race. Using Newton's laws of motion, explain how the swimmer achieves the initial forward motion.   **3 marks**

 b) Describe what has happened to the swimmer at point A and explain the motion that occurs.   **3 marks**

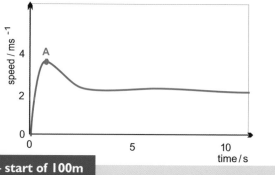

figure 7.35 – start of 100m swim race

16) Tennis players have to change direction quickly during a match to recover to the centre of the court. Figure 7.36 shows a tennis player just after hitting a forehand and then starting to recover to the centre of the court in the direction shown.

 Draw a pin diagram of the tennis player as he pushes off the court surface to recover to the centre of the court, showing all forces acting on the tennis player at this point. All forces must be clearly identified.

 Explain the factors that affect the horizontal force at this point. Apply Newton's second law of motion to explain the effect of this force on the player.   **10 marks**

figure 7.36 – a tennis player moves between strokes

moving

17) How do the following technologies aid analysis and feedback for improving sporting performance?

 a) Video and computer software analysis.
 b) Force plate technology.
 c) Wind tunnels.   **9 marks**

Answers link: http://www.jroscoe.co.uk/downloads/as_a1_revise_pe_ocr/OCRAS_A1_ch7_answers.pdf

SKILL ACQUISITION

CHAPTER 8: *Classification of skills and methods of practice*

Characteristics and definitions of skill

The term **motor skill** is used to describe a **technique** within a game or sport (for example, passing, hitting, catching, controlling a ball), or in reference to **the sport itself** (diving, tennis, hammer throwing), or a **quality** possessed by a sportsperson. The characteristics of skill (see figure 8.1) are that it should be co-ordinated, controlled, with good technique, efficient, or pre-determined by practice or the observation of others performing the skill perfectly. As such the skill will be well-learned, efficient and consistent. The beauty or pleasing nature of a skill is its aesthetic quality (figure 8.2).

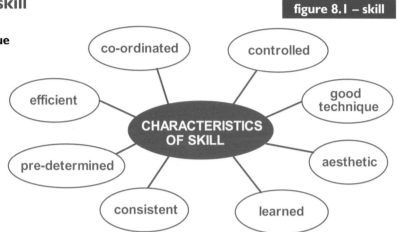
figure 8.1 – skill

Difference between motor and perceptual abilities

Characteristics of ability

figure 8.2 – squash, a skilful activity

Ability (see figure 8.3) is the foundation for skill learning. A successful sportsperson must be born with a number of relevant abilities. An ability is **genetically determined**, since we are born with our abilities, which means that it is **innate** and **enduring** – it is part of our constitution and will last all our lives. For example, some children can quickly pick up skills (such as catching a ball or riding a bike), whereas other children take much longer and are less successful at any given skill.

Gross Motor ability (mainly physical)
This involves the body coordination of large muscle groups, enabling running, rolling, sitting up, or riding a bike.

Psychomotor ability (mainly cognitive)
This is the ability to process information about how and when we move. For example, fast reaction time is an ability, a rugby player must react quickly to an oncoming player who changes direction. Other examples are speed of movement and decision making.

Perceptual ability (mainly sensory)
This is the ability to sense and interpret sensory inputs or information. For example, the awareness of the positions and actions of opponents which enables anticipating play 'reading the game'.

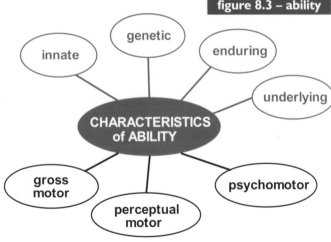
figure 8.3 – ability

Ability is an **enduring** trait. We largely hold on to our abilities throughout our lives, for example, riding a bike.

General ability
This does not really exist - we have specific abilities.

Specific abilities
This refers to the fact that skills require different abilities. For example, gymnastics involves balance, strength and flexibility.

Groups of abilities
A good sportsperson may have many different groups of abilities. For example, a good all round sportsman could have different specific abilities such as good hand-eye co-ordination and balance which could be transferred to lots of different sports activities.

Difference between skill and ability

Skill is acquired. Skills must be **learned**, which can require an extended process including the copying of expert models. On the other hand, **ability** is an **enduring** trait which can last throughout a person's life, and is genetic in basis. Abilities underpin and contribute to skills. For example, someone with good natural balance, shoulder and hip flexibility, and upper body and wrist strength, has all the abilities necessary to perform a handstand. But practice would be required to actually perform the skill of the handstand.

Types of skill

A **psychomotor skill** is a voluntary body movement with a pre-determined end result, for example, hitting a ball with a bat. **Fundamental psychomotor skills** are basic skills that are learned when young. They form the basis of more complex movements, for example, jumping.

A **perceptual skill** is about being able to interpret information quickly at a given time and to make an appropriate decision. For example, a goalkeeper in football assessing the movement of an opponent approaching. A **cognitive skill** is about being able to make sense of a problem and to solve it. These skills affect perception.

Classification of skills

All skills are on a classification continuum. There are several types of continuum:

The difficulty continuum

Simple skills are straightforward skills with few subroutines requiring little concentration and cognitive activity on the part of the performer, for example, walking or running. **Complex skills** are complicated skills requiring a lot of attention or practice, the complexity of which can be perceived differently by different individuals. Complex skills require a large number of (interlinked) subroutines, some of which may be habitual and learned, which affects the ease with which the performer performs the skill. For example, a gymnastic floor exercise. See figure 8.4.

figure 8.4– difficulty continuum

SIMPLE					COMPLEX
sprinting	throwing		gymnastic tumble	snooker	gymnastic floor exercise

Environmental influence

The environmental influence continuum deals with a range of skills labelled open to closed. **Open skills** are predominantly perceptual, with no clear beginning or end, are affected by environment, are externally-paced, in response to many actions of others. For example, receiving a pass at soccer or hockey. On the other hand, **closed skills** are predominantly habitual, with a clear beginning and end, and are not affected much by environment. For example, an athlete performing a shot-putt. See further examples in figure 8.5.

figure 8.5 – the environmental influence continuum

OPEN						CLOSED
soccer goal save	soccer pass	tennis stroke		tennis serve	soccer penalty	shot putt

Pacing

The pacing continuum deals with self-paced and externally-paced skills. **Self-paced skills** are those in which the performer has control over movement, for example, serving in volleyball. **Externally-paced skills** are those in which the environment has more control, for example, blocking in volleyball. See figure 8.6 for further examples.

figure 8.6 – pacing continuum

EXTERNALLY-PACED					SELF-PACED
yachting	tennis receiving serve	soccer game	diving	tennis serve	weight lifting

Muscular involvement

The muscular involvement continuum deals with **gross** and **fine** skills. **Gross skills** are those that use large muscle movements, for example, weight lifting. **Fine skills** are those that use small muscle movements, for example, darts. See further examples in figure 8.7.

figure 8.7 – muscular involvement continuum

GROSS						FINE
weight lifting	javelin throw	netball pass	cricket stroke	golf shot	ten pin bowling	darts/ snooker

Continuity

The continuity continuum deals with **discrete, serial** and **continuous skills**. Discrete skills are those that have a clear beginning and end, for example, taking a penalty kick at soccer. **Serial skills** are those that have a number of discrete elements linked together. For example, the triple jump in which the hop, step and jump are linked into one movement. **Continuous skills** are those that cannot be split up very easily into subroutines, for example, a hockey player dribbling a ball. See further examples in figure 8.8.

figure 8.8 – continuity continuum

DISCRETE		SERIAL	CONTINUOUS	
weight lifting	javelin throw	high jump	basketball dribble	running

figure 8.9– organisation continuum

LOW ORGANISATION		HIGH ORGANISATION	
swimming stroke	cycling	gymnastic move	pole vault

The organisation continuum

Skills with low organisation are uncomplicated and have little organisational structure and whose subroutines tend to be discrete and may be practised separately. For example, swimming. **Skills with high organisation** have a complex organisational structure with subroutines which are closely linked and cannot be practised separately (the skill must be practised as a whole). They require far more attention and concentration to be performed successfully. For example, the pole vault. See figure 8.9 for further examples.

The skill continuum

All skills have elements of **all** the classifications. For example, a golf swing may be predominantly a closed skill but it can be affected by strong weather conditions which would be an open skill characteristic. The swim start in figure 8.10 could be said to have gross and closed characteristics, but is it also self-paced and discrete?

Most skills have characteristics which make them near one end of a classification continuum. For example, a batsman in cricket as he plays a shot can be seen to be performing more of an open skill than a closed skill (he has to adapt to the speed and direction of the ball). But the cricket shot does have elements of closed characteristics too. The player has learned particular shots and almost automatically puts them into operation when the ball approaches at different speeds, with different spin, and in different directions.

figure 8.10 – swim start, gross and closed skill?

Types and methods of practice

This reflects the ways in which a skill **can be taught** to facilitate learning and maximise performance.

Factors affecting choice of method are: the **type** of skills to be taught, the **complexity** of the skill, the **classification** of the skill, the **environment**, the **ability** level of the **performer**, and the **motivational** level of the performer.

See figure 8.11 for the different methods of organisation of skill practice, and figure 8.12 on page 125 for the details of how the different methods are organised.

figure 8.11 – organisation of practice

The whole method

In this method, the skill is **practised in total**. The method should be preferred **where the skill or task**:

- Is of low complexity or is a simple task.
- Has high organisation.
- Consists of interrelated subroutines.
- Has discrete skills of short duration (the movement is rapid or ballistic).

figure 8.12 – practice methods
WHOLE METHOD whole practice only
PART METHOD part A - part B - part C - part D practiced separately
PROGRESSIVE PART METHOD part A - B - parts AB - part A - B - C - parts ABC - part A - B - C - D - whole ABCD
WHOLE - PART - WHOLE METHOD whole (ABCD) practiced - then parts A - B - C - D practiced separately - then whole (ABCD)

This method should be preferred **where the skill or task**:

- Cannot be broken down into parts.
- Or requires temporal or spatial coordination.

Examples of skills or activities where the whole method would be appropriate are:

- Somersault or tumble in gymnastics.
- Dart throw.
- Snooker or pool shot.
- Tennis serve figure 8.13.
- Soccer penalty kick.

The **performer**:
- Would be experienced.
- Has high levels of attention.
- Is in the later stages of learning.
- Is older and highly motivated.
- Uses distributed practice (page 126).

figure 8.13 – Andy Murray - tennis serve - whole method

The part method

In this method, the skill as a whole is **broken down into parts** for practice. The part method should be preferred **where the skill or task**:

- Has high complexity.
- Is of low organisation.
- Has independent subroutines.
- Has slow or serial tasks, where the skill as a whole is of long duration.
- Or for dangerous skills.

Examples of skills or activities where the part method would be appropriate are:
- Triple jump in athletics figure 8.14.
- Full trampoline routine with ten different moves.
- Clean and jerk in weight-lifting.

The **performer**:
- Is a beginner.
- Has limited attention span.
- Is in the early stages of learning.
- Is having problems with a particular aspect of a skill.
- Has limited motivation.
- Uses massed practice (page 126).

figure 8.14 – triple jump - best by parts

The progressive part method

In this method, parts are practised separately, then combined into slightly bigger elements for practice, which in turn can be combined into the whole movement or bigger parts for further practice and so on. This method is suitable for:

- Complex tasks or skills.
- Chaining of complex skills learned independently.
- Skills which have limited attentional demands.
- Skills which require coordination of spatial/temporal components.
- Skills which have a good **transfer** to the whole movement.

The whole-part-whole method

This method is a **combination** of whole and part methods having the advantage of flexible application to almost any task and situation depending on the stage of learning of the performer and the task difficulty. A learner would first practise the whole movement and identify difficult components, which would then be practised separately. These difficult components might be different for different people. When sufficiently fluent, the parts can then be re-combined into the whole for further practice.

Practice Conditions - variable practice

Variable practice (see figure 8.15) is a method in which practice **conditions are varied** to encourage the formation of **the patterns in the brain which enable a sportsperson to perform skills with fluency and competence**. Practice activities would include a number of different activities which could be performed in different ways. Conditions should be as **realistic** as possible in **as many situations** as possible, as near to the **competitive** or match situation as possible. The method is relevant to **open skills**.

Distributed practice

Distributed practice is a method in which training sessions include **rest intervals** which could involve mental practice. Sessions would be short and spread over time with recovery periods between. Good for the **beginner** and most **skill learning**, gives **time to recover** physically and mentally and is good for potentially **dangerous** situations.

Massed practice

Massed practice is a method in which practice is done with **no rest intervals** with sessions **long in duration**. In this method, a single training session will last a relatively long time, and all the activities are performed one after the other. This method is good for 'grooving' of skills and to encourage an **habitual** response, is good for **discrete skills** of short duration, but can lead to **fatigue** and boredom and there may be elements of **negative transfer**.

Fixed practice

Fixed practice involves **repeatedly practising** a whole skill in order to strengthen the performance of skills and their storage in the performer's brain. This type of practice takes the form of **learning drills** that underpin sports techniques and is most suitable with discrete, closed skills. For example, learning the kick serve in tennis or rotational shot put technique. Fixed practice is used during all stages of learning from beginner to elite levels of performance.

figure 8.15 – practice conditions

Practice questions

1) Tackling in football would be best classified as which type of motor skill?
   a. closed skill.
   b. fine skill.
   c. continuous skill.
   d. open skill.

2) Skills involving large muscle groups and less precise movements are best classified as which type of skill?
   a. gross skills.
   b. open skills.
   c. fine skills.
   d. continuous skills.

3) When should teachers introduce whole method of learning for students?
   a. when the skill is high in complexity and low in organisation.
   b. when the skill is low in complexity and high in organisation.
   c. when the skill is low in complexity and low in organisation.
   d. never.

4) Massed practice is the most appropriate practice method to use when:
   a. the learner needs to practice the same task in a number of different ways.
   b. the learner practices a set task without any change.
   c. the learner's motivation is low.
   d. the task is simple and can be fully learned in one session.

5) Which of these schedules of practice sessions represents the most distributed practice session?
   a. 2 x 4-hour a week for 2 weeks.
   b. 4 x 2-hour a week for 2 weeks.
   c. 2 x 2-hour a week for 4 weeks.
   d. 2 x 1-hour a week for 8 weeks.

6) If you were watching a number of performers in sport, what characteristics would you expect the movements of a skilled performer to have?   4 marks

7) By using examples from sport, explain what is meant by fundamental psychomotor skills and why they are so important.   4 marks

8) a)   Why is the shot put often regarded as a closed skill?   2 marks

   b)   Using passing skills in a team game, explain what is meant by an open skill.   4 marks

   c)   Give one example from sport of each of the following and state why you have chosen your example:
        continuous skills, serial skills, discrete skills.   3 marks

Practice questions

9) The diagram in figure 8.16 shows a profile for the racing start in swimming scaled across four different continua representing the skill characteristics of the movement.

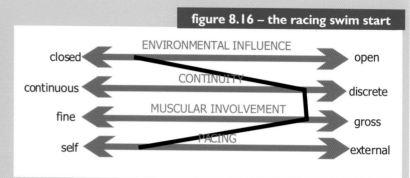

figure 8.16 – the racing swim start

a) Referring to the profile, describe the swim racing start in terms of each of the four characteristics shown.   4 marks

b) Using this same profile chart, sketch a profile which would describe the characteristics of a table tennis serve.   3 marks

c) Explain why you have chosen your particular characteristic for muscular involvement and environmental conditions.   4 marks

d) Explain how your profile for the table tennis serve might assist a coach in planning practices for players learning this skill.   5 marks

10) a) Explain the difference between massed and distributed practice.   2 marks

b) Justify the choice of practice conditions for a training session of a sport of your choice.   6 marks

c) Name two characteristics of the task, and two attributes of the learner which might lead you to decide which method (massed or distributed) of practice to use.   4 marks

11) Generally a skill should be taught as a whole as far as possible. Give reasons for this. Some skills need to be split up into parts to be taught effectively. What are the advantages and disadvantages of this type of skill presentation?   10 marks

Answers link: http://www.jroscoe.co.uk/downloads/as_a1_revise_pe_ocr/OCRAS_A1_ch8_answers.pdf

CHAPTER 9: *Transfer of skills, learning theories and stages of learning*

The term **transfer** (figure 9.1) describes the influence of one skill on the performance of another.

Positive transfer

This type of transfer occurs when **learning** in one task is enhanced by learning in **another task**. For example, learning a golf stroke may be enhanced by virtue of the fact that the player is a good cricketer.

Negative transfer

This occurs when the learning of a new task is **interfered** with by the knowledge of a similar activity. For example, the flexible use of the wrist needed for badminton may interfere with the firm wrist needed for tennis.

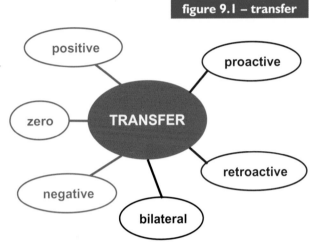

figure 9.1 – transfer

Proactive transfer

This type of transfer refers to the influence of one skill on a skill **yet to be learned**. For example, having learned the forehand drive in tennis, the action is then modified to the forehand drive with top spin.

Retroactive transfer

This type of transfer is where there is a negative influence of one skill on a skill that has **previously been learned**. For example, a hockey player learns the flicking skill which may have a negative effect on the previously learned push (the push pass may be lifted unnecessarily).

Zero transfer

This describes the situation where **no transfer at all** may occur even between skills which appear to be similar. For example, learning at squash may have zero transfer from weight training.

Bilateral transfer (limb to limb)

This is the transfer which takes place from **one limb to another**, sometimes called **lateralisation**. For example, a soccer player learns to kick a ball with the non-preferred foot, the actions are learnt through reference by the brain to the preferred foot.

Principles and theories of learning movement skills

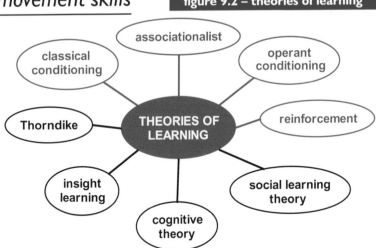

figure 9.2 – theories of learning

Operant theories - the S-R bond

See figure 9.2 for a summary of the theories of learning.

Operant theories are a form of Associationalist theory which states that learning occurs as a result of the **association** or connection between a **stimulus** and a **response**, this stimulus-response connection is called the **S-R bond**.

Operant conditioning

The connection between stimulus and response is due to **conditioning**, which is a form of **training** which makes a certain behaviour into a **habit** (**habitualised** - unvarying). Such a habit is an ingrained and learned behaviour which becomes part of a person's **automatic** response to a stimulus.

A sports example of this would be the instant reaction of a soccer goalkeeper to a penalty taker's strike depending on the penalty taker's stance or body position.

Since **learning** involves a **change of behaviour**, learning takes place when a **connection** is made between stimulus and response.

An example of this could be the baton passing routine during a sprint relay. An incoming runner would shout 'hand', and the outgoing runner would present his or her hand to receive the baton. The shout is the stimulus, the reaching out of the hand the response. Eventually, the response is automatic (and learnt) and the baton will always be passed successfully.

Operant conditioning is concerned with **modifying behaviour** and hence **response** to a specific situation. This is the work of **Skinner** who used pigeons to whom he gave food if they pecked at and then hit a table tennis ball with their beaks.

Eventually, by developing the **reinforcement** (giving of food) when the desired response was achieved, the pigeons were able to knock a ball back and forth between them. This is based on **trial and error**, with the correct response **reinforced** as described below under Thorndike's laws.

This can be used to learn from a **demonstration** that teaches how to perform the skill (shaping), and then **reinforced** after the performer has performed the skill successfully (through knowledge of results). For example, suppose a rugby player kicks when he or she should pass the ball.

By rewarding (reinforcing using praise) every time the player passes, gradually the player learns to pass the ball (behaviour has been modified). The learner may not know **why** the response is correct only that it will be **rewarded**. To be effective, a reward will **closely follow** a correct response, and a coach will be concerned **to strengthen a correct S-R bond**, and weaken an incorrect S-R bond.

Thorndike's laws

Thorndike's laws (see figure 9.3) are concerned with **strengthening the S-R bond**, and hence the concept of reinforcement, and therefore a part of conditioning theory.

figure 9.3 – Thorndike's laws

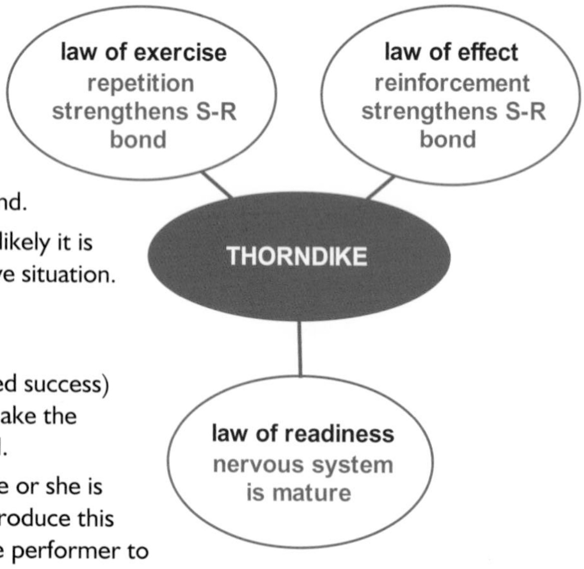

- **The law of exercise** explains that **repetition** strengthens the S-R bond.

  For example, the more a discus thrower practises throwing the more likely it is that this correct throwing technique will be repeated in the competitive situation. So **practice** is very important.

- **The law of effect** uses **reinforcement** (by praise, reward or observed success) which strengthens the S-R bond. Satisfying **reinforcers** (ones which make the learner feel good) increase the likelihood of a response being repeated.

  For example, if the thrower feels that the movement is correct then he or she is more likely to repeat the movement. A **trial and error** process can produce this effect, since **success** reinforces a response, whereas **failure** forces the performer to try new methods to achieve success.

- **The law of readiness** says that learning can only occur when the **nervous system** (and muscular system) is **sufficiently mature** to allow the appropriate S-R bond to happen.

  For example, the more a thrower is physically and mentally prepared to perform a throw then it is more likely to be performed well. People should learn **simple basic skills** (and become **basically fit**) **before** attempting to learn more complex skills. Also the performer needs to be **psychologically ready**.

Cognitive theories

Cognitive theories are concerned with **understanding** and **insight**, and are the work of **Gestaltists** (German scientists who showed the importance of perceiving a problem in its **entirety**). **Intervening variables** are the factors which come between the stimulus occurring and a response being selected.

The learner is involved in the process by absorbing **information** from various sources to understand the 'whole picture'. He or she needs to know **when, where and why** to use a skill, not just how to perform the skill, and must be able to draw on **previous experiences** and knowledge. He or she must recognise **important cues** (within a game situation) to **understand** the skill learning problem and how it should be tackled. This might be termed **insight learning**.

For example, a tennis serve should be practised as a whole not broken down into parts. Another example is hockey players being encouraged to think about marking strategies against twin centre forwards. This would be a problem to be solved which gives the players more insight and eventual understanding of the problems.

Bandura's social learning theory

This theory (see figure 9.4) describes learning by **copying** others (**observational learning**).

In this theory, the performer is more likely to copy '**significant others**', those who are seen as **high status role models**.

- **Demonstration** of the skill (by **significant others**), is followed by the learning process which includes **attention** (the learner takes note of the demonstration).
- **Retention** (the learner remembers the demonstration).
- **Motor reproduction** (the learner attempts to copy the movement), and is **motivated** to do so.
- Finally the learner produces a **matching performance** (successful reproduction of the skill).

The learner copies because he or she wishes to be accepted by others or to be held in **high esteem**. Skills are often copied to achieve the **success** that others enjoy and to be **praised**.

Observational learning

Observational learning is at the heart of social learning theory (see figure 9.5). Learning takes place via **watching** and then **imitating** what is seen. Imitation is **more likely** if the model is seen as relevant, complies with social norms, and is similar in age or ability. Also, imitation is more likely if the behaviour of the learner has been reinforced, and the performance of the model is seen as successful.

For example, the techniques and tactics of a successful tennis player are most likely to be copied, the behaviour and techniques of a top soccer player are most likely to be imitated.

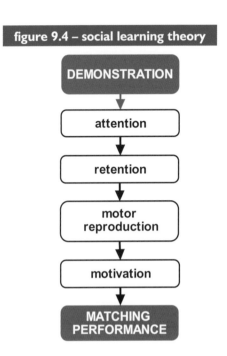

figure 9.4 – social learning theory

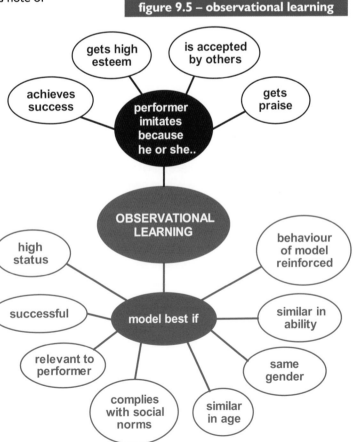

figure 9.5 – observational learning

Reinforcement of movement behaviours

Reinforcement (see figure 9.6) is concerned with ensuring the correct response is repeated.

Positive reinforcement

Positive reinforcement uses rewards or praise to achieve the desired result. For example, a footballer might receive a bonus for scoring a goal or an amateur gymnast might be praised by the coach for a good performance.

Negative reinforcement

This means withdrawing rewards. For example, the same footballer may not receive a bonus when he fails to score a goal, the gymnast would not be praised if he or she performed inadequately.

Punishment

Punishment means inflicting retribution on a learner who performs incorrectly. This breaks a bond between the learner's learning process and an incorrect performance. For example, the footballer might be dropped from the team after he fails to score a goal, or a player is sent from the field if he or she fouls an opponent.

Stages of learning - Fitts and Posner

The **phases of movement skill learning** (see figure 9.7) are:

Cognitive

The **cognitive (early)** phase, in which the learner attempts to understand the skill, begins to look at techniques and memorise what is required, begins to practise and repeat the skill according to a simple model, and learns by trial and error. In this phase **guidance** would tend to be predominantly visual, with manual or mechanical guidance also being used, as basic body positions and movements are learnt. Here **feedback** involves reinforcement of success by the coach, with mistakes corrected by reference to the model. This phase applies to the novice player who can require a lot of support in order to achieve success.

Associative

The **associative (intermediate)** phase, in which the learner will understand the skill, and movement patterns will be more fluent and established (can be repeated at a reasonable level without much thought). In this phase **guidance** is more likely to be visual and verbal with some manual guidance to illustrate specific body positions or movements. The coach will give a lot of detail within this guidance. Here **feedback** involves the learner associating the 'feel' of the activity (via kinaesthesis) with the end results. This phase applies to the competent performer who still requires full support from a coach to correct mistakes.

Autonomous

The **autonomous (final)** phase, in which movements are well integrated and automatic, with the learner able to perform without conscious effort. The performer can now give attention to the environment and wider cues about play (such as the position and movements of opponents). **Guidance** would not need to be extensive, but highly specific to situations which the performer would already have realised need attention. Verbal guidance would be the predominant method, with **feedback** being mostly via the learner being able to judge performances and make corrections by him or herself (often with the aid of video analysis of the performance). This phase applies to the player who can perform by him or herself, who can make decisions about tactics without prompting, and whose skill under pressure is stable.

The details of guidance are discussed in chapter 10 on page 135 onwards.

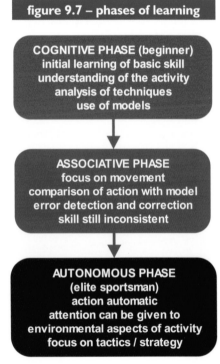

figure 9.6 – reinforcement

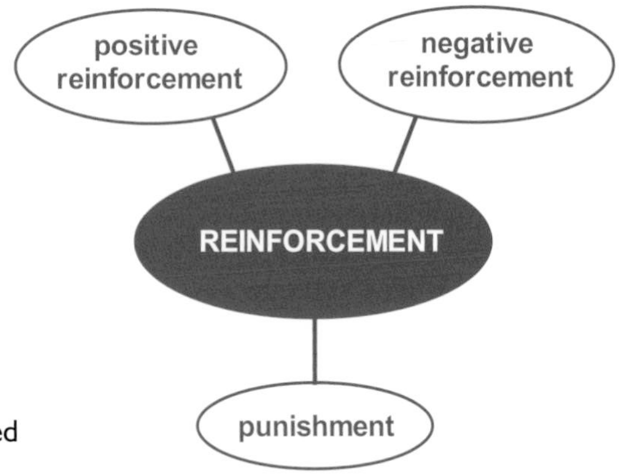

positive reinforcement

negative reinforcement

REINFORCEMENT

punishment

figure 9.7 – phases of learning

COGNITIVE PHASE (beginner)
initial learning of basic skill
understanding of the activity
analysis of techniques
use of models

ASSOCIATIVE PHASE
focus on movement
comparison of action with model
error detection and correction
skill still inconsistent

AUTONOMOUS PHASE
(elite sportsman)
action automatic
attention can be given to
environmental aspects of activity
focus on tactics / strategy

Practice questions

1) Due to the different wrist action involved in tennis and badminton, a person who has learned the forehand in tennis before learning the forehand in badminton often experiences what kind of transfer?
   a. positive transfer.
   b. negative transfer.
   c. proactive transfer.
   d. bilateral transfer.

2) The critical activity in the associative stage of learning is to:
   a. develop an understanding of the task.
   b. refine the motor skill and associate specific environmental cues with specific movements develop a basic movement pattern.
   c. make small adjustments to the skill to improve performance.
   d. learn by copying others.

3) Performance changes tend to be largest in which stage of learning?
   a. cognitive.
   b. associative.
   c. autonomous.
   d. a. and c.

4) Within Fitts and Posner's cognitive phase of learning the key aim is to:
   a. organise a more efficient movement pattern.
   b. make the actions automatic.
   c. understand the skill.
   d. focus on the established movement patterns.

5) A gymnast is preparing for a major competition and has been practising the routine over and over again for several months. Which of Thorndike's laws explains the effects of practice on performance?
   a. the law of effect.
   b. the law of readiness.
   c. the law of exercise.
   d. a. and c.

6) Explain four different types of transfer of learning.   4 marks

7) a) Using a practical example, explain what is meant by the term 'transfer' in skill learning. How can transfer be detrimental to performance? Give a practical example.   5 marks

   b) How can a teacher or a coach ensure that as much positive transfer takes place as possible in a training session?   5 marks

8) Figure 9.8 shows the improvement in performance of a gymnast over a period of time.

   a) Name the stages **A**, **B** and **C** shown on this chart and explain their significance to the gymnast.   6 marks

   b) Identify the characteristics of a performer in phase **C**.   4 marks

   c) How might the type of mental practice change in the last phase of learning?   4 marks

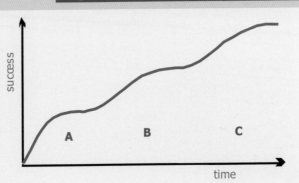

figure 9.8 – performance of a gymnast

Practice questions

9) According to Fitts and Posner, learning passes through three stages. Use an example from one of your practical activities to describe the key characteristics of each of these stages.   5 marks

10) a) Explain how you would use operant conditioning to teach a sports skill of your choice.   5 marks

   b) Describe what is meant by reinforcement and give examples of different types.   4 marks

11) a) Using examples from sport explain what is meant by the S-R bond.   4 marks

   b) Explain how a coach in a sport could ensure that a correct response follows a particular stimulus.   5 marks

12) Stimulus-response bonding has been used to explain how a physical skill can be learned. What is a stimulus-response bond and how can a Physical Education teacher ensure that it is strengthened when teaching swimming or athletics?   6 marks

13) A coach reinforces good performances in training with praise. Why does this reinforcement work rather than punishing poor performance? Explain what is meant by reinforcement and punishment in this case.   5 marks

14) A Level. Using Thorndike's laws, discuss how producing a satisfying effect in a particular situation becomes more likely to occur again in that situation, and responses that produce a discomforting effect become less likely to occur again in that situation.   20 marks

Answers link: http://www.jroscoe.co.uk/downloads/as_a1_revise_pe_ocr/OCRAS_A1_ch9_answers.pdf

CHAPTER 10: *Guidance and feedback*

Guidance methods

See figure10.1 for a summary of methods of guidance.

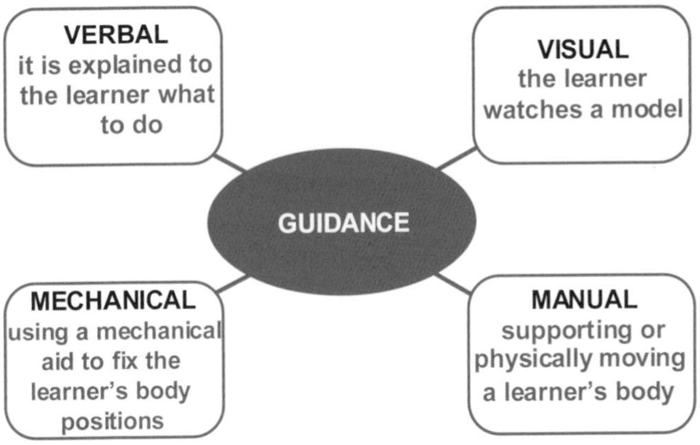

Visual guidance

This method works mainly through **demonstration** (by **video** or poster, by human **live** model, or by demonstration of techniques by a **coach** or teacher).
This demonstration should:

- **Be realistic**, **appropriate** and **not too complex**.
- Emphasise **relevant** aspects of a skill and be **repeated**.

Visual guidance is very important in the **cognitive** early stage of learning:

- The **learner** should be **attentive** and **retentive**, and should be **capable** of **matching** the demonstration (performer at the appropriate level of learning).
- The performer would learn by **watching** and **imitating** a **model** who should be of **high status** (figure 10.2) and technically correct.
- **The coach** should **reinforce** correct copying of skills.

Advantages of visual guidance

- Visual guidance provides a mental picture of a required skill.
- Enables the parts of a part learning process to be seen clearly.
- Encourages observational learning by drawing attention to relevant cues.

Disadvantages of visual guidance

- Visual demonstration may not be clear or may be too quick to be followed, and bad habits could be developed.
- An accurate demonstration may not be available.

Verbal guidance

This method is used often to **accompany visual** guidance and is used more with **competent** performers at a later stage (the autonomous stage) of learning. The amount of verbal guidance must be **controlled** and the **quality** of this guidance is important for effective coaching or teaching. Verbal guidance can be used for **conditioning** a response (giving reinforcement), which is useful for situations that require quick decisions. Players prefer coaches who give plenty of feedback (figure 10.3). This type of guidance can create a mental image. Tactics can be explained, and technical information, key points and cues highlighted.

Advantages of verbal guidance

- Can be controlled by the coach.
- Can be used to motivate a performer and reinforce a correct response.
- Can be used to explain why certain actions are necessary, and highlight relevant cues.
- Can be used to quickly identify errors which then can be corrected.

Disadvantages of verbal guidance

- Can overload beginners with information.
- The language used may be too complex for beginners.
- This could lead to learners **losing concentration**.
- Not as useful when used by itself, therefore should be combined with other forms of guidance to be effective.

figure 10.1 – types of guidance

VERBAL
it is explained to the learner what to do

VISUAL
the learner watches a model

GUIDANCE

MECHANICAL
using a mechanical aid to fix the learner's body positions

MANUAL
supporting or physically moving a learner's body

figure 10.2 – visual guidance - model of high status

figure 10.3 – verbal guidance

Manual guidance

This method (figure 10.4) uses **physical support** (as in a coach supporting a gymnast during an asymmetric bar movement or performing somersaults), or **placing** limbs in correct positions (as for a novice thrower). This helps with **kinaesthetic** awareness, is useful for giving **confidence**, particularly for **beginners**, and is useful for **safety** reasons.

figure 10.4 – manual guidance

figure 10.5 – mechanical guidance

Mechanical guidance

This method uses a mechanical **aid**, for example:
- Stabilisers on a bike (see figure 10.5).
- Flotation devices for swimming.
- Belay ropes for climbers.
- Somersault rig for trampolinists.

Advantages of manual/mechanical guidance

- Can be used safely.
- Can be used to give confidence.
- Can be used to break down a skill into parts which then can be practised separately, for example holding a swim float in one's hands to practice leg kick in swimming.

Disadvantages of manual/mechanical guidance

- Can restrict a movement and create over-reliance on a device, for example the extra wheels on a stabiliser bike.
- Can restrict the kinaesthetic awareness of the movement of a skill, which will then be not similar enough to the real thing.

Feedback

Feedback is a term which describes the way in which information is received by a performer about a performance either just completed, or sometimes during the performance itself.

Intrinsic feedback

This form of feedback takes place when the feeling of a movement tells a performer whether it was successful or not (see figure 10.6). Part of this is **kinaesthetic** and is provided by the **proprioception** within joints and muscles which tells a person of the muscle tension and joint angles during a movement. This is an **ability** which is usually a part of the person from birth, and is genetic and enduring. A person who has more effective kinaesthetic feedback about movements made by his or her body is more likely to be a successful sports performer.

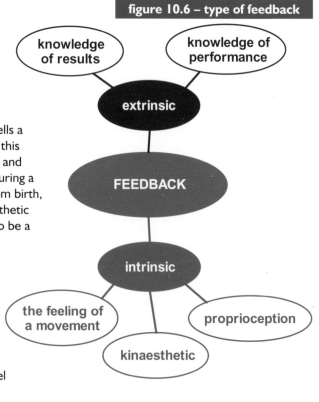

figure 10.6 – type of feedback

knowledge of results

knowledge of performance

extrinsic

FEEDBACK

intrinsic

the feeling of a movement

proprioception

kinaesthetic

Advantages of intrinsic feedback

- Performer is independent since the feeling comes from within him or herself.
- Can be used for reinforcement, since a good feeling can be linked to an outcome, for example how far a javelin has been thrown.
- Can be used for error detection as a movement is in progress, by the comparison of the shape of the skill with the perfect model stored in the memory.
- If the performer is in the **autonomous stage** of learning, a performance is likely to be more accurate, and reinforces itself.

Disadvantages of intrinsic feedback

- This type of feedback may not be accurate when a performer is in the **early cognitive stage** of learning, since he or she would not be experienced enough to relate the feeling to a correct response.

Extrinsic feedback

Extrinsic feedback is from an external source to the performer that can affect performance, and either **motivate** or demotivate the performer depending on the quality of the feedback.

This has two forms in which the first is **knowledge of performance**:
- Where information is obtained about a performance. For example, its **quality**, **rhythm** or **aesthetics** from a coach, video (figure 10.7), or from the press or TV.

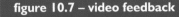

figure 10.7 – video feedback

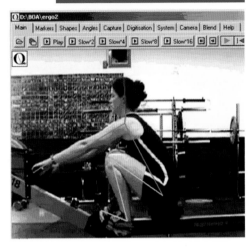

The second form is **knowledge of results** in which a performer has:
- Information about the **outcome** of a performance.
- Success or failure, or the distance, height or time performed.
- Information can be from a number of sources, the coach, video, or press and TV.

Advantages of extrinsic feedback

- Provided the feedback is given accurately, it gives reinforcement of correct or incorrect aspects of a performance.

Disadvantages of extrinsic feedback

- This type of feedback may demotivate a performer if he or she does not understand the feedback.
- Does not encourage as much kinaesthetic awareness, and the performer therefore can become over reliant on the coach.

Feedback dependency

Feedback dependency occurs when some performers can become **dependent** on feedback:
- For example, from a coach or significant other about the quality of performance or technical competence.
- If this feedback is withdrawn or cannot be given then performance **can deteriorate**.
- This might occur in a field event athlete in a major games who cannot function without feedback from a coach about his or her technique, and who therefore will fail.

figure 10.8 – positive feedback

Positive feedback

Positive feedback is feedback which gives information aimed at a **constructive** development of performance. It uses positive reinforcement, **praise** and **encouragement** about good performances, and the knowledge from poor performances which gives insight about **errors and their possible correction**. For example, a coach who praises a performer and encourages him or her to repeat the skills being praised will be giving positive feedback (figure 10.8).

Advantages of positive feedback

- Provided the feedback is given accurately, it gives reinforcement of correct or incorrect aspects of a performance on its own.
- Can build self esteem and confidence in the performer.
- Important for performers in the **early cognitive stage of learning** to give positive reinforcement of the S-R bond.

Disadvantages of positive feedback

- Some performers can become overconfident, and a performance can become weaker, because an incorrect S-R bond can be created.
- Some performers do not respond well to too much praise, and hence ignore the feedback, resulting in a reduction in performance.

Negative feedback

This type of feedback is information which could **depress performance** and would consist of negative reinforcement or negative criticism about **poor** performances. For example, in this case, a coach who repeatedly feeds back information about faults, and gives little help about how to correct them would be giving negative feedback.

Advantages of negative feedback

- If negative feedback is used sparingly (particularly in the **autonomous stage of learning**) it could refine and improve performance.

Disadvantages of negative feedback

- This type of feedback may demotivate a performer especially if he or she is in the early cognitive stage of learning.
- Does not encourage a performer especially if the feedback is inaccurate or unfounded.

figure 10.9 – squash requires feedback

Feedback used in sport

In the case of a squash player (figure 10.9), in open play the skill is an **open** one (movements are altered according to the position and direction and action of the other player, the stroke played, and the subsequent direction and speed of the ball).

Feedback to the player occurs during the movement, and he alters his position, stance, movement pattern and stroke outcome in response.

Part of this feedback is **kinaesthetic**, in that his position, speed and posture are sensed by the orientation of his limbs and tension in his musculature, and changes are then made according to the sensations and feelings from this – in response to the game situation.

Practice questions

1) Which is the best type of guidance a coach could use when coaching an advanced skilled performer?
   a. visual.
   b. mechanical.
   c. verbal.
   d. manual.

2) Visual guidance is a very important tool when learning a new motor skill.
   Which one of the following possible answers should be considered prior to using visual guidance?
   a. visual guidance can overload beginners with too much information.
   b. visual guidance should be used in conjunction with verbal guidance.
   c. visual guidance should be used during the autonomous stage of learning.
   d. visual guidance should be used during the cognitive stage of learning.

Practice questions

3) What is the best description for how visual feedback could be used during the later stages of learning?
   a. to enable the performer to attend to more detailed and lengthy bouts of verbal feedback.
   b. to gradually phase out extrinsic feedback in order to reduce the effects of feedback dependency.
   c. to provide concurrent feedback during the movement.
   d. give the performer time after feedback before practicing the skill again.

4) Feedback about the outcome of performance is known as which of the following?
   a. concurrent augmented feedback.
   b. terminal augmented feedback.
   c. knowledge of performance.
   d. knowledge of results.

5) Knowledge of performance (KP) is feedback about:
   a. result or outcome of performance.
   b. winning or losing.
   c. the process of skill performance that led to the outcome.
   d. the result of movement from internal sources.

6) a) Why is visual guidance particularly suitable for learning a new skill?   2 marks

   b) Why can verbal guidance be of limited use on its own?   2 marks

   c) What are the advantages of verbal guidance?   3 marks

   d) When are manual or mechanical guidance best used?   4 marks

7) a) Other than visual guidance, what other main methods of guidance are there?
      Give a practical example for each.   6 marks
   b) How would you optimise the use of visual guidance in teaching motor skills?
      What are the drawbacks of this method?   4 marks

8) a) Identify two different mechanical items which might assist movement skill learning.   2 marks

   b) Give reasons for the use of these mechanical items to help a learner come to
      grips with a motor skill.   4 marks

   c) Identify two disadvantages of using a mechanical aid to enhance skill development.   2 marks

9) a) Define the term feedback, and briefly describe three functions of feedback.   4 marks

   b) How would you make feedback effective when teaching a motor skill?   4 marks

10) Distinguish between intrinsic and extrinsic feedback.   2 marks

11) Using figure 10.9 on page 138, what feedback might a coach give to the player
    (in the black kit) who has just played a forehand drive and is attempting to read
    his opponent's next shot.   3 marks

12) Explain how feedback differs through the associative and autonomous stages
    of learning as a performer makes progress.   4 marks

Practice questions

13) Explain how feedback in a sports skill learning situation helps the
sportsperson improve performance.

4 marks

14) When we play sport we are given many different types of feedback by
different people and they come in different forms. Evaluate the use of
positive and negative feedback in sports performance.

6 marks

15) Discuss the idea that improvement in skill performance is dependent
upon the nature and frequency of feedback provided by the coach.

10 marks

Answers link: http://www.jroscoe.co.uk/downloads/as_a1_revise_pe_ocr/OCRAS_A1_ch10_answers.pdf

SPORT PSYCHOLOGY

CHAPTER 11: *Personality, attitudes and motivation*

Personality theories

Personality

Personality is the term which describes the **unique** characteristics of an individual which makes him or her act as they do. Knowledge about personality is important to ensure **optimum** sporting performance.

Figure 11.1 outlines the main ideas various theorists have used to explain and describe personality and its features.

figure 11.1 – features of personality

- TRAIT innate and enduring
- extroversion introversion
- SOCIAL LEARNING behaviours are learnt by observation and copying
- **PERSONALITY**
- neurotic stable
- INTERACTIONIST a mixture of trait and social learning
- type A type B

Trait theories

Trait theories use the idea that a person has always had a feature of his or her personality, and always will have. Such features will be **general** (covering all situations), **underlying** (inside of and part of the person), **enduring** (long lasting), and include **predispositions** (inclinations or motives formed earlier). Such predispositions will tell you how a person will behave when faced with certain situations. For example, the prospect of failure such as losing an important sporting match or competition.

Most trait theories use labels for features of behaviour, and you should remember that such labels (attached to a person) would be intended to last for ever. Some labels for aspects of personality are:

- **Extroversion** (including liveliness, sociability, impulsiveness, activity, excitability).
- **Introversion** (including isolation, independence, shyness, quiet).
- **Stability** (including unchanging behaviour patterns).
- **Neuroticism** (including the fact that behaviour may change unpredictably).

Eysenck identified a **two dimensional** view of personality as four primary types:
- A **stable extrovert** would be talkative, outgoing, easy going, carefree, and showing leader qualities.
- A **neurotic extrovert** would be restless, aggressive, excitable, and changeable.
- A **neurotic introvert** would be anxious, sober, rigid, or pessimistic.
- A **stable introvert** would be careful, thoughtful, controlled, reliable, and even-tempered.

At a later date Eysenck added a third scale of **psychoticism** as a measure of how tough-minded a person is, assessed in a test called Eysenck's personality questionnaire.

figure 11.2 – which features of Chris Hoy's personality have led to him becoming a multiple Olympic champion?

Types A and B personalities

Table 11.1 – **differences between personality types A and B**

type A characterised by:	type B characterised by:
impatience.	relaxed and patient.
works at a rapid pace.	allows time for tasks to be completed.
higher levels of stress.	low personal stress.
strong desire to succeed.	less competitive.
easily aroused and shows anxiety in stressful situations.	calm and unflappable in most situations.
lacking in tolerance.	tolerance of others' mistakes.
has a need to be in control.	delegates easily.
makes decisions quickly without much preparation or thought.	prepared to wait and assess all options when decisions need to be made.

Trait theories

Which set of characteristics would enable you to predict who would become the next British Olympic champions (figure 11.2).

Cattell is another trait theorist who identified a much larger number of personality traits which he measured in a questionnaire called Cattell's 16PF.

Social learning theories

Social learning theory explains behaviour in terms of the reaction to specific situations. The main point of social learning theory is that we learn to deal with situations by **observing others** or by observing the results of our own behaviour on others and by **modelling** our own behaviour on what we have seen. Athletes learn **behaviour** by watching others. This is in addition to the idea of being able to learn skills by watching then copying others (this is the social learning theory of skill development).

Bandura says that behaviour is determined by the situation. In other words there is social comparison, and a person will behave the same way as the peer group. Social approval or disapproval determines our responses since such behaviour is reinforced or penalised by **the peer group**.

Vicarious conditioning is the learning of emotional responses through observational learning. For example, learning to become angry after a valid referee decision has gone against him or her by watching other players do the same.

Interactionist theories

Interactionist theories (figure 11.3) are those which assert that a combination of trait and a person's situation or environment builds up a person's personality, and that traits determine behaviour but can be modified by situations. **Lewin** was the theorist who stated that behaviour is a function of both the person (personality P) and the environment (E), and put this in the mathematical form:

$$B = f(P,E)$$

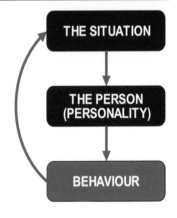

figure 11.3 – the interactionist model of personality

THE SITUATION

THE PERSON (PERSONALITY)

BEHAVIOUR

Example of the interactionist theory approach

A young field event athlete shows promise, but worries about competing in important competitions and underperforms in these situations. Her coach works with her on anxiety management strategies and her next competition sees a personal best.

The innate (**trait**) factors of the athlete's personality cannot be changed by a coach, so the coach must therefore get her to view her **anxiety** (which could be a trait which emerges whenever undue stress is placed on her) in terms of the specific situation of the next competition. The anxiety could be channelled into positive images of her technical model, rejecting poor efforts as due to external factors (for example, the weather or the wind), and building on positive images of successful technical elements achieved. The athlete can then build success by focusing on factors other than her own anxiety.

This enables her to adjust her behaviour according to internal factors such as rhythm and fluency, and this strategy should enable the athlete to remove the stress from the situation and hence reduce anxiety - even if she competes poorly.

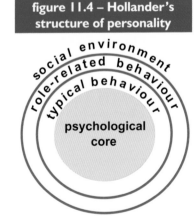

figure 11.4 – Hollander's structure of personality

social environment
role-related behaviour
typical behaviour
psychological core

Hollander's structure of personality

Figure 11.4 outlines the structure of personality as proposed by Hollander.

In this model:
- The **psychological core** (the inner core of beliefs) describes the beliefs and values that remain more or less permanent. For example, a sportsman's belief that fair play underlies his attitude on the field of play.
- **Typical behaviour** describes the way in which an individual responds in certain situations, for example, to stop fighting at the bell during a boxing bout.
- **Role-related behaviour** describes the fact that in other situations we may behave differently, for example, striking our opponents after the bell when annoyed or frustrated. This is the most changeable aspect of personality.
- **Social environment** describes how the behaviour and expectations of others affect our role. For example, a player argues with the referee because others have done so and he or she has got away with it before.

Personality testing or measuring

The profile of mood states (POMS)

This sports-specific questionnaire asks questions which determine the mood of a sports performer and attempts to relate this to the quality of performance. Results are plotted on a chart similar to figure 11.5. Moods are an important aspect of personality which may influence sports performance. The moods assessed by this test are:

- Tension.
- Depression.
- Anger.
- Vigour.
- Fatigue.
- Confusion.

From figure 11.5 you can see that elite sportspeople show low tension, depression and confusion, and they also show high vigour. Unsuccessful sportspeople show high tension, depression, fatigue and confusion, and lower vigour than the elite athlete.

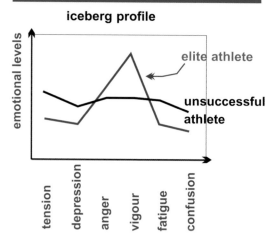

figure 11.5 – profiles of mood states for good and poor performers

Attitudes

Attitudes are combinations of **beliefs** and **feelings** which lead us to think and behave **positively** or **negatively**.

Attitudes are combinations of beliefs and feelings about objects, people and situations (called attitude objects) which predispose us to behave in a certain way towards them. They are learned or organised through experience, and are evaluative (lead us to think and behave positively or negatively) about an attitude object. Sporting attitude objects would include lady bodybuilders as in figure 11.8 on page 145. Attitudes tend to be deep seated and enduring, but can change or be changed.

Components of attitude, Wood's triadic model

This model is outlined in figure 11.6, which lists the **cognitive**, **affective**, and **behavioural** components of attitude.

Factors affecting formation of attitudes

The major factors affecting formation of attitudes are outlined in figure 11.7.

Additionally, **conditioning** (for example, the use of rewards such as praise) will tend to strengthen attitudes, and **social learning** will have the same effect, in which people will learn by observing and imitating significant others.

Familiarity with an attitude object can change an attitude towards that object.

Prejudice

Prejudice is a prejudgement of a person, group, or situation, usually based on **inadequate** information, or inaccurate or biased information. This prejudice tends to reinforce **stereotypes**. For example, women are often excluded from male dominated sports clubs or events (historically golf, rugby and snooker clubs have been guilty of this).

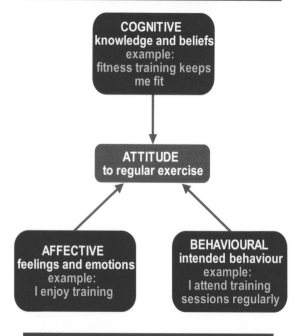

figure 11.6 – Wood's triadic model of components of attitude

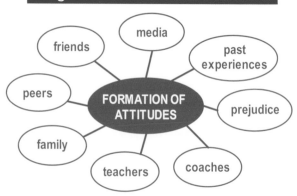

figure 11.7 – formation of attitudes

Sport stereotypes

In the general population, people form attitudes which are negative stereotypes about certain groups participating in sport.

For example:
- Women in strength, endurance and contact sports, figure 11.8.
- Participation of the disabled in physical activity.
- Older age groups' interest and ability at sport.
- Participation of particular ethnic groups in specific sports or positions within teams, for example:
  - The black quarterback in American football.
  - The white sprinter.
  - The black skier or swimmer.

Changing attitudes

Sometimes, a coach or sport leader will want to change an attitude of a sports player or performer, particularly if this person displays aggression or negative feelings towards a colleague. There are two generally accepted ways of tackling this.

Attitude change by persuasive communication

In order for this method to be effective, the subject (the person whose attitude is hopefully to be changed) must pay attention, and must understand, accept and retain the message being given. The coach must be expert and be trustworthy, and the message must be clear, be unambiguous, be balanced between emotion and logic, and be balanced between pros and cons.

Attitude change by cognitive dissonance (theory due to Festinger)

Cognitive dissonance occurs when two completely different and contradictory facts affect the behaviour of a sportsperson. The most clear example of this is when a successful sports performer knows that to maintain his or her success, he or she must maximise the use of his or her lungs, and knows therefore that smoking is bad, yet continues to smoke because he or she likes the sensations produced.

In order to change the attitude of such a person (to smoking), he or she must be consistent between cognitive, affective, and behavioural components, and must realise that there is a conflict between the two behaviours (fitness and smoking). At this point, cognitive dissonance will occur and force the performer to change an attitude to smoking (or perhaps to participation in top level sport!). This is because Festinger's theory is based on the principle that people intrinsically want their attitudes and beliefs to be in **harmony**, so they change their habits to **avoid dissonance**.

Motivation (figure 11.9)

A **motive** is seen as a cause of behaviour which **energises**, **directs** and **sustains** the behaviour. It can be explained as a **drive** to **strive** to meet the needs of the situation in which a person finds him or herself. The strength of such a drive (or motive) depends on the **person** and the **situation**. Different people will have different types and strengths of motives (drives) to meet the needs of the situation. In a sporting context, the term **motivation** implies the driving and striving to **succeed**, to **win**, to **improve performance**, and to **pursue goals** (having set them in the first place).

figure 11.8 – participation in some sports has a negative stereotype with some members of the public

figure 11.9 – motivation

Intrinsic motivation

Intrinsic motivation (figure 11.9 page 145) is the term which describes the **internal** drives or feelings that make us do things. These feelings come from **within** the performer and involve **enjoyment** of the performance, **satisfaction** of performing, **pride** and the feeling of **well-being** from a job well done.

Extrinsic motivation

Extrinsic motivation (figure 11.9 page 145) describes the feelings coming from rewards **externally** derived (from outside the performer).

These rewards could be **tangible** such as prizes, money, or awards. For example, a gymnastics badge, or wanting to win at basketball because a trophy may be won, or an Olympic medal. Or rewards could be **intangible**, such as approval, praise or recognition from others. For example, attaining a world record initiates praise by the media, initiates national recognition, and reinforces the glory of the situation. Raising social status is a further intangible reward which would reinforce extrinsic motivation.

Arousal

Arousal is a term which describes the level of **inner drives** and which forces the sportsperson to **strive to achieve**. It needs to be **under control** and at the **right level** depending on the task. This striving is linked with the concept of motivation.

Drive reduction theory

This theory (figure 11.10) explains why it is sometimes necessary to **vary or renew** the need to learn to stimulate motivation.

The theory says that the **need to learn** to solve a problem, to learn a skill, or to achieve mastery inspires **motivation**, the **drive** to succeed at the task. This leads to the performer **achieving** the desired outcome (action) which in turn leads to a **reduction in drive** (motivation) to achieve the **same outcome** (since it has already been achieved). This is known as **inhibition**.

The theory explains why people give up sport when it becomes routine, and why changes in for example training venue, training partner, coach or manager, can renew motivation to succeed and continue with a high level of commitment of time and effort.

figure 11.10 – drive reduction

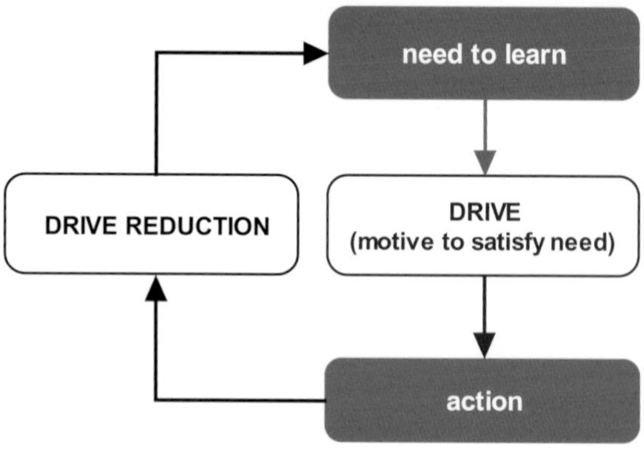

need to learn

DRIVE REDUCTION

DRIVE
(motive to satisfy need)

action

Motivational strategies

These ideas should aim at avoiding or **reducing drive reduction** (reduce **inhibition** of motivation) by changing the **importance** of a task (raise its **status**), or **matching** the task to the performer's needs ('you need to do this to be able to progress towards the Olympic Gold'). Jason Kenny and Laura Trott (figure 11.11) have won 10 Olympic Golds between them.

figure 11.11 – shared motives for elite success

Developing and enhancing motivation

Motivation is a combination of personal characteristics and situational aspects.

Motivation is **highest** when:
- The performer is keen to **participate**.
- The performer is keen to **learn**.
- The performer is keen to **perform**.
- The performer is keen to **perform effectively**.
- The motivational **climate** is right.
- The training programme is **interesting** and **varied**.

Enhancing motivation

Motivation is **reduced** by:
* **Routine**.
* **Competition between motives**.

People:
* Have **multiple** motives.
* **Share** motives.
* Have **unique** motivational profiles.
* Need **variation** in **training** and competition.
* Need **variation** in **intensity** and competitiveness.
* Need **structured coaching** and teaching environments.

Motives change over time, and teachers and coaches are important motivators.

Practice questions

1) Which one of the following is not included in the definition of personality psychology?
   a.   it deals with adaptations to the environment.
   b.   it deals with how traits influence the environment.
   c.   it deals with how the environment influences traits.
   d.   all of the above are included.

2) Type A and Type B personality theory describes two contrasting personality types.
   Which of the traits are characterised by personality Type A?
   a.   delegates easily.
   b.   works at a rapid pace.
   c.   tolerance of other's mistakes.
   d.   strong desire to succeed.

3) An athlete has been given some new information from the coach which radically changes
   the athlete's training programme and which is contrary to the athlete's current attitudes
   and ideas. Which attitude theory explains the athlete's reaction?
   a.   cognitive dissonance.
   b.   attitude formation.
   c.   persuasive communication.
   d.   drive theory.

4) Which one of the following choices best describes extrinsic motivation in sports performance?
   a.   a swimmer has been selected to compete for Great Britain in the Olympic Games and
        is overjoyed at this news.
   b.   an athlete reviews his long-term goals in order to progress and maintain motivation.
   c.   a gymnast rehearses a floor routine in order to perfect a competent performance.
   d.   the coach praises the athlete for a good competitive performance.

5) Which one of the following is an intrinsic motive for participating in the role of a leader
   in a physical activity?
   a.   getting paid for leading a physical activity session.
   b.   running sessions to get a qualification.
   c.   to please parents.
   d.   to enjoy leading a physical activity session.

Practice questions

6) a) What do we mean by the term personality?
       Why is it important for sports psychologists to know about personality?   3 marks

   b) Eysenck identified two dimensions of personality as in figure 11.12.
       Describe the trait approach to personality. What do the traits extroversion and stability mean?   4 marks

7) a) From figure 11.12 describe the characteristics of players **X** and **Y**.   4 marks

figure 11.12 – dimensions of personality

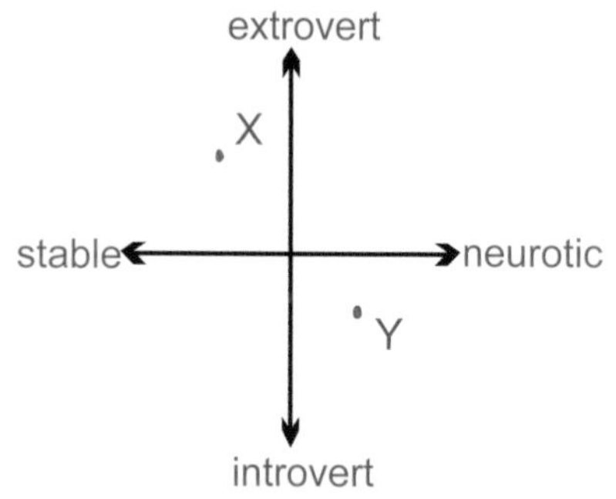

   b) By using an example from sport, outline the social learning
       approach to personality.   3 marks

   c) What do we mean by the interactionist approach?   2 marks

8) Hollander (1971) viewed personality as a structure with layers
   of influence. Using examples from sport, explain Hollander's
   structure of personality.   8 marks

9) List six ways in which a coach might use personality theory
   to help an athlete during training or competition.   6 marks

10) Discuss theories that are used to explain personality,
    and apply them to sporting situations.   10 marks

11) a) What do we mean by the term attitude?   1 mark

    b) We often refer to someone as having a positive attitude in sport.
        Using Wood's triadic model describe the characteristics of a positive attitude.   3 marks

    c) What factors influence our attitudes?   4 marks

12) a) If you wished to change a young person's negative attitude to sport into a positive one,
        what strategies would you employ? Use psychological theory to back up your answer.   4 marks

    b) What do we mean by the term prejudice and how does it manifest itself in sport?   4 marks

13) a) What do you understand by the term motivation?   2 marks

    b) Explain the difference between intrinsic and extrinsic motivation, giving sporting
        examples to illustrate you answer.   4 marks

    c) How could a coach use the different types of motivation with a group of beginners?   2 marks

14) Using figure 11.10 on page 146, explain drive reduction theory.   4 marks

Answers link: http://www.jroscoe.co.uk/downloads/as_a1_revise_pe_ocr/OCRAS_A1_ch11_answers.pdf

CHAPTER 12: *Arousal, anxiety and aggression*

Arousal

Arousal is a state of **mental** and **physical preparedness** for action. This is the level of inner drives which forces the sportsperson to strive to achieve. It needs to be under control and at the right level depending on the task and is closely related to **anxiety**. The symptoms of arousal are:

- A faster **heart rate**.
- Faster **breathing rate**.
- **Sweating**.
- Ability to focus (**concentrate**).
- Response to danger (**fight or flight** adrenaline response).

The **reticular activating system** (RAS) is a system within the brain which causes arousal. Extroverts have lower levels of intrinsic arousal than introverts, hence extroverts seek situations of high arousal whereas introverts seek low arousal situations.

Theories linking arousal and performance

Hull's drive theory

This theory (see figure 12.1) describes the **simple** situation where the **higher** the **arousal** level, the **higher** the achievement or **performance** level.

This theory applies to gross skills like weight lifting and sprinting. The theory also states that the more arousal, the more likely that a **well-learned** skill (a **dominant response**) will be reproduced. This means that older more deep-seated skills will tend to be produced when a person is very aroused rather than newer less well-learnt skills practised more recently. The implication of this is that a highly aroused performer will need to focus very hard and direct his or her attention very strongly towards a **desired response**, particularly if this response includes recently learned elements. Otherwise the state of arousal will cause the person to regress to an older, less desirable but dominant response. This theory explains why in some sporting activities, a sportsperson who **tries too hard** (and who therefore is in a state of high arousal) fails to reproduce his or her best performance.

Inverted U theory

In **inverted U theory** (figure 12.2) there is an **optimum arousal** level. As arousal increases, performance increases up to a certain point, if aroused more than this, the performance will **go down**.
Optimum arousal depends on:

- **Type of activity**, for example, **gross** skills (like weight lifting) require **high arousal**, whereas **fine** skills (like snooker) require **low arousal**.
- The **skill level of the performer**, the more skilful the performer the **higher** the optimum arousal level could be.
- The **personality of the performer**, in which the more **extrovert** the performer, the **higher** the arousal likely to have to be attained by the performer to produce **optimum** performance.

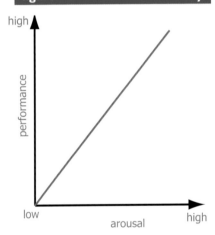

figure 12.1 – Hull's drive theory

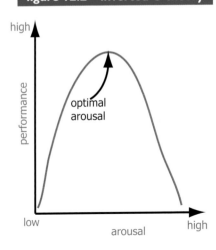

figure 12.2 – inverted U theory

Effects of arousal on technique

- The **point of optimum arousal** is of crucial importance to the learning and stability of a sportsperson's technique.
- Technique is the sequence of actions which enables a performer to successfully perform the skill of his or her event.
- Trying too hard (overarousal) can cause a performer to change his or her technique in an uncontrolled way - with a resultant loss of performance.
- This can be made worse by the anxiety which would accompany a major event - such as a major at tennis or an open at golf.

Anxiety affects arousal, and these theories can also apply to how anxiety affects performance.

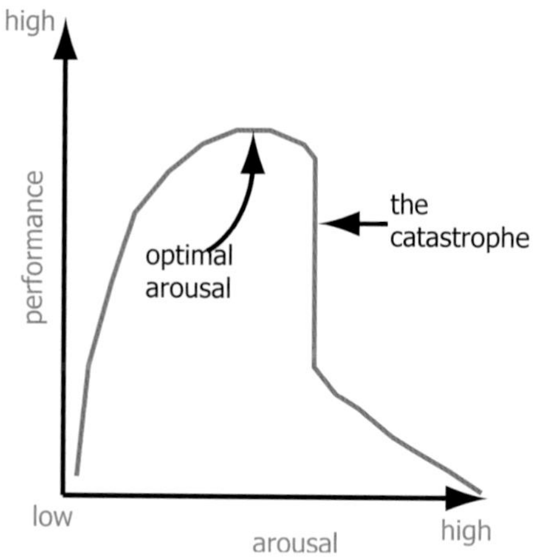

Catastrophe theory

Catastrophe theory (see figure 12.3) is a variation of inverted U theory in which performance **increases** as arousal **increases**, but if **arousal** gets **too high** a **complete** loss of performance occurs (the catastrophe). The performance line on the graph plummets rapidly towards disaster. This almost always happens when the performer tries too hard!

For example, the golfer who tries too hard and completely misses the fairway from his drive at the 18th hole when in a winning position, or the gymnast who completely messes up her previously well-executed routine in a national final.

figure 12.3 – catastrophe theory

Anxiety is linked to arousal

Anxiety can be explained as an emotional state similar to fear, associated with:
- **Somatic** (**physiological**) arousal or anxiety - connected with raised heart rate, raised breathing rate, sweating and so on.
- **Cognitive** (**psychological**) arousal - worry and negative feelings about the situation, feelings of nervousness, feelings of **apprehension**.

Anxiety is closely linked to arousal, since an anxious person is more likely to become aroused than a calm person. Hence the various theories linking arousal with performance (drive, inverted U, catastrophe) can also apply to link anxiety with performance.

It can have **behavioural** consequences - in which a person will experience:
- Tension.
- Agitation.
- Restlessness.

Trait anxiety - A-trait (Speilberger)

Trait anxiety is an inbuilt (**trait**) **part of the personality** which gives a person:
- A tendency to be **fearful** of unfamiliar situations.
- A tendency to perceive competitive situations as **threatening**.
- A tendency to respond to competitive situations with **apprehension** and **tension**.

STUDENT NOTE

The Sport Competition Anxiety Test (**SCAT**)
Martens recognised the need to measure anxiety in response to a sporting competition and devised a self-report psychometric questionnaire called the Sport Competitive Anxiety Test (SCAT) to find out how athletes felt prior to competition. This has proved reliable for predicting **A-trait anxiety** levels.

State anxiety - A-state

State anxiety is an emotional response to a **particular situation**, characterised by feelings of nervousness and apprehension which is often **temporary** - as you might expect if the anxiety is related to a certain situation which of course will change as daily activities change.

Choking and anxiety

High arousal can cause a performer to have negative thoughts and hence anxiety. **Negative thoughts of failure** or lack of success can creep in if a performer is **over-aroused**. These thoughts can affect the performer's confidence and create an almost complete inability to perform skills properly. This is **choking** and is an aspect of inverted U theory.

Examples are:
- The snooker player who misses an easy shot when in the final frame of an important match.
- The golfer who misses the fairway from the tee when in the lead in a competition.
- This particularly applies to sports which use a fine skill.
- Choking can be controlled by cognitive management techniques.

Symptoms of anxiety

Table 12.1 – **symptoms of anxiety**

physiological symptoms	psychological symptoms	behavioural symptoms
increased heart rate.	worry.	rapid talking.
increased blood pressure.	feeling overwhelmed.	nail biting.
increased sweating.	inability to make decisions.	pacing.
increased breathing rate.	inability to concentrate.	scowling.
decreased flow of blood to the skin.	inability to direct attention appropriately.	yawning.
increased oxygen uptake.	narrowing of attention.	trembling.
dry mouth.	feeling out of control.	raised voice pitch.
		frequent urination.

Zone of optimum functioning

Hanin worked out that the optimum level of arousal is not always at mid-point of the inverted U, and that best performance will vary between sportspeople. For example, some athletes will peak at low arousal, and other athletes will peak at medium or high arousal.

Also, an athlete's best performance will be in a **zone** (not just a point of optimum performance - figures 12.4 and 12.5), and different athletes will have **different zones of arousal** for optimum performances. This will depend on **personality**, **skill** or **task** and degree of **habit**.

Habit is defined as the strength and **permanence** of a correctly learned skill.

figure 12.5 – Usain Bolt in the zone

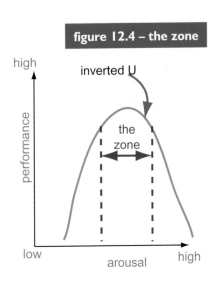

figure 12.4 – the zone

Aggression in sport

- **Aggression** (figure 12.6) involves arousal and anger and intention to harm outside the rules.

- **Assertion** has no intent to harm and uses legitimate force within the rules, displays unusual effort, and may carry unusual energy. This is sometimes called **channelled aggression** (figure 12.7).

- **Hostile aggression** has the intent to harm.
  The goal is to harm with arousal and anger involved.

- **Instrumental aggression** has the intent to harm with the goal to win. This is used as a tactic and is commonly named '**dirty play**'. There is no anger involved and is illegal in all sports except boxing and other martial arts sports.

Theories of aggression

- **Instinct theory** (due to Lorentz, figure 12.8) suggests that aggression is innate and instinctive - caused by a 'survival of the species' response to situations as they arise. In this theory, sport releases built-up aggression, and the aggressive response is cathartic - it gets the aggression out of the system, and purges the person of aggressive intent.

- **Frustration aggression theory** (due to Dollard) states that aggression is caused by frustration as the sportsperson is being blocked in the achievement of a goal. This causes a drive towards the source of frustration.

- **Social learning theory** (due to Bandura) suggests that aggression is learned by observation of others' behaviour. Then imitation of this aggressive behaviour is reinforced by social acceptance of the behaviour.

- **Aggressive cue hypothesis** (due to Berkowitz) states that frustration causes anger and arousal which creates a readiness for aggression. The aggression itself can be initiated by an incident during the performance or game (the cue), so that the aggression is a learned response. For example, a player sees a colleague fouled then decides to join in.

figure 12.6 – aggression - the details

intention to harm another participant, player, spectator or umpire

verbal aggression if intended to embarrass or hurt

outside the rules of the sport

AGGRESSION

not including accidentally injuring or harming

not including eyeballing or intentionally damaging equipment

figure 12.7 – aggression or assertion?

figure 12.8 – theories of aggression

frustration

social learning

THEORIES OF AGGRESSION

instinct

aggressive cue

Deindividuation

The theory of deindividuation concerns the fact that people sometimes behave differently when by themselves, as compared with behaviour in a football crowd. The contrast between the behaviour of people in their workplace as compared to when on the terraces, has often been observed.

Responsibility for aggression

Responsibility for aggression lies within the factors listed in figure 12.9. Influential others can exert a moderating influence on the performer, but the performer must accept that aggression is wrong, and modify behaviour accordingly. **Reinforcement** of good behaviour will be important to ensure behavioural change.

Causes of aggression

- **Physiological arousal** in which anger towards another person causes an increase in arousal. This is because the sportsperson is highly motivated.
- **Underdeveloped moral reasoning** in which players with low levels of moral reasoning are more likely to be aggressive.
- **Bracketed morality** in which there is a double standard of condoning aggressive behaviour in sport, but not in life in general. This way of dealing with aggressive behaviour may hinder a player's moral development.

Other causes of aggression

- High environmental temperature.
- Home or away - reaction to a hostile crowd.
- Embarrassment.
- Losing - excessive pressure to win.
- Physical pain.
- Unfair officiating.
- Playing below capability.
- Large score difference - frustration at poor performance.
- Low league standing - low self-esteem.
- Later stage of play (near the end of a game) - fatigue and niggles.
- Reputation of opposition (get your retaliation in first).
- Copying the behaviour of others.

Strategies to reduce aggressive behaviour

Governing Bodies

Governing Bodies are responsible for **player codes of conduct** which should involve coaches, players and officials. They will:
- Use strong officials where appropriate.
- Alter rules of games and implement punishment (remove league points, use sin bins and so on).
- Reward non-aggressive acts (for example, the FIFA fair play award).
- Encourage use of suitable language.
- Attempt to reduce media sensationalism in connection with aggression on or off the field of play.

A coach education programme is essential to reduce and control aggressive behaviour among players.

Coaches and players

- Coaches and players (figure 12.10) should promote ethical and sporting behaviour.
- They should control aggressive behaviour using stress management strategies and **relaxation techniques** among players.
- Coaches should initiate **self-control** strategies, and attempt to reduce levels of arousal in players.
- Both coaches and players should maintain a **healthy will-to-win** without winning being everything, and set **performance goals** rather than outcome goals.
- Coaches should **remove players** from the field if it is determined that he or she is at risk of aggression.
- Their tactic would be to enable **channelling of aggression** towards a performance goal, and to use **peer pressure** to 'avoid letting the side down'.

figure 12.9 – responsibility for aggression

figure 12.10 – controlling aggression?

Practice questions

1) Which of these is not a theory of arousal in sport?
   a. inverted U.
   b. excitement-arousal.
   c. drive.
   d. catastrophe.

2) What are the two fundamental problems that bring aggression to sport?
   a. reinforcement and anxiety.
   b. anxiety and frustration.
   c. anxiety and fitness.
   d. reinforcement and frustration.

figure 12.11

3) In figure 12.11 two players clash during a game, but are not penalised
   for their actions as there was no intent to harm each other. What type
   of behaviour does the picture portray?
   a. hostile aggression.
   b. instrumental aggression.
   c. assertion.
   d. foul play.

4) Which one of the following is a good example of a performer
   controlling their emotions during physical activity?
   a. shouting at a team mate for playing poorly.
   b. playing more aggressively because your team is losing.
   c. accepting a decision by the official which you think is wrong.
   d. only fouling when the referee is not looking.

5) A thrower prepares for a qualifying competition, but suffers from
   stress and tries too hard and so performs badly. Which theory explains this behaviour?
   a. catastrophe theory.
   b. multi-dimensional anxiety theory.
   c. inverted U theory.
   d. drive theory.

6) The catastrophe theory is used to explain a golfer's disastrous failure to
   win a match having been 3 strokes in the lead coming up to the last green.
   Explain this situation and why this theory might be useful in preventing a repetition.   4 marks

7) A number of PE students are attending trials at their chosen sport.
   Describe the Inverted U theory and explain how it might affect a
   student's performance at the trials.   5 marks

8) a) What is the difference between state and trait anxiety?   2 marks

   b) What coping strategies should the anxious performer draw upon?   5 marks

9) a) Discuss the possible relationships between anxiety and performance in sporting activities.   7 marks

   b) High levels of arousal have often been linked with stress. Sketch a graph showing
       the relationship between the performance of a complex skill and level of arousal.   2 marks

   c) Add a second curve to your graph showing how performance of a simple skill might
       be affected by arousal.   2 marks

Practice questions

10) With reference to sporting performance, explain how cognitive and somatic anxiety differ. — 5 marks

11) Discuss Hull's drive theory and the inverted U hypothesis as explanations of the anxiety-performance relationship. — 10 marks

12) Under-arousal can lead to poor performance. Discuss methods an athlete could use to increase his or her level of arousal to optimal levels. — 8 marks

13) a) What do we mean by the term aggression in sports psychology?
   Give an example from a sport or game which would illustrate your answer. — 2 marks

   b) Using examples from sport, briefly describe the differences between aggression and assertion? — 2 marks

   c) Some team players display unwanted aggression. What are the possible causes of such aggression? — 4 marks

14) Explain in detail what is meant by social learning when applied to aggression.
   How can aggressive tendencies be eliminated in a sports situation? — 10 marks

15) a) The aggressive cue hypothesis (Berkowitz 1969), is a theory which explains why aggression may be experienced by sports performers. Using an example from sport, describe the aggressive cue hypothesis. — 4 marks

   b) Using examples from sport, explain the frustration aggression hypothesis. — 4 marks

16) A Level. Discuss how theories of aggression can be applied to sport. — 20 marks

Answers link: http://www.jroscoe.co.uk/downloads/as_a1_revise_pe_ocr/OCRAS_A1_ch12_answers.pdf

CHAPTER 13: *Social facilitation, groups and goal setting*

Social facilitation

Social facilitation concerns how people other than the performer can influence a sportsperson's attitudes and behaviour.

The effect that the presence of spectators has on the way sportspeople play or perform can be positive (called **facilitation**), or negative (called **inhibition**). For example, a crowd (figure 13.1) encourages a team playing well (positive or facilitation), or the crowd jeers at a team playing poorly (negative or inhibition).

Facilitation

Facilitation of a performance by an audience tends to lead to the fact that high arousal leads to improved performance by a highly skilled or extrovert performer. Gross or simple skills tend to be improved by audience effects. See the link between arousal and performance in Hull's drive theory (page 149 figure 12.1).

Inhibition

Where the presence of an audience **inhibits performance**, high arousal tends to lead to reduced performance by novices whose skills are not well-learned. This also applies to introvert performers. Fine and complex skills requiring great concentration will also tend to have performance levels reduced by negative audience effects.

Different types of audience

Passive others (social facilitation) are audience and co-actors, whilst **interactive others** are competitors.

Co-actors

Co-actors are a passive form of audience involved in the same activity and at the same time as the performer, but not competing directly. For example:

* Officials, umpires or referees.
* Members of a player's own team.
* Ball-boys (figure 13.2) or helpers during a performance.

Factors affecting performance

* **Size of audience** - larger crowds create more arousal.
* **Proximity of audience** - the closer the audience the greater the arousal.
* **Intentions of the audience** - can be positive or negative. If spectators are negative about a player (shouting or jeering) this may suppress arousal or increase arousal depending on the personality of the performer.
* **Skill level** or **difficulty** of the task - performance improves for a well-learned skill and decreases if the skill is not well-learned.
* **Personality** of the performer - extroverts perform better when aroused, but introverts can be over-aroused.

figure 13.1 – effects of audience?

figure 13.2 – ball-boys as co-actors

Zajonc's model

Zajonc's theory says that the mere **presence of others** creates **arousal**, which then affects performance negatively if a skill is poorly-learnt (early in the learning curve - figure 13.3).

In this case, arousal causes an incorrect response because the incorrect response is dominant.

On the other hand, if a skill is **well-learnt** (later in the learning curve), then **arousal** causes a **correct response** because the correct response is dominant.

Effect of the type of task on facilitation or inhibition

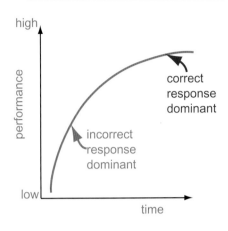

figure 13.3 – a learning curve

- An audience may facilitate the performance of an **extrovert**, but diminish or inhibit the performance of an **introvert**.

- **Beginners** (who have by definition low and unpractised levels of skill) will be affected more by an audience than experts (who by definition have well practised and stable skills).

- A task having **simple skills** (such as power lifting) will be improved by an audience, even if the skills are not habitual, compared with the performance of **complex skills**. Again this depends on whether or not the skill is habitual (well practised) or not. This is the reason that elite performers (with a well practised habitual skill) perform complex skills well on the top stage such as the Olympic Games.

- **Fine skills** need lower levels of arousal (produced by an audience for example), whereas **gross skills** could be improved by increased arousal. The difference between snooker and weight lifting (figure 13.4).

figure 13.4 – fine skills or gross skills?

Evaluation apprehension

This theory (due to Cottrell - figure 13.5) explains that an **audience is perceived as evaluating** (assessing the value or worth of) performance. This **causes anxiety** - which in turn causes arousal.

The distraction effect

Baron's distraction-conflict theory says that **distraction** is an aspect of concentration (or **lack of concentration**). **Attentional focus** is very important for the effective sportsperson and if this is disrupted then he or she is distracted from his or her task.

Audience and evaluation apprehension can act as a distraction. The sportsperson needs therefore to practise in distracting circumstances, and practise switching attentional focus when faced with potentially distracting circumstances.

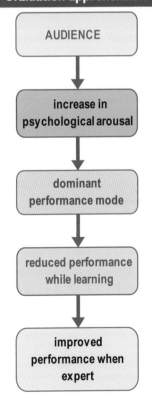

figure 13.5 – the process of evaluation apprehension

AUDIENCE

↓

increase in psychological arousal

↓

dominant performance mode

↓

reduced performance while learning

↓

improved performance when expert

Homefield advantage

Home or away effect on performance concerns the fact that more teams win at home than away. A crowd may be judged as supportive or hostile (facilitation or inhibition), and high levels of anxiety caused by hostility may reduce performance.

figure 13.6 – World Cup 1966 - Wembley, 97,000 spectators, homefield advantage?

The environment of their own stadium or playing situation is familiar to home teams, therefore home players are more comfortable. This limits anxiety and enables a worry-free and hopefully successful performance (figure 13.6).

Strategies for coping with social inhibition

Strategies include:
- Stress management.
- Mental rehearsal.
- Selective attention (away from evaluators).
- Lowering the importance of the situation.
- Training with an audience present.

Dynamics of groups and teams

A **group** consists of two or more people **interacting** with one another so that each person influences and is influenced by the others. A group will have a **collective identity** and a sense of **shared purpose**, and is a **social aggregate** involving **mutual awareness** and **potential interaction** with structured patterns of **communication**. For example, a crowd at a soccer match, a soccer team or parents watching their children swim.

Successful groups:
- Have a strong collective identity in which members have an opportunity to **socialise** and who **share goals**, **ambitions** and **ownership** of ideas.
- Will have members who are able to **communicate effectively** (on the same wavelength).
- Will have strong **cohesion** (see below).
- Have members who **value relationships** within the group.

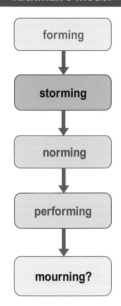

figure 13.7 – Tuckman's model

forming

storming

norming

performing

mourning?

Formation of groups

Tuckman's model for group formation

Tuckman's model says (figure 13.7) that groups are formed in four stages, with a possible fifth stage occurring afterwards. These are:

- **Forming**, in which group members get to know each other, they find out about the task or objective of the group, and they show respect for one another (before starting to work together). During this stage, the coach **tells the group** what to do.

- **Storming**, in which group members argue and compete with each other, and different types of leader emerge. During this stage, inexperienced group members may refuse to compromise, and a team may fail. The coach must **drive the team** through the stage.

- **Norming**, in which group members agree how to work together, and rules are developed with acceptable behaviour defined. Members begin to trust one another, and the accepting of criticism and new ideas are developed. During this stage, leaders emerge and take responsibility, and the coach becomes a **consultant**.

- **Performing**, in which the group works as a unit, and the team reaches the performance stage when hard work leads to the achievement of the team's goals. Group members are **interdependent**, and the more skilful or experienced members make decisions independently. During this stage, there is consultation (by the coach), leadership is devolved and accepted, and authority and direction are accepted in times of stress. Dissent can be used to improve performance, as members argue and reach agreement on the best way forward at difficult moments.

The possible fifth stage is:
- **Mourning**, as a group breaks up and members go their separate ways. This is almost the inevitable eventual outcome when a number of highly independent and articulate individuals are members of a group.

Group cohesion

Cohesion points at the way in which group members **gel** together, or feel **collective affection** for one another, or feel a strong **sense of sharing** whatever it is that the group does. It is the extent to which members of a group exhibit a desire to **achieve common goals** and **group identity**. The two themes of cooperation and coordination are strong elements of this idea.

- Sometimes this can mean selection of less skilled but more co-operative players for a team.
- Unfortunately, friendship groups can have negative effects.

Cohesion has both **task** and **social** elements:
- **Task cohesion** is about people who are willing to work together (see figure 13.8) whether or not they get on personally, hence the group would have the potential to be successful. Task cohesion is more required for success than social cohesion.
- **Social cohesion** covers the notion that teams with high social cohesion but low task cohesion are less successful.

On other words, a team will like socialising together and enjoying each other's company, but the greatest success will be achieved when the task the team faces (winning in the cup final for example) is large and dominant.

figure 13.8 – cohesion is important for some teams

Carron's model

This model (figure 13.9) outlines **four** factors that affect the development of cohesion:

- **Environmental factors** which bind members to a team, for example, contracts, location, age, eligibility. To make cohesion stronger, you should avoid a star system and provide opportunities for socialising.
- **Personal factors** which feature characteristics that members believe are important, and include motives for taking part. To optimise on cohesion, a coach should give opportunities for motives to be realised, and develop ownership feelings and social groupings within the team.
- **Leadership factors** which are about the behaviour of leaders and coaches. Coaches should use all leadership behaviours to influence different individuals.
- **Team factors** relating to the group, including team identity, targets, member ability and role, creation of team short-term and long-term goals, and the rewarding of individual and team efforts. These factors reflect all the characteristics of the group, norms and stability factors.

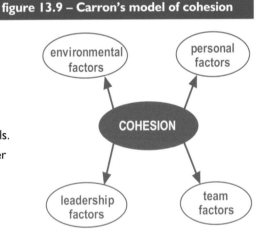

figure 13.9 – Carron's model of cohesion

environmental factors

personal factors

COHESION

leadership factors

team factors

This model also differentiates between **group outcomes**, which include the stability and performance of the team, and **individual outcomes**, including member satisfaction and individual performance.

Steiner's model of a group or team

Steiner produced a model to show the relationship between the performance of a team and the individuals.

Actual productivity = potential productivity – losses due to faulty processes

Actual productivity is a team's level of achievement on a specific task. For example, a rugby team reaching the semi-final of a cup competition.

Potential productivity is the best possible level of achievement of a cohesive team for this rugby team to win the cup competition.

Steiner's model of a group or team

Losses due to 'faulty' processes are coordination and motivational problems which the team face, which reduce the level of cohesion and as a result lower the level of achievement.

'Faulty' processes fall into two categories:
- **Coordination problems** (for players) occur if there should be a high level of interaction between players, but one (or more) player is being selfish or aggressive, or if a defence is not working together, and hence overall team performance suffers.
- **Motivational problems** in which groups tend to make individuals perform below their own best potential.

The Ringlemann effect

- **Motivational problems** occur because people seem to work less hard in a group than they do on their own. For example, in rowing, times of winning double sculls are often only slightly faster than single sculls.
- The **Ringlemann Effect** refers to this fact of average individual performance decreasing with increasing group size.

Social loafing

figure 13.10 – social loafing

- Hence individuals appear to **reduce their effort** when in a group (figure 13.10), and can **hide their lack of effort** amongst the effort of other group members. The term **social loafing** ascribes the reason for this as being due to motivational losses.
- **Motivational losses** occur because individuals may not share the same motives. This leads to loss of group cohesion, for example, some players may play a game for social reasons, others in order to win.
- It can be eliminated if the contribution of an individual **can be identified** as with **player statistics** (American football, rugby league, cricket, basketball).
- The **need** for interaction between players varies between sports.
- **Cooperation** between players can be significant in eliminating social loafing.

Coaching strategies used to develop group cohesion

- Put together a group with **high potential productivity** whilst trying to minimise losses due to faulty processes.
- **Minimising losses** could be achieved by organising practices so that all team members are certain of their role, over learning set plays in order to get the timing right and manipulating the use of rewards to optimise motivation levels.
- Coaches should not just pick the best players for a team, but those who are most likely **to get on with each other**.
- **Measure** both group and individual performances. If people know they are being monitored, they will conform.
- Use **Peer Pressure**. If most of the group aren't of similar disposition, then this should help.
- Give **Feedback**. It is possible that the loafer is unaware of his or her behaviour. The coach should provide positive feedback, focusing on observations, the impact, and what actions will be taken to remedy the situation.

Goal setting and SMART goals

figure 13.11 – goal setting

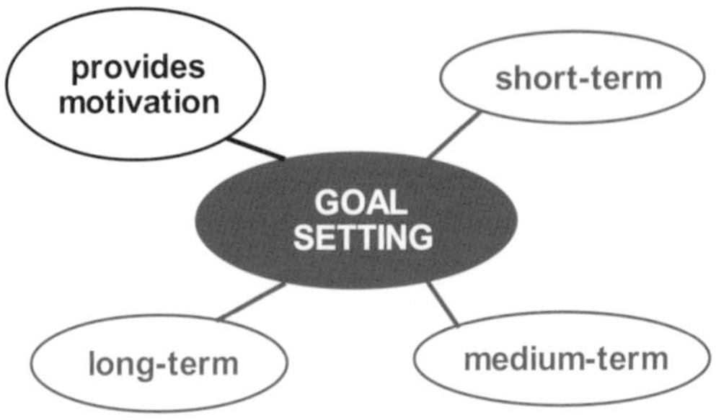

provides motivation • short-term • GOAL SETTING • long-term • medium-term

Many research studies have validated the link between goal setting and performance.

The main function of goal setting (figure 13.11) is to increase **motivation**. The feeling of satisfaction gained from achieving a goal brings about this motivation. Goal setting can also be used as a means of **managing anxiety** or stress.

Goals can be **short**-term, **medium**-term or **long**-term. Short-term goals can be used as targets for single training sessions, or what can be expected after a period of training. Long-term goals may or may not be achieved, but are placed in the background of a performer's mind and can underpin everything he or she does. Kelly Holmes had the ambition (goal) of getting an Olympic gold, and she **eventually** did this – twice! This goal motivated Kelly to keep going through injury and disappointment, to keep her training through bad weather and good times.

S.M.A.R.T goals

SPECIFIC
> directly related to a sporting situation.

MEASURABLE
> progress can be assessed.

ACHIEVABLE
> by the performer, coach and manager.

RECORDED
> written down and used to monitor performance - when achieved, the goal is ticked, and another written goal is set.

TIME-PHASED
> a date is set for completion.

figure 13.12 – goal achieved

For example, the **smart** goal of running a 400 metres in 48 seconds. This would be achieved after 5 racing attempts, agreed by both performer and coach, assessed at an 80% success rate, providing an exciting challenge, with a record of training and racing times. Performance is **monitored** via the setting of goals.

Jack Laugher and Chris Mears (figure 13.12) achieve a long-term goal by winning the gold in sychronised diving in Rio.

Goal setting

Goals (figure 13.13) should be:
- **Easily** attained initially and therefore **realistic**.
- **Incremental**, a little bit at a time.
- **Challenging** but **achievable**.
- **Progressively** more difficult.
- **Training goals** should be planned around **overall goals**.

Goals are either:
- **Outcome oriented**:
- Towards the end result of the sporting activity.
  For example to win a race.
- **Performance oriented**:
- Judged against other performances, and related to improvement and enhancing the performer's current standard.
  For example to beat his or her best time.
- **Process oriented**:
- To obtain an improvement in techniques.

figure 13.13 – goals should be?

easily attained • realistic • outcome oriented • GOALS • incremental • performance oriented • challenging • process oriented • achievable • progressively more difficult

Effective goal setting

figure 13.14 – effective goals

Goals (figure 13.14) should be:

- Stated **positively**.
- **Specific** to the situation and the performer.
- **Time phased**, to be achieved in one week or two months for example.
- **Challenging and aspirational**.
- **Achievable and realistic**.
- **Measurable**, so that you can actually say exactly whether or not a goal has been achieved.
- **Negotiated** between sportsperson and coach.
- **Progressive**, from short-term to long-term.
- **Performance oriented** rather than outcome oriented.
- **Written** down.
- **Reviewed** regularly (with downward adjustment if necessary - in the case of injury).
- **Achievement oriented** rather than failure oriented.

Failure to achieve goals should be followed by the resetting of goals to maintain the performer's **self-esteem**.

Goal setting and performance

- Gives the performer an aim or **focus**.
- Increases **motivation** when the goal is accomplished, and promotes **persistence** to achieve the goal.
- Increases **confidence** levels (increases **self-efficacy** - the situation specific self-confidence).
- Controls **arousal** or anxiety levels.
- Focusses **efforts in training** on game or competitive situations.

Practice questions

1) According to Cottrell (1965) the effect that others have on a performance is dependent on whether the performer perceives the others evaluating his or her performance. A subsequent rise in arousal levels was said to result from:
   a. social facilitation.
   b. evaluation apprehension.
   c. social inhibition.
   d. the dominant response.

2) Tuckman suggested the formation of a group occurs in a specific order
   a. forming, storming, norming, performing.
   b. norming, performing, forming, storming.
   c. performing, forming, storming, norming.
   d. storming , norming, performing, forming.

3) Which one of the following is the best example of a SMART goal set to improve performance of an official in a physical activity?
   a. to learn the rules of the game and to give the right decisions in the next match.
   b. to get fitter and to keep up with the run of play.
   c. to learn the signal for offside by this time next week.
   d. to talk to the players after the game to get feedback on performance of the official.

Practice questions

4) Goal setting is useful for performers in many ways. Which of the following choices does not support this statement?
   a. confidence is increased.
   b. evaluation and feedback are immediate and focused.
   c. uncertainty is increased.
   d. practices are structured.

5) Which of the following statements represents Steiner's model of group effectiveness?
   a. actual productivity = potential productivity – gains due to faulty processes.
   b. actual productivity = potential productivity – losses due to faulty processes.
   c. potential productivity = actual productivity – gains due to faulty processes.
   d. potential productivity = actual productivity – losses due to faulty processes.

6) a) What is meant by social facilitation and what is its main effect?   3 marks
   b) What effects can be experienced by an individual if there is an audience present?   5 marks

7) a) Using figure 13.5 on page 157 and examples from sport, explain what is meant by evaluation apprehension   5 marks
   b) Briefly outline the causes of evaluation apprehension.   2 marks

   c) As a coach of an individual who is affected adversely by the presence of an audience, how would you
      help him or her to overcome negative influences?   4 marks

8) Two groups of male sportspeople (of the same age) undertook an arms-length weight hold endurance test. Success at this exercise was measured by the length of time the weight was held. Table 13.1 shows the average times for group 1 (who did the exercise alone) and group 2 (who did the exercise in the presence of an audience).

Table 13.1 - **average time for strength exercise**

	group 1 no audience	group 2 with audience
average time held in seconds	46.5	50.5

   a) What effect (if any) did the audience have on the performance of the exercise?   1 mark

   b) How would you account for this effect (or lack of effect)?   4 marks

   c) The audience in this exercise (for group 2) was not known to the participants.
      Explain any effect you think there would be if the audience was known to the group.   6 marks

9) a) What is meant by cohesion in the context of teams?   4 marks

   b) Explain what is meant by social loafing by using examples from sport.   3 marks

   c) What advice would you give a coach of a team to ensure maximum productivity?   5 marks

10) Elite performers sometimes train on their own and sometimes as part of a group.
    How would you distinguish between a group and a collection of individuals?   3 marks

11) Psychologist Bruce Tuckman first came up with the memorable phrase 'forming, storming, norming and performing'. How is this phrase used to describe the path that most teams follow on their way to high performance?
                                                                                                                  8 marks

Practice questions

12) a) Explain the Ringlemann effect, and its related term, social loafing.   4 marks
    b) How can social loafing be reduced?   3 marks

13) Describe Carron's conceptual model of cohesion.   4 marks

14) a) Explain Steiner's model of group performance:

    Actual productivity = potential productivity – losses due to faulty processes   6 marks

    b) What factors stop a team performing to its true potential?   6 marks

15) A Level. Discuss and apply to sporting situations, theories that affect formation and development of group cohesion. What strategies could a coach use to develop group cohesion?   20 marks

16) According to Carron (1982) the following factors influence group cohesion.
    For each factor give an example to explain how this happens.
    a) Environmental factors.
    b) Leadership factors.
    c) Personal factors.
    d) Team factors.   8 marks

17) a) Identify five characteristics of goals which a performer might set to achieve an aim.   5 marks
    b) Explain how outcome goals and performance goals can affect motivation, anxiety and stress.   4 marks

18) a) Show what is meant by short-term goals and long-term goals by using examples from sport.   4 marks
    b) What are the main positive effects of setting goals in sport?   2 marks
    c) As a coach how would you ensure that your goal setting was as effective as possible?   6 marks
    d) How does performance profiling assist in goal setting?   3 marks

19) Explain the meaning of the acronym S.M.A.R.T. in relation to goal setting.   7 marks

20) Explain the many important factors that have to be taken into account when setting goals.
    What effect does goal setting have on performance?   10 marks

Answers link: http://www.jroscoe.co.uk/downloads/as_a1_revise_pe_ocr/OCRAS_A1_ch13_answers.pdf

Popular recreations

The culture of the English lower classes before the late 19th century was linked with social conditions. The lower classes/peasants were badly paid, often work was seasonal, they worked as farm labourers, lived in poverty, had poor health and very basic housing. This formed the basis of recreation and pastimes available to them.

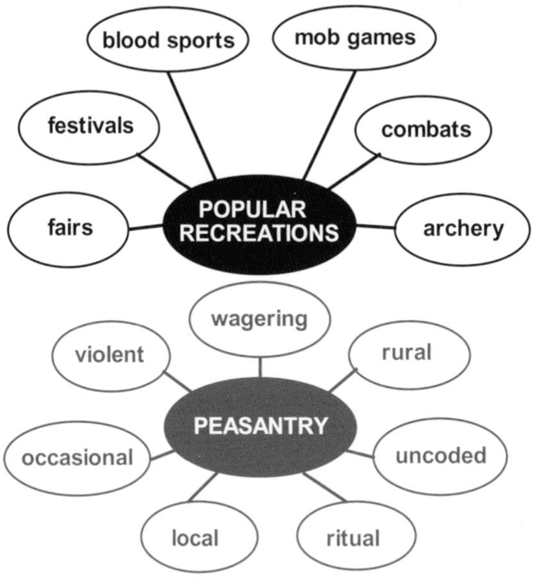

Characteristics of recreation and pastimes pre-1850 (figure 14.5)

- They were **occasional** because there was limited free time.
- They were **local** because there was limited **transport**, other than walking, horses or oxen were used to pull carts or traps.
- They were **uncoded** (figure 14.6) because the peasantry was often **illiterate**.
- They were **ritualised** because of the influence of older pagan and existing church influences.
- Any recreations of a sporting nature were often in the context of village fêtes or **fairs** held on holydays.
- The activities were often **violent and cruel** (figure 14.7), because life was hard and harsh at that time.
- **Wagering** was a primary feature of life at this time, and wagers would be made on the outcome of any contest.

Many of these activities have survived both at an aristocratic and popular level, but many have been either curtailed or reformed. Nor is there the clean separation between the two groups (upper and lower classes) within our present democracy.

Among the **upper class sports**, coursing, if allowed at all, is limited to only two dogs and is tightly controlled, hunting is now legally restricted and shooting is strictly controlled.

- Popular recreations like **baiting** have long since been made illegal (cock fighting was made illegal in 1849).
- **Festivals** are more respectable.
- **Archery** (figure 14.8) has changed from military combat practice to a codified target sport.
- And **mob football** has only survived in rural areas which escaped the impact of reform.

The **socio-cultural influences** which brought about the evolution of the various pastimes of the middle ages are summarised in figure 14.13 (page 170).

The changes which led to modern versions of existing sports will be explained later with the focus on the mid 19th century development of **public school athleticism** and **rational sport**.

figure 14.5 – popular recreations

blood sports · mob games · festivals · combats · fairs · **POPULAR RECREATIONS** · archery

wagering · violent · rural · occasional · **PEASANTRY** · uncoded · local · ritual

figure 14.6 – mob football as a lower class pursuit

figure 14.7 – bull baiting, brutal but exciting

figure 14.8 – archery as preparation for war

How did women fit into the evolution of sporting pastimes in this period?

In pre-industrial Britain, **lower class women** living in rural communities participated in the management of the agriculture of the time as well as their men - within the strict purpose of creating and then feeding their families. When holydays and fayres came along, women were able to participate in terms of **smock races** (see figure 14.9) and other events. Just as athletic men were wrestling, boxing, and shooting in organized contests to display their physical prowess, healthy young, unwed women could do the same in the smock race. Competition was fierce, attracting large audiences, and there were occasions when some women took part in the mob football type of activities which most of the working rural population seemed to enjoy during this period.

Some festivals such as the horse racing on Epsom Downs, were occasions when **upper class women** could parade in their finery - a tradition still upheld today.

But formal sporting structures for women seemed to be restricted to cricket in which there was a flourishing County Championship played in county grounds (in which men would normally play) provided by the aristocracy as in figure 14.10 portraying a women's county match in 1811.

figure 14.9 – women's smock race

figure 14.10 – women's cricket 1811

The growth of regulation of sport between 1700 and 1850

Some sporting activities had been evolving during this period, mostly because they were played and were organised by the gentry who had the space and time to play them.

Also, the Church provided frequent feast days and a suitable space for gatherings. This period saw the early organisation of cricket (rules in 1727), horse racing (jockey club formed in 1752), prize fighting or bare-fist fighting (Broughton's rules in 1743) as spectator attractions and commercial enterprises. Note that the major commercial feature of these activities was the **wagering** accepted as part of the proceedings.

Evolution of sport

Some sports developed from the **occupation** of participants, for example, competitive rowing, which grew from the work of ferrymen taking passengers across the River Thames (figure 14.11).

Pedestrianism, the forerunner to track athletics, evolved from competition between lower class footmen carried in the coaches of the wealthy, who were wagered by their masters to reach a destination first. Scottish landowner, Robert Barclay Allardice (founder of Barclay's bank) in 1809 – drew a crowd of about 10,000 for 1000 miles walked in 1000 consecutive hours - again **gambling** on the outcome became a major feature of these events.

Unfortunately, **trickery** became commonplace – with professional athletes using false names and race fixing to fix a wager.

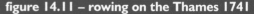

figure 14.11 – rowing on the Thames 1741

In the middle ages before 1700, it was usual for landowners to arrange for their subjects to learn to swim for safety reasons when land adjoined rivers or open water. King Charles II established a series of fashionable **swimming** contests on the Thames and the first open air swimming bath was built in London in 1784.

Mob games

Most such games (figure 14.12) involved kicking, handling or throwing a ball, but some involved striking with a stick or club, and some were played with a roll of sacking or approximately spherical wooden block. Goals were a relatively late development, with most games attempting to retain possession or gain territory. By 1600, a ball was made of a pig's bladder encased in leather, and there were special shoes with hobnails on the toes and soles to protect the players' feet but not shins.

The fact that so many people participated in each game (for example, all the villagers or townspeople divided somehow into 'sides'), with people able to use any force or violence ensured that the 'mob' name for the activity was justified. The violence of the games was outlined in a 1555 poem:

Bruised muscles and broken bones
Discordant strife and futile blows
Lamed in old age, then crippled withal
These are the beauties of football.

figure 14.12 – a mob game

The violence sometimes led to deaths, and the banning of the games by various monarchs, such as King Edward III of England, in 1363: 'moreover we ordain that you prohibit under penalty of imprisonment all and sundry from such stone, wood and iron throwing; handball, football, or hockey; coursing and cock-fighting, or other such idle games'. This stance was also followed by King Henry IV in 1409 and 1410 and King James I of Scotland in 1424.

The characteristics of mob football more or less followed the characteristics of popular recreation as in figure 14.15 (page 170), which were:

* **Local** - Village v Village, community based.
* **Uncoded** - Simple rules, local rules, based on the word of mouth, simple, natural.
* **Violent** - Uncivilised, regular deaths not skills based.
* **Occasional** - Often annual on festival days or holydays.
* Played by **lower class males**, a way to show manliness.
* Unlimited **number** of players (figure 14.6 page 167).
* **Rural** - Occasionally in towns.
* Often **restricted** - illegal, curtailed.
* **Wagering** - betting on the outcome.

Attempts were made to curtail mob games but some in rural areas have survived, for example **The Alnwick Shrovetide Football Match** is one of the few surviving games of mob football still being played today. The fixture between the parishes of St Michael and St Paul was first recorded in 1762. The game has **few rules** and involves **large teams** of roughly 150 players on each side and attracts hundreds of spectators. The goals are decorated with greenery and stand about 400 yards apart.

Education and law and order

The type of pursuits that the two-tier class system participated in reflected their educational backgrounds.

The **lower classes** were **uneducated** and **illiterate** (poor children got what education they could in Sunday Schools). Lower class pursuits were simple and unsophisticated, as reflected in the characteristics of mob football described above.

The educated **upper class** pursuits were more refined, as reflected in the rules that governed sports such as real tennis, hunting and croquet.

Law enforcement and policing was based entirely locally, which often included provision for paid watchmen or constables to patrol towns at night, while rural areas had less formal arrangements. The characteristics of mob games and bare knuckle fighting reflected this unruly and lawless society.

Transport

Transport for the working class was on foot and by horse and cart and so they stayed in the local vicinity. The upper classes had horse drawn carriages and so could travel further and get to sporting facilities such as real tennis courts or to Epsom Downs for the horse racing.

The social and cultural factors which shaped sport in Britain after 1850

The development of **physical education** and **sport** reflected changes in British society (figure 14.13). Hence we place **social and cultural** changes in the context of elitist **institutions** like the **English public schools**.

The major changes which occurred in society influenced participation in sport today. We will now discuss how society changed during the period over which the industrial revolution occurred, as it influenced **development and change** in English institutions.

The early 19th century marked the beginnings of **three social revolutions** in England:

- The **agrarian revolution** (figure 14.14) which involved the gradual movement of workers from the countryside to the larger towns, caused by:
    - The emergence of a **gentry** class.
    - The **enclosure** of much of the countryside.
    - The growth of the **Methodist** movement.
    - The gradual increased significance of **respectability** in early Victorian society.
    - The **poor wages** of the rural working class.
    - The gradual **mechanisation** of tenant farms.

- The **industrial revolution**, in which this mechanisation meant that:
    - People: started to migrate into towns and villages and away from the land.
    - Work became available in the factories for this surplus labour, hence the industrialsation of the economy.
    - This gave increased power to the middle classes.
    - And better wages for some of the industrial working class.
    - And greater prosperity for the country at large.

- The **urban revolution**, which marked a massive rise in the population, as industrial and commercially well-placed towns grew in size and national significance.

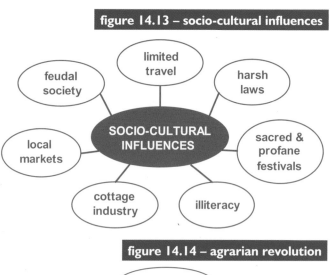

figure 14.13 – socio-cultural influences

SOCIO-CULTURAL INFLUENCES: limited travel, harsh laws, sacred & profane festivals, illiteracy, cottage industry, local markets, feudal society

figure 14.14 – agrarian revolution

AGRARIAN REVOLUTION: enclosure, growth of Methodists, respectability, low wages of rural workers, mechanisation of farms, emergence of gentry

Popular and rational recreation

These two strands of development towards modern sport had the characteristics identified in figures 14.15 and 14.16. Popular and rational recreation were not totally different. They both involved **physical activity**, they were both **competitive** and they were both **enjoyable** and **fulfilling**. They both had features of **ritual** and **festival** and both had elements which can still be seen in modern sport.

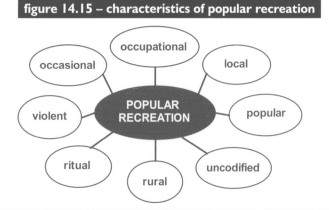

figure 14.15 – characteristics of popular recreation

POPULAR RECREATION: occupational, local, popular, uncodified, rural, ritual, violent, occasional

figure 14.16 – characteristics of rational recreation

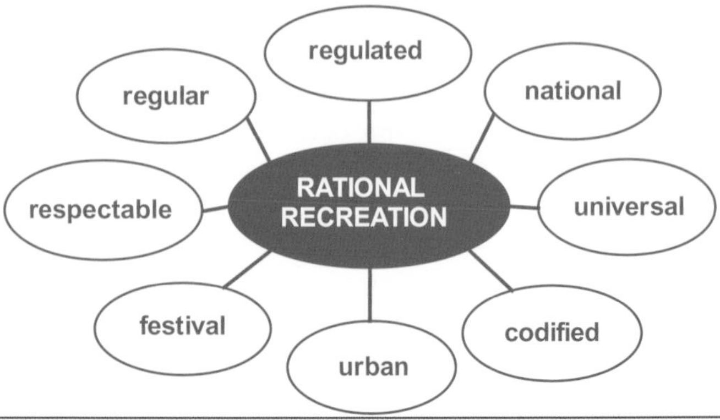

RATIONAL RECREATION: regulated, national, universal, codified, urban, festival, respectable, regular

Table 14.1 – **the cultural factors which influenced the conversion of popular sports into rational sports**

popular	rational
agrarian.	industrial and urban.
feudal.	emergent middle class.
limited travel.	railways.
illiterate.	elementary education.
cottage industry.	factories.
payment in kind.	wages.
limited free-time.	regular free-time and the Saturday half day.
markets.	shopping centres.
harsh laws.	law and policing.
church festivals.	muscular Christianity - athleticism.
fields and rivers.	parks and baths.

The effects of industrialisation on the development of rational recreation

Industrialisation had the effect of improving three major **developmental** factors in society, these were:

- **Communication**: the sporting press (rather than just current affairs) was established. Receiving results quickly kept spectators interested in their favourite sport, and newspapers were transported by rail.

figure 14.17 – 1859 - excursion to Brighton for 3s 6d

- **Transport**: better transport meant fixtures could be played in different towns thus leagues and competitions became more developed. Factory owners would arrange excursions to the coast (figure 14.17), hence workers' morale was maintained. Rail travel was vastly improved with the arrival of steam power, so spectators and racehorses could be transported to different events. Also, as cycling grew more popular, road improvements were demanded.

- **Technology**: clothing was made by machines in the mills, and sport specific clothing and footwear became available. More sophisticated timing devices (stop watches) and other sport equipment (balls, racquets, athletic equipment) made sport more fair and more competitive. Printing presses were used to produce the popular press as literacy amongst the working class improved. The electric telegraph meant results of games could be distributed faster, to more places.

The effects of urbanisation and industrialisation on sport

- There was **less open land-space** for pre-industrial games to take place.
- **Transport** - lower class countryside-based people were deterred from travelling to towns for sport because transport from where they lived was poor. Rough roads or tracks were available to horse drawn carts, walking or on horseback.
- **Long working hours** in factories decreased leisure time.
- **Low wages** meant that there was little disposable income available for participation in sport.
- **Women** and **children** were used as cheap labour.
- Workers were too **tired** for leisure activities.
- The **12 hour working day** meant that it was dark before and after work in the winter months.
- The **1847 factories act** reduced the working day to 10 hours, hence slightly more time for leisure activities, which encouraged the growth of factory teams.

The effects of education on sport

- In the 1800s, learning became available even to the poorest people, particularly after the **1870 Education Act** which established '**board schools**', and the act of 1880 which made education for all children between the ages of 5 and 10 compulsory. This was partly aimed at reducing child labour in factories.

- More people became **literate** and **aspirational** towards their futures as wider opportunities in the management and operation of factories became available.

- The fact that more people were able to read and therefore understand the rules of a sport or game produced greater participation in sport.

- The **industrial middle class** gradually increased in size and asserted their rights to boarding school education, hence increasing their opportunity to participate in sport. But the poorest people living in slums and working long hours in factories did not have the same opportunity.

- Whilst the growth of middle class sport was noticeable in membership levels at clubs, in working class culture it was more evident in increasing levels of spectatorship. Unlike the middle class, they had no physical education which might have encouraged them to participate in greater numbers.

The development of professional sport

Popular recreation was normally centred on the **lower class**, with **aristocratic** or **gentry** sports co-existing alongside peasant sports. Normally, **patronage** by the gentry not only determined whether the popular activities and **festivals** flourished in a community, but it was also why they were allowed to continue well after levels of industrialisation and urbanisation had increased. The key factors were:

- The significance of **wagering and possible corruption**.
- The **limited free time** available to the urban lower class and agricultural labourers.
- The **minimal pay** for workers who were on the bread-line.
- The **lack of transport** except for the wealthiest classes.

As a result, the **occasional festival** and **fayre** offered the chance to **earn money prizes** through sporting competition to young people with talent and bravery. If they were good enough, they could increase their income by travelling to different fairs and wakes to compete in combat sports like single stick play, wrestling or running events. In addition to prize money, there was always **wagering** where you could risk money on backing yourself to win or lose!

Amateurism and professionalism in the 19th century

- The distinction between amateurs and professionals in so far as sport is concerned was mainly on a **class basis**.
- In cricket, the '**gentlemen**' were the amateurs who played for the fun, the '**players**' were professionals - usually employed by the gentlemen.
- 'Players' started as the employed groundsmen who prepared the pitches, but also played for the teams.
- This was deemed the correct way of paying professional players in what was essentially an amateur sport.
- In **rugby**, it was expected that players would not be paid and were therefore amateur.
- This changed in 1895 when the Rugby League was formed, but Rugby Union remained amateur until 1995.
- **Soccer** became a professional sport in 1885, because players were mostly working class.
- Factory owners encouraged the formation of **work's teams** and benefited from a fitter workforce.
- **Athletics**, **swimming** and **rowing** remained strictly amateur until the 1980s.
- **Tennis** had both amateur and professional factions until the 1950s, when the Lawn Tennis Association (LTA) and Wimbledon began to pay winning players, and the sport was unified.

Women's sport in the 19th century - the gender issue

- Historically, sport was a male pastime. Sport had evolved from violent activities undertaken by males in connection with the need to prepare for war (fencing, jousting, stave fighting, archery, wrestling and fist fighting), and since hunting and horse riding were gentry pastimes, women tended not to be involved until a later date.
- The **middle classes** did not expect their wives to work, but increasingly they were allowed to play as long as the activities were private and genteel. As a result croquet, lawn tennis and golf were acceptable.
- **Working class women** did not generally have the time, money or provision for sport until the end of the 19th century.

Women's sport in the 19th century - the gender issue

Victorian attitudes to women led to females being excluded from rational sport on the grounds that:

- It was too manly.
- It could endanger childbirth.
- **Victorian fashion**, among upper and middle classes (restrictive clothing), prevented freedom of movement and so discouraged women from vigorous activity.
- It was not expected that Victorian women should display their bodies, or be competitive and sweat!

Nineteenth century public schools and athleticism

The **characteristics** of the 19th century public schools included the facts that they were for the **sons of the gentry** and they were **boarding, fee paying**, and **non-local** establishments (figure 14.18).

- The non-local feature of these schools was very important in that the developments that occurred in the schools became spread across the nation.

- There were also scholars from poorer families and by the 1870s the number of schools had increased to accommodate an emergent middle class.

The **Clarendon Commission** was a Royal Commission established in 1861 to investigate the state of nine leading public schools in England. Following reforms, seven boarding schools were the centre of a subsequent **expansion of boarding schools** as middle class copies appeared throughout the country.

- There was a delay before similar selective high schools emerged for **upper and middle class girls** (figure 14.19).

- By the end of the nineteenth century, there was public or grammar school access for wealthy and bright boys and girls. The schools had an active policy of **athleticism (goodness, manliness, restraint** and **discipline)** perceived character building qualities.

- Other reforms also occurred such as a broader curriculum, reduced flogging, and control of school sport by the Sixth Form.

- The characteristics of these schools are identified in the model (in figure 14.18), where each component had a positive effect on the growth of athleticism.

figure 14.19 – cricket in an early girls' academy

Athleticism

Athleticism was originally defined as '**a muscular Christian view of manliness reflecting physical endeavour and moral integrity**' (honour, truthfulness and sportsmanship). By the end of the 19th century, athleticism had become so popular that some authorities felt that it was undermining other educational values. Hence a second critical definition was given as '**the exultation and disproportionate regard for games, which often resulted in the denigration of academic work and in anti-intellectualism**'.

The growth of this movement is best broken up into **three stages**.

Stage one – schoolboys' recreations

- There is a link between developments in the schools and changes in society. At the beginning of the 19th century, **transport** was limited to carts, stage coaches and wagons. Only the **very wealthy** had the **time, money** and **transport** to travel any distance.

- As a result they were the only people with the tradition of sending their sons to boarding schools. It is important to mention that at this time the daughters of the very wealthy either had governesses or went to **academies** near to home (figure 14.19).

- **Recreations** within this first stage followed local folk customs and practices.

Stage one – schoolboys' recreations

- With game laws in place, hunting and shooting were controlled by the upper classes, and traditional festivals were held in the towns and villages on occasional **holydays** and chartered fair days.

- The upper class played a courtly role and the lower classes made the most of a festival day, which of course was a day off from the grind of work.

The **boys** therefore took local **folk activities to school**, so that there were regular fights, mob games (figure 14.20), cricket (of course), swimming in the river or open pools, and boating. Very few schools had hounds, so the young boys became the **hares** and the seniors chased them labelled as **hounds**. This was the basis of the '**boy culture**' within which these schools flourished.

figure 14.20 – mob games in a public school

Stage two – Arnold and Christian gentlemen

By 1830, a **new breed of headmasters** were **reforming** their schools and starting to link Christianity with the Ancient Greek model of **Mind, Body and Spirit**. They chose to link the energy identifiable in the games and sports with education. The Headmaster would have led the revised programmes, with prefects and junior members of staff establishing basic rules. House matches allowed healthy, social competition.

Social control (figure 14.21) was an important objective of this process. It was an attempt to reduce the bullying and lawlessness in the schools and the effect of the boy culture outlined above. Dr Thomas Arnold is known to have led this reform, but much of his reputation comes from the book Tom Brown's Schooldays, rather than research evidence. In the eyes of Arnold and others, the **desire to produce Christian gentlemen** was central and the moral code of **fair play** was introduced at this stage.

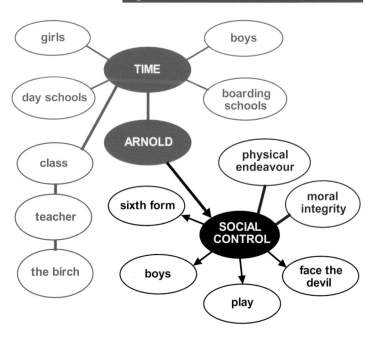
figure 14.21 – Arnold and social control

Stage three – Corinthian athleticism and the emergence of rational recreation

With more regular play of games and sports, **written rules** were established. But because this was an internal programme, each school devised its own version of rules depending on the facilities available. At this time only the game of **cricket** had a set of **universal rules** across several different schools throughout the country (figure 14.22). **Football** and **fives** rules were different in each school. **Swimming** was popular wherever there were lakes, ponds or rivers available, as in the Duck Puddle bathing pool at Harrow (figure 14.23).

figure 14.22 – inter-school cricket by 1851

figure 14.23 – the Harrow School Duck Puddle

Stage three – Corinthian athleticism and the emergence of rational recreation

At Eton, **boating** was encouraged instead of swimming in the Thames, but Shrewsbury and Eton established safety rules that only those boys who could swim, could row.

As the schools and society changed to meet the energy and reforming zeal of Victorian England, so the lesser gentry and **industrial middle class** presumed the right to public boarding school education. They were not allowed into the Clarendon Schools and so they built new ones. These new schools had extensive sports facilities, were built in attractive spa towns and other wealthy areas, and were linked by the new **railway** system.

Middle class developments

*   The middle classes were not only wealthy and industrious, they wanted the status previously reserved for the gentry and they felt that the **public schools** would at least give that to their sons.

Women's public schools

*   Meanwhile, with some upper class women gaining access to Oxbridge, these women opened boarding schools for their daughters.
*   This was eventually taken up by the middle class with a **girls' high school** opening in every major town.

Sport in public schools

Sport in public schools was now **widespread**, as teachers moved schools to obtain headships and took the notion of sport as part of a school with them. But certain idiosyncrasies remained, such as soccer and rugby having separate codes and fives having several versions. **Regular play** and **written codes** evolved as senior boys continued with sport at the **universities** and, as **old boys**, they continued to encourage athleticism in their old school and in amateur sport.

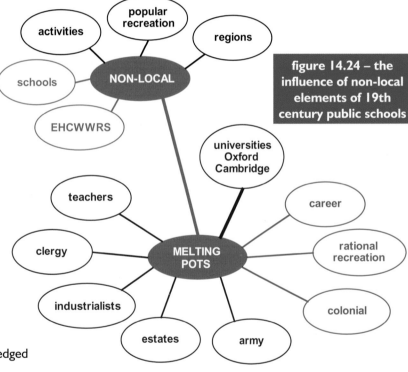

figure 14.24 – the influence of non-local elements of 19th century public schools

*   For example, a group of **university graduates** discussed the rules of football. They accepted the divide between the two codes of association and rugby, and established the **governing bodies** of the Football Association (FA) in 1863, the Rugby Football Union (RFU) in 1870, and the Lawn Tennis Association (LTA) in 1888.
*   The notion of the **gentleman amateur** continued, while several games had acknowledged the place of the **professional** performer.
*   In **cricket** and **association football**, the professional player and club were controlled by middle class administrators, who accepted the code of **physical endeavour and moral integrity** as the basis of all modern games and sports. Hence the nineteenth century public schools had a major part to play in the development of most modern day sports and games.

Some cultural changes, such as working class free time, elementary education and the emancipation of the lower class female, took more time. But the cultural changes were under way, and perhaps sport led the way.

Girls' schools started with callisthenics and girls also played organised games based on similar principles to the boys. Established men's games were generally avoided. The girls played **hockey** and **lacrosse** (figure 14.25) in the winter and **lawn tennis** in the summer, but cricket was often limited to junior girls.

figure 14.25 – lacrosse as a girls' game

Spreading the message

'**Melting pot**' is a concept that is used to describe how a combination of different things produces a new outcome. And so the mixing of all the factors via the public schools (shown in figure 14.24 page 175) formed the basis of the early amateur governing bodies and the birth of rational recreation. A large number of these boys returned to teach in the public schools after graduation, and spread the new rules to the next generation of schoolboys. Hence inter-school matches and competitions were held according to the new unified rules, and the word was spread.

With the lead coming from university graduates, there was a focus on the things men had learnt at school and university. These men were experienced **all-round** sportsmen, often getting '**blues**' in several sports at university. They formed **elite clubs** (for example, Leander for rowing and the Corinthians for cricket and soccer), setting a high standard of sportsmanship. This process was the basis of early **amateur governing bodies** and the birth of **rational recreation**. See figure 14.24 (page 175) for an outline of the factors affecting the birth of rational recreation via the public schools.

Development of the sporting press

The gradual emergence of the sports journalist can be traced against a background of an expanding newspaper industry. The 1850s saw the gradual lowering and then abandonment of punitive newspaper taxes.

A steady improvement in living standards, increasing educational opportunities and a growth in disposable incomes, combined with urban expansion, led to the emergence of a reading public of commercial proportions.

Advances in rail transport together with technological innovations in printing and the telegraph system eased the way for a rapid expansion in newspaper production and a classless readership.

The establishment and development of clubs, NGBs, a sporting calendar for spectator and player, and a dramatic increase in the range of sports available and in the number of people who played and watched them, led to the introduction of the sports column and then the sports page. This also partly led to the growth and development of rationalised sport due to the newspapers contributing to free publicity and sports coverage.

Practice questions

1) Sport has remained a major recreational activity in the UK since the 19th Century. The majority of sports were rationalized in the 19th Century. Which one of the following is a characteristic of rational recreation?
    a. violent.
    b. rural.
    c. respectable.
    d. occasional.

2) Which one of the following best describes the cult of athleticism?
    a. character building qualities.
    b. reduced flogging.
    c. playground control by sixth form.
    d. codes of honour and loyalty to school.

3) Social class in pre-industrial Britain influenced the types of sporting activities a person would engage in. Which one of the following pursuits was associated with both the upper and lower classes?
    a. prize fighting.
    b. pedestrianism.
    c. hunting.
    d. mob games.

4) Mob games are no longer played regularly in the United Kingdom. What social factor caused the decline of mob games in the 19th century?
    a. lack of space in urban areas.
    b. hygiene issues.
    c. reduction in the working week.
    d. wagering.

Practice questions

5) Which one of the following best explains how the development of the railways helped the growth of association football?
   a. rules standardised the FA (formed in 1863) teams which had to play to the same rules.
   b. leagues cups fixtures and competitions developed.
   c. supporters could watch their team and supporters clubs grew.
   d. literacy and the sporting press increased popularity.

6) What were the characteristics of popular recreation?   6 marks

7) What do you understand by the terms codified, regulated, and respectable in relation to rational recreation?   6 marks

8) Public schools, such as Rugby and Eton, played an important part in the development of rational games in society from mid 19th century onwards. Explain the role played by 'old boys' of such public schools in the development of rational recreation.   4 marks

9) Why were Oxford and Cambridge Universities able to make such an impressive contribution to elite sport in the late 19th century?   6 marks

10) Participation in sports and games was a key feature of 19th century public schools. Describe three factors which lead to increased participation in physical activity by young people in public schools in Stage three of development (the 'cult' of athleticism). How do these factors continue to impact upon participation and performance in physical activity in schools today?   10 marks

11) Modern sports are partly a result of changes that occurred in the 19th century. How did English public schools influence the technical development of games?   3 marks

12) A Level. Explain the emergence of physical endeavour and moral integrity in 19th century public school athleticism and discuss the issues which threaten it in today's sport.   20 marks

13) Describe Mob football as an example of popular recreation.   4 marks

14) How did sport spread from the English public schools in the late 19th century?   3 marks

15) How did 19th century public schools contribute to the technical development of 'rational recreation'?   3 marks

16) How did social class influence participation in sports and pastimes in both pre-industrial and post-industrial Britain?   8 marks

17) What factors, other than improved transport, influenced the emergence of rational sport after 1850? Discuss how the impact of these social and cultural factors shaped sport in Britain.   10 marks

18) Many NGBs of sport were set up in England between the late 1800s and early 1900s. Why was it necessary to form these governing bodies and why did some of them prevent professional athletes from competing in their sport?   6 marks

19) Describe and explain the effect that the industrial revolution had on sport after 1800.   5 marks

20) Define the terms 'Gentleman Amateurs' and 'Playing Professionals'.   2 marks

21) Discuss the sporting opportunities available to females in the 19th century.   4 marks

Answers link: http://www.jroscoe.co.uk/downloads/as_a1_revise_pe_ocr/OCRAS_A1_ch14_answers.pdf

CHAPTER 15: *Emergence & evolution of modern sport between 1900 & present*

By the early 1900s some well established spectator sports already had major organised events during the year which amounted to a season in or near London. These have continued throughout the twentieth century: the Oxford and Cambridge Boat Race on the Thames in March, The Oxford versus Cambridge Rugby match at Twickenham also in March, the Derby Day horse race at Epsom in April, and the Wimbledon Lawn Tennis Championships in July. Elite performers came from the upper and middle classes as did most of the spectators, who had the free time and money. These events are still well attended and popular events a century later and with television coverage and modern technology are viewed by even more people today. The social setting within which cultural and sporting developments occurred in the first half of 20th century Britain is summarised in figure 15.1.

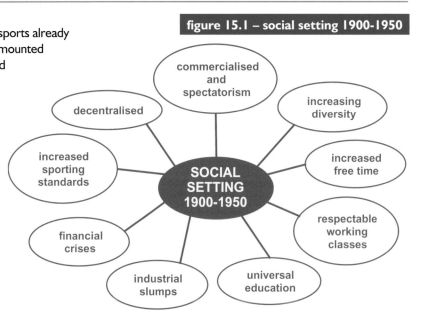

figure 15.1 – social setting 1900-1950

The code set by the governing bodies held true to the amateur ethic until the 1980s, when they reluctantly allowed amateur rules on financial aid to be revoked. Today, **professionalism** has taken over the status of most sports.

Governing bodies for all sports became established as independent bodies which regulated their sports. Apart from setting out the rules for a sport, the **regulations** had to take into account the changes such as professionalism which were being demanded by the sportspeople they represented.
Regulations had to account for player violence, changes in clothing and equipment, and in the ways in which sport as a whole was becoming financed by commercial sponsorship and TV rights.

Fair play, sportsmanship, gamesmanship and cheating

Nevertheless, governing bodies continue to also represent grass roots development which has remained amateur. However, with media coverage showing regular examples of **gamesmanship and cheating**, it is increasingly difficult to maintain the importance of **sportsmanship** in sport. In spite of this trend in society, the teaching of **fair play** is still a basic principle underlying the role of sport in society.

Amateurism and professionalism, class, law and order

The twentieth century brought a further reduction in the elitism of **amateurism** as there was a gradual change from the 'gentleman amateur' tradition that had dominated most Victorian sports to a new professionalism, but this varied considerably between different sports. In the early part of the century, though the **barrier** between amateurs and professionals remained strong, several sports like athletics and swimming opened their doors to amateurs from **all classes**. Women had their own governing bodies and they also broadened the definition of amateurism.

Amateurism changed in meaning as defined by governing body regulations:

*   Firstly, to a **no financial gain** regulation.
*   Then to the justification for **legitimate expenses** where this later included **lost time**.
*   And eventually, **funding** and **sponsorship** were allowed to help in the achievement of excellence.
*   The owners and managers of the embrionic factories of the early 1900s were the new middle classes who spread their knowledge of sports to their workforce, hence the formation of factory teams like Arsenal, the members of which were paid as part of the workforce.

Professional football in England was largely a working class northern game before 1914, but all the current London clubs had been established by then.

Amateurism and professionalism, class, law and order

Meanwhile, **professional** performers were getting higher wages and prize money. The idea of professionals being lower class all but disappeared as middle class competitors were also attracted by the rewards and kudos.

The social setting

The social setting within which cultural and sporting developments occurred in the first half of the century are summarised in figure 15.1 (page 178).

- **Professional soccer players** playing in the then English first division in 1948 were restricted to £8.00 per week as a cap on wages (figure 15.2).
- In 1957, John Charles (figure 15.3) became the first British soccer player to transfer into the Italian Football League for a transfer fee of £65,000. By the end of the 20th century, player wages reached £50,000 per week, with transfer fees in excess of £25 million.
- The expansion of professional sports was financed by the **spectators** who paid to watch games.
- This was possible because the **working conditions** of working men began to include Saturday afternoons off.
- Most **spectators** at professional soccer games were **men** who were able to spend some money at the turnstiles to support their local team.

The **Hillsborough disaster** of 1989 was a human crush at Hillsborough football stadium in Sheffield resulting in 68 deaths among spectators. The resulting **Taylor Report** recommended that all top division stadia in England and Scotland phase out the usual terraces. In order to stage events carrying more than 5,000 spectators, stadia must be all-seater, which therefore included all football league soccer clubs, most of the professional rugby league grounds, and other sporting venues.

Law and order in the 21st century

NGBs **rules and regulations** have changed considerably as technology, the impact of social media and global media evolve.

One worrying result of fiercer professional competition in the 21st century, particularly in rugby union and football,
is an increase in on-field violence, the growth of which can be explained by:
- Pressures exerted by **media scrutiny**.
- Obsession with **winning** brought about by the greater availability of large prizes.
- **Failure** of governing bodies to develop an adequate framework of regulation and control.

This increase in violence and tendency for people to break the rules of competition has initiated the following facts:
- Many **schools fear litigation** as do clubs where spectator and player injuries occur.
- The Crown Prosecution Service (CPS) and policing are committed to taking a robust stance towards dealing with **football related disorder** and **hooliganism** as witnessed during the European Football Championships held in France in 2016.
- The CAS (**Court of Arbitration for Sport**) is an independent institution, based in Lausanne, involved in resolving legal disputes in the field of sport. For example, CAS dismissed the appeal filed by the Russian Paralympic Committee, see below.

Leading up to the 2016 Olympic Games, the organising committee (the IOC) of the Olympic Games decided not to issue a total ban on Russian athletes after doping regulations supervised by RUSADA (the **Russian Anti Doping Agency**) were found not being implemented at the instigation of Russian State authorities. However, the organising committee of the Paralympic Games decided on a **blanket ban** for all Russian Paralympic Athletes. The Russian Paralympic Committee filed an appeal against this decision, which was later turned down.

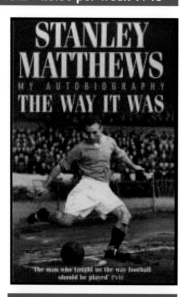

figure 15.2 – £8.00 per week 1948

figure 15.3 – John Charles, £65,000 in 1957

EMERGENCE AND EVOLUTION OF MODERN SPORT BETWEEN 1900 AND THE PRESENT

Social class in the 21st century

The concept of the social class system still affects British society in the early-21st century as it is still influenced by factors of **wealth, occupation** and **education**. However, increased opportunities for the working classes to enter a university education has created a more fluid society.

Social mobility can also be achieved through sports. For example, Denise Lewis OBE (figure 15.4) was brought up by her mother in a terraced house in Wolverhampton. She joined Birchfield Harriers at age 13 and went on to win a gold medal in the heptathlon in the Sydney 2000 Olympics. After retiring she has featured on 'Strictly Come Dancing' and currently works as a sports commentator for the BBC.

figure 15.4 – Denise Lewis

Today, elite sport operates on global professional circuits, such as the IAAF athletics Diamond League, and therefore elite sportspersons can benefit from prize money. **Tennis** has maintained its **middle class** roots, because costs such as coaching fees and court hire are out of the range of most working class parents. This has a direct impact at elite level since the placing of potentially gifted athletic people from lower socio-economic backgrounds does not happen, and therefore denies them access to the sport..

Government intervention - Economic depression late 20th century

The 1970s saw a decline in heavy industry such as coal mining and the resulting economic depression characterised by the **3 day working week** (implemented by the Conservative Government) which limited commercial consumption of electricity to three consecutive days each week. The resulting inflation and unemployment created major social problems and imposed financial constraints that may have impacted on live spectator audiences.

Government intervention – a negative impact on playing facilities

10,000 **playing fields were sold off** under the 1979-1997 Conservative governments thereby reducing opportunities for school children to participate in sports. In 1999, the UK Government financed a £125 million scheme to **'bring back our playing fields'** aimed at addressing the shortfall in playing fields and the need to increase sports participation. Despite this investment in 2010 school playing fields continued to be sold off at a rate of one every three weeks under the Coalition government. Today this is perceived by sceptics as squandering our Olympic legacy of 2012.

Funding for Sport

The **National Lottery** was introduced in 1994 and today the **World Class Performance Plan** with means-tested grants of up to £30,000 a year on a rolling four-year basis has had a huge economic impact for elite GB sportspeople and young talented performers to train and compete within their chosen disciplines. **Lottery and exchequer funding** finance the infrastructure of organisations such as Sport England, the British Olympic Association (BOA) and Paralympic Association, so that they can prepare well in advance of major global games. The impact of Lottery funding for GB sport has reaped its rewards as shown by Great Britain medal tallies of 47, 65, 67, at the Beijing, London and Rio Olympic Games respectively and at other major global championships. Mo Farah is an example of home grown identified talent having recently achieved the double/double in winning the 5,000 and 10,000 metres at the London and Rio Olympic Games.

Commercial activity in professional sport continued to grow inexorably during the post war period, so that by the 1980s it had attained the status of big business within the UK and global markets.

Transport

In 1900, almost every vehicle on the streets of Britain was **horse-drawn**. For longer distances, there were **steam trains** which transported sports fans to away fixtures.

By 1914 **buses and electric trams** had become popular ways to travel. There were **few motor cars** as only wealthy people could afford them. Trains, buses and trams transported the predominantly working class male fans to away fixtures.

From the mid 20th century to present day, the development of **road links,** motorways, a **car ownership** society and **cheap air fares** (as the wealth of the nation has increased) have provided competitors and fans easier and cheaper travel to sporting competitions. For example, in the 2016 Virgin Money London marathon 39,000 runners (many of whom had travelled great distances) were at the start line, many raising money for charities.

Education in the 20th century and its effect on sport

Starting with the **Education Act of 1902** - establishing Local Education Authorities - **the 1918 Act - raising the school leaving age** to 14, and the intervening First World War, many Government activities progressed the education of young people.

Over the previous century, many schools had been built (for the common people) - Board Schools, Grammar Schools and other secondary schools all of which had sport facilities of one sort or another - in the interests of the health and strength of the population. This was the notion of 'ready for war' following the drastic losses of the Boer War in the late 19th Century, and the major losses of men in the First World War.

Education in the 20th century

Grammar Schools in the 1920s and 1930s were fee paying - apart from those few local children who 'passed the scholarship' to gain entry. The **1944 Education Act** established the tripartite system of Grammar Schools, Secondary Technical Schools, and Secondary Modern Schools, with a strict 'intelligence test' to gain entry to the grammar schools which would no longer be fee paying. About 1200 such schools were converted from the old system, with 179 becoming a new form of secondary school, the **Grant Maintained School** maintained by the Ministry of Education rather than the Local Authorities, with free access to some able local students who were admitted by entrance exam or interview. Comprehensive schools were also allowed by this Act, although very few such schools were either newly created, or transferred from the old Grammar Schools.

By 1960, the Grammar Schools had extensive playing field provision but not so extensive indoor provision of for example sports halls or swimming pools. The per capita financial provision for the Grammar Schools was roughly double that for the Secondary Modern Schools in the context of provision for the most able students. Approximately 25% of the school population went to Grammar Schools and between one quarter and one third of these Grammar School pupils went on to higher education, with approximately 6% of the total 18 year old population going on to university or other forms of higher education. Thus the elite nature of this educational system was established. **Apprenticeships** (consisting of up to 5 years working at a low level in industry 'learning the trade') catered for the large number of able school leavers who did not go to University.

In 1965, Comprehensive Schools were established by the then Government as the main delivery system for secondary education. The point of this was to provide equal funding for all pupils, with funding being withdrawn for schools which continued to insist on selection at 11 plus. Many schools were built at this time containing some excellent sporting facilities and hence greater opportunity for sports development for all secondary age pupils. In 1973, the school leaving age went up to 16, and by 1997 the secondary school provision was extended to include specialist schools, such as **Sport Colleges** (but also Language and other specialist subject Colleges).

Education in the 21st century

The Labour Government under Tony Blair established **academies** through the **Learning and Skills Act 2000**. The main reasons for this policy were to address the needs of state schools most in need of urgent repair, and to drive up educational standards.

Most academies are secondary schools (figure 15.5) along with a few primary schools. Until 2010, many school buildings were funded from the **private finance initiative** (PFI) and boast joint school and community sports facilities.

In the late 20th century, examinations in PE at GCSE, A level and BTEC Sport became popular and the first teaching of the new syllabuses began in September 2016. At university level there are many PE/Sport degrees and allied subjects on offer to undergraduates.

figure 15.5 – academy school 2015

Education in the 21st century

Some academies have retained their Sports College status and many schools have embraced new initiatives: for example, in 2011 the government created **school games organisers** (SGOs) who supported the delivery of the **School Games** and **Change4Life** (eat well, move more, live longer) which focuses on families with children aged 5 to 11 who are at greatest risk of becoming overweight or obese. In 2016 there are roughly 450 SGOs across England, attracting additional government funding which is no longer ring-fenced. The point of this policy is to enable autonomy and diversity in respect of sport provision in school. There are five 'core tasks' designed to provide a focus for an SGO's work programme. The core tasks for 2015-16 include:

- **Participation**: drive school participation in School Games competition and increase the number of young people taking part in competition.
- **Competition for all**: develop competitive opportunities for all, including the least active. This can be measured using the Inclusive Health Check tool, available to complete via a dashboard.
- **Clubs**: increase regular participation in club sport: involve the least active through Change4Life Sports Clubs and increase links to local clubs.
- **Workforce**: broaden participation opportunities through volunteering and workforce roles.
- **Performance**: establish key performance indicators, target delivery and regular progress reviews.

Initiatives within England, such as the School Games (established in 2011 supported by lottery and exchequer funding), have engaged able and disabled youngsters from grass roots level through intra-school competition to the **Sainsbury School Games** national finals. By 2012 there were 8,341 participating schools.

At the **elite level**, more than a third of British medal winners in the 2012 London Olympics were from private schools, which educate 7% of the school population.

There were some 450 sports colleges by 2010, each attracted funding from the government to support sporting activities in the schools and hence improved sports provision in their locality. The aim of developments of Britain's educational system since then has been to expand opportunity for all children regardless of ability or aptitude.

Gender

Traditionally, women have participated in sport less than men. The legacy of the Victorian era (page 173) continued into the early part of 20th century. The position of women improved gradually and grudgingly during the post war period and is only now approaching anything like parity with men.

Most of the older sports, such as rugby and cricket, were considered to be male territory, whereas more recent recreational activities such as swimming, cycling, tennis and archery became equally accessible to both sexes and club membership in these sports often showed a predominance of women. The Rugby Football Union (RFU) and Football Association (FA) finally recognised the growth of female participation in their sports in 1994 by granting associate status to the women's governing bodies.

Combat sports, such as boxing and wrestling, are still generally deemed undesirable for women but are becoming more popular. Womens' rugby is becoming increasingly widespread, even though in many cases women have only associate membership in male clubs.

Equally, removal of discrimination of women in athletics has now led to full participation in triple jump, hammer throwing, steeplechase, and pole vault. These athletic events and womens' boxing, wrestling and rugby are now in the Olympic Games, with Nicola Adams (double Olympic Champion, figure 15.6) as an example of an expanding Boxercise movement.

figure 15.6 - Nicola Adams, double Olympic winner

Gender

Womens' soccer (figure 15.7) is increasing its participation - led by the USA in which soccer is the major female sport.
- Perhaps this is because soccer is not met by the same gender prejudices as female soccer in Europe.
- School, collegiate and national level female soccer teams have all seen a massive increase in number of players in recent years.
- Also, England's women won the bronze medal in the 2015 women's World cup for soccer, hence there has been a big increase in participation and media coverage of women's soccer in the UK.

figure 15.7 - women's soccer is increasing

Participation trends in the UK in the 21st century

Participation trends in the UK have been documented over a period of several years. The most recent trends have been surveyed in the **Active People Survey (APS) 5-7**, carried out for Sport England in conjunction with NGBs, Local Authorities, Higher and Further Education Institutions, Charities, Olympic Organisations and other funded partners, to ensure that sporting opportunities are created in every community in the country. This has the fundamental aim of increasing participation and improving performance at all levels of English sport.

These surveys analyse how **participation** varies from place to place and between a range of different demographic groups in the population such as gender, ethnicity, social class, age and disability.

A number of other important measures are also captured by these surveys, such as the proportion of the adult population (aged 16 and over) who are taking at least 30 minutes of moderate intensity sport three times a week, current levels of club membership, the number of people who are currently in receipt of tuition and coaching, the levels of involvement in organised sport or competition and also overall satisfaction with levels of sporting provision in the country.

figure 15.8 – school children experience a wide range of sports

Participation trends in the 21st century

The data in table 15.1 is from the **Active People Survey** 7 by Sport England showing once a week participation in funded sports.

Table 15.1 – **participation trends from 2006 to 2013 for various sports - numbers playing at least once per week**

Sport	2006	2008	2012	2013
Swimming	3,273,800	3,244,300	2,824,800	2,892,200
Athletics	1,353,800	1,612,100	1,994,200	1,958,000
Football	2,021,700	2,144,700	2,198,300	1,939,700
Cycling	1,634,800	1,767,100	1,934,600	1,866,100
Golf	889,100	948,300	908,000	772,800
Badminton	516,700	535,700	538,800	499,000
Tennis	457,200	487,500	420,300	424,300
Equestrian	314,600	341,700	325,500	300,800
Squash and racketball	299,800	293,900	281,100	257,700
Bowls	251,900	277,800	231,400	223,900
Cricket	195,200	204,800	211,300	189,400
Basketball	158,300	186,000	149,400	172,300
Rugby Union	185,600	230,300	197,500	166,400
Netball	111,700	118,800	148,000	150,900
Boxing	115,500	106,800	139,200	150,100
Angling	*	*	141,000	131,500
Table Tennis	69,400	75,600	107,300	112,200
Weightlifting	107,800	118,400	86,100	106,600
Snowsport	127,400	120,600	80,800	106,400
Hockey	93,900	99,800	106,800	92,100
Mountaineering	67,000	86,100	91,600	87,800
Sailing	64,000	89,900	56,900	61,400
Gymnastics	*	*	51,100	49,100
Rugby League	73,700	82,000	58,100	48,700
Canoeing	36,500	43,500	42,400	38,500
Rowing	39,300	54,900	48,600	35,800
Volleyball	32,700	48,400	27,400	34,900
Taekwondo	19,000	23,500	26,200	23,100
Judo	17,200	18,700	23,600	19,900
Rounders	16,500	25,900	19,200	16,400

The active people survey

Samples from this survey are given in table 15.2. From other aspects of this survey:

* 15.5 million adults in 2015 played sport at least once a week, which is 1.4 million more than in 2005/6.
* Most adults – 58% – still do not play sport.
* **Gender** has a big influence on sports take-up, and currently (2015) 40.6% of men play sport at least once a week, compared to 30.7% of women.
* At a younger age, men are much more likely than women to play sport, but this difference declines sharply with **age**.
* 54.8% of 16-to-25-year-olds take part in at least one sport session a week, compared to 31.9% of older adults (26 plus).
* More **disabled** people are taking part in sport – latest results (2015) show 7.4% are playing sport regularly, up from 6.1% in 2005/6.

Table 15.2 – **participation trends from 2005 to 2015 for various demographic groups - % of total England groups**

3 sessions per week of at least 30 min duration %	2005/06 %	2007/08 %	2008/09 %	2009/10 %	2010/11 %	2011/12 %	2012/13 %	2013/14 %	2014/15 %
male	19.1	20.3	21.0	20.7	20.8	21.3	21.7	21.6	21.1
female	12.4	13.6	13.3	13.4	13.0	14.3	14.3	14.1	14.3
age 16 - 25	29.6	31.3	31.9	30.9	30.6	30.2	31.4	32.4	31.1
age 26 - 34	21.6	22.7	22.9	22.3	22.4	24.4	23.3	23.2	23.0
disabled	6.1	6.9	6.4	6.9	7.3	8.1	8.2	7.4	7.4
people in education	*	*	*	27.9	27.3	28.5	28.3	29.3	29.3
white British	15.4	16.8	16.8	16.8	16.6	17.5	17.6	17.6	17.3
black minority	17.4	17.3	18.7	18.2	17.8	19.4	19.6	18.9	19.3

* Data unavailable, question not asked or insufficient sample size.

Implications for the health of the nation from this survey

* Most **preventable diseases** are attributed to modified behaviours that relate directly to physical inactivity, dietary excess and obesity.
* **Life-extending benefits** of physical activity correlate more with preventing early mortality than improving overall life span.
* The greatest **reduction in death rate** from cardiovascular disease occurs when going from sedentary to a moderate fitness level.
* Hence **mass participation programmes/initiatives** encourage members of the public to participate actively in sports with the objectives of promoting good health, self-realisation, community development and social cohesion.

Globalisation of sport

Globalisation of sport refers to the spreading of the knowledge and customs of sport across the world.

This happened by various means depending on the sport, but in the case of sports originating in England or the UK, as mentioned earlier, graduates from the Oxbridge melting pot (page 175) of ex-public school boys (between 1840 and 1900) procured jobs and careers across the World in the former British Empire, and spread their games and pastimes accordingly. Hence cricket and rugby developed in Australia, India, Pakistan, New Zealand and South Africa from this formative history.

These countries (and others) eventually organised competitions between themselves, until such '**test matches**' became regular fixtures. Up until 1950, travel to such events was by boat (taking 4 to 6 weeks to travel to Australia from the UK).

Globalisation

The term **globalisation** therefore describes the growing role of sport in most societies across the World:

- The **infrastructure** (sports stadia, indoor and outdoor facilities).
- The involvement of people in sports activities.
- The **commercialism** and money involved.
- The **media** (print and electronic), and so on.
- **Industry** (clothing, footwear and equipment).

Modern sport is bound up in a global network of interdependent chains that are marked by global flows and uneven power relations. People across the globe regularly view satellite broadcasts of English Premier League and European Champions League matches, where the best players drawn from Europe, South America and Africa perform. Players use **equipment** – boots, balls, uniforms etc - that are designed in the West, are financed by multi-national corporations such as Adidas and Nike, and are hand-stitched, in the case of soccer balls, in Asia using child labour. This equipment is then sold, at significant profit, to a mass market in our towns and cities.

Global media sport complex (figure 15.9)

The global media sport complex has five dimensions:

- The international **movement of people** such as tourists, migrants, guest workers and superstars of the various sports.
- The **technology** dimension is created by the flow between countries of the machinery and equipment produced by corporations.
- The **economic** dimension centres on the rapid flow of money on the international trade in personnel, prize money and endorsements around the world.
- The **media** dimension entails the flow of images and information between countries that is produced by newspapers, magazines, radio, film, TV, video, satellite, cable and the internet (social media).
- The **ideological** dimension is the flow of values centrally associated with state or counter-state ideologies and movements.

figure 15.9 – global media sport complex

The West is dominant in terms of the design, production and marketing of sports equipment, and innovations emerge within the West. Sport federations tend to be controlled by Western officials and global sport tournaments are usually located within the West.

White, male groups control and regulate access to global sport, and the same groups control how indigenous peoples both resist these processes and recycle their own cultural products (if at all). For example, the Haka, or chant performed by the All-Blacks (New Zealand Rugby Team) just before a match is an element of Maori culture in New Zealand, and has been reincorporated globally within Rugby Union.

Migration patterns of performers

Athletes are on the move. In some sports this involves **sport labour movement** from one country to another within or between continents. In other sports athletes assume an almost **nomadic migratory lifestyle**, constantly on the move from one sport festival to another, for example, the tennis and golf international circuits.

Migration patterns of sporting labour have developed globally since the 1990s, particularly since the introduction of the clubs' licences to contract players and with the professionalism and organisation in male professional team sports.

Historical reasons for migration

Up to around the 1960s, migration used to be local within the boundaries of a country (and hence **geographical** in nature - figure 15.10). But with the increased role of the media (such as TV contracts, sponsorship and overseas investors) professional football clubs have increased their wealth and status, resulting in increased labour mobility – for example, within the EU there is greater European integration and so easier to move location and work.

Recent indication is that elite female football players are becoming part of the network of global migration.

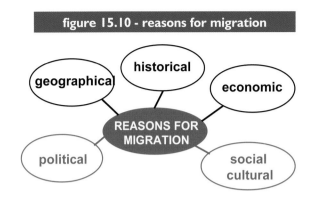

figure 15.10 - reasons for migration

Economic reasons for migration

Huge transfer fees are paid for elite global male football players to the extent that many of the UK's premier league clubs such as Manchester United and Arsenal, are predominantly made up of overseas players. More than half of the English Premier League clubs (the corporations) are owned by foreign businessmen, and are perceived as non-profit making, but highly valued as 'global investors' of multi-national enterprises.

Facility investment is also partly responsible for player and coach migration – for example, NBA has built state-of-the art basketball arenas in China which are attracting global talent.

The entire revenue of the US Big Four sports of football, baseball, basketball and ice hockey represents only a small percentage of the US economy, but is perceived as a very important part of **cultural** lifestyle.

Global sport stars, such as Usain Bolt and Andy Murray, obtain sponsorship, advertise products, and are exposed to extensive media hype, which enhances their financial worth to a sponsor.

Geographical reasons for migration

Many of the transfers within the football, rugby and other sports are close to home and so the cultural and social transitions for both players and family are not too difficult.

During the 2014-15 season Canada attracted 31 international players to its NBA league - Canada is perceived as a great place to live.

Political reasons for migration

World leaders are also passionate about sport, for example Barack Obama's love for basketball adds further global appeal and attractiveness, national identity and acceptance of African Americans within global markets. Changing political systems and the associated redrawing of political boundaries has also contributed to an increase in sport labour migration, the exodus of Russian hockey players to the NHL was a prime example of this movement.

Social and cultural reasons for migration

New global migration and mobility patterns have altered **cultural composition** to create cosmopolitan communities and intercultural acceptance within communities, teams and clubs.

Note the 2016 PFA awards for the player of the year (premiership) was Riyad Mahrez of Leicester City Football Club, who is a Frenchman of Algerian background. The significance of this is that the vote was made by all the professional footballers in the Premiership, hence showing his acceptance into the community of players.

Other facts about sporting migration

Elite performers are supported by elite coaches, agents and national governing bodies (NGBs) across the globe. **Global coaches** attract elite sports stars with the athlete travelling to the coach for training blocks. For example, Rana Reider (US track and field coach – currently based in Holland) oversees a diverse group of sprinters, jumpers and hurdlers including Shara Proctor, Martyn Rooney, Christian Taylor (2012 and 2016 Gold medallist triple jumper), and Dafne Schippers (2015 World championship gold medallist 200m, figure 15.11).

figure 15.11 - Dafne Schippers

Media involvement

Sports events have become global spectacles and are far and away the most watched television programmes in the world. For example, 30 billion viewers watched the 2006 Soccer World Cup and 4.7 billion viewers watched the 2008 Beijing Olympics. Superbowl reaches around 160 million viewers across the globe every year.

This global following attracts publicity and sponsorship and networks that encourage global migration.

Sporting greats such as David Beckham, Ronaldino, and Michael Jordan are now recognised and admired the world over as icons, with their skilful performances and ability to enhance the reputation (shop window effect) and desirability for other sports performers to migrate to their sporting locations and clubs.

Commercial pressure impact

- Over the years governing bodies have had to adapt to commercial pressures in order to maintain their status.
- Governing bodies have changed **rules** as a result of commercial pressures. Innovations such as the golden goal in football and the use of Hawkeye in tennis and cricket create more excitement for spectators, which increases the sport's popularity and hence the commercial revenue for both sponsors and the governing bodies.
- With the increased reward/prize for winning, it has become essential that the correct calls are made by umpires/referees.
- **TV commercial breaks** in play enable sponsors to advertise their products and so interruption of play is often controlled by such commercial breaks.
- **Deals** made between governing bodies and the media can favour certain sports such as the alliance between Adidas and FIFA Initiatives.

Practice questions

1) Creating new sport programmes for girls and women is one of the recommended strategies for changing the way we do sports. The advantage to this strategy is that new programmes:
   a. provide new settings for women to learn to be tough competitors.
   b. can be organised to challenge traditional gender ideology.
   c. effectively exclude men from all positions of responsibility.
   d. give women opportunities to dominate other women on and off the field.

2) We often talk about sports performers playing fairly. Which of the following options best describes gamesmanship?
   a. playing within the written rules.
   b. it's not whether you won or lost that matters, it's how you played the game.
   c. the intention to compete to the limit of the rules and beyond if you can get away with it.
   d. fair, generous and polite behaviour, especially when playing a sport or game.

3) The story of 20th century English sport has been the widespread erosion of amateurism. Which of the following is not responsible for this change?
   a. television broadcasting.
   b. influence of internationalism which offers the governing bodies the prospect of enhanced prestige for their sports.
   c. opportunity to become a salaried professional.
   d. sheer joy of winning.

Practice questions

4) Which one of the following is mainly responsible for globalisation in sport?
   a. increased participation.
   b. the sporting media.
   c. cheap air fares.
   d. gender equality.

5) Identify a key factor that has enhanced participation patterns among girls and women in team sports.
   a. increased health and fitness.
   b. positive use of free time.
   c. improvement in social skills.
   d. equal opportunity.

6) Identify a key factor which may negatively disadvantage working class sporting opportunities for young children.
   a. sports facilities.
   b. coaching.
   c. sports clubs.
   d. poorer health.

7) Explain three social or cultural factors that inhibit an athlete's progression to elite level.　　　　3 marks

8) What social and economic barriers to sport and leisure do women face in the 21st century?　　　　4 marks

9) UK educational opportunities have improved during the 21st century. Discuss the impact on sports participation.　6 marks

10) There are many reasons for the growth and change in leisure time and recreational activities during the 20th and 21st century in the UK. Discuss.　　　　6 marks

11) a)　Discuss the development of Saturday Half-Day and the emergence of working class sport.　　　　4 marks

    b)　Account for the delay in the opportunities for the working class to be able to play games such as lawn tennis　4 marks

12) Identify and explain the factors that can influence an individual's participation in sporting and recreational activities
　　　　4 marks

13) From table 15.2 on page 185, compute the difference for 3 sessions per week of at least 30min duration between the improvement in males and females between 2005 and 2015. Are the policies for gender equality in the UK working?
　　　　4 marks

14) From table 15.2 on page 185, compute the percentage trend for participation at 3 sessions per week as between black minority and white groups in the UK. How would you amend public policy to improve participation of both groups?
　　　　6 marks

15) The opportunity for sporting and recreational activities has varied since the 19th Century. Why were many National Governing Bodies, such as the Football Association, established in the 19th century?　　　　3 marks

16) Over the years sports governing bodies have had to adapt too many external pressures in order to maintain their status with the sporting arena. How and why has this happened?　　　　6 marks

17) a)　What is meant by the term globalisation in the context of sport?　　　　2 marks

    b)　How are national cultures and cultural identities being affected by processes of globalisation of sport?　6 marks

18) Over the years the global sports sector and global media sector have developed a self-interest relationship. Discuss.
　　　　10 marks

Answers link: http://www.jroscoe.co.uk/downloads/as_a1_revise_pe_ocr/OCRAS_A1_ch15_answers.pdf

CHAPTER 16: *Global sporting events*

The modern Olympic Games

STUDENT NOTE

The Olympic Games is the most significant attempt to establish globalisation within sport. Therefore you will need to be able to structure an analysis of the Olympic Games, giving points for and against the possibility of successfully achieving sports organisation at world level. This should use examples from various Olympic Games. In this way you can present a feasibility study.

figure 16.1 – Athens 1896

Baron **De Coubertin**, founder of the Modern Olympic Games, visited English public schools including Rugby during the 1870s. He was impressed with athleticism in these schools and the linking of physical endeavour with moral integrity. He also visited the Olympian Games held at **Much Wenlock**, inspired by Dr Penny Brookes. De Coubertin believed that it was the character developed by exercise and games that would be the key to the re-building of France after the Franco-Prussian War. De Coubertin's Olympic dream was achieved in 1896 in Athens, when 311 athletes from 13 countries contested nine sports (figure 16.1).

The issue of **professionalism** has always been contentious in Olympic sport. It revolved not just around whether sportsmen were paid, but whether they were gentlemen. Early Olympians would have been white, middle or upper class and wealthy. Hence money was not an issue - they could afford to do it!

The Olympic motto

The Olympic motto is 'Citius, Altius, Fortius' which means swifter, higher, stronger.

The Olympic creed and charter

The **Olympic Creed** was put forward in 1908: **'The most important thing in the Olympic Games is not to win but to take part, just as the most important thing in life is not the triumph but the struggle. The essential thing is not to have conquered but to have fought well'**.

The **Olympic Charter** contains the principles, rules and byelaws adopted by the IOC (the International Olympic Committee) and states '**Olympism** is a philosophy of life, exalting and combining in a balanced whole the qualities of body, will and mind. Blending sport with culture and education, Olympism seeks to create a way of life based on the joy found in effort, the educational value of good example and respect for universal fundamental ethical principles'.

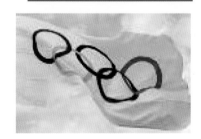

figure 16.2 – Olympic flag

Olympism consists of 6 fundamental principles that are based on Coubertin's original beliefs that the Olympic movement could enhance human development and are as follows:
- Personal excellence.
- Sport as education.
- Cultural exchange.
- Mass participation.
- Fair play.
- International understanding.

Olympism abides by three essential values:

Excellence - this value means '**do your best**' in sport and life. This means to chase your own personal goals with determination and effort. The Olympic creed makes the point that the most important thing is not winning, but taking part, to do your best in everyday life and benefitting from a healthy body, mind and strong will.

Friendship - this value refers to the construction of a better and more peaceful world through **solidarity**, **team spirit**, **joy** and **optimism**. The athletes express this value when they hold strong ties with team members and opponents.

The Olympic creed and charter

Respect - this value represents the ethical principle that should **inspire** all those who participate in the Olympic Games. It includes respect for oneself and one's body, respect for others, for the rules and for the environment. The respect value also refers to **fair play** that every athlete should practice, as well as the obligation to **avoid doping**. It is an essential value to apply not only at the Games, but in day-to-day life.

These statements revolve around an **ideal** notion of human behaviour including the fact that athletes should be free to participate irrespective of race, colour or creed. Mass access to sport requires that **constraints** upon cultural and sub cultural groups should be removed. But in order for minority groups to have equality they must also have **access** and **provision**. **Access** can be denied by a numerically superior culture, self-imposed cultural constraint, and economic and topographical limitations.

The major issue, therefore, is the **exclusion** of racial minorities from existing opportunity, or the failure to **extend provision** to all **Olympic Solidarity** Programmes. The various IOC commissions are responsible for education and provision in areas of need, which are funded these days by income from television rights. The **IOC** is the organising group for the Olympic Games, and decides policy and placement of Games.

The Summer Games are every fourth year, multiples of four: 1992, 1996, 2000, 2004, 2008 Beijing, 2012 London, 2016 Rio de Janeiro, and 2020 Tokyo. The Winter Games are also every fourth year offset by two years from the Summer Games 1994, 1998, 2002, 2006, 2010 Vancouver, 2014 Sochi, Russia, and 2018 Pyeongchang, South Korea.

The Olympic family

All members of the Olympic Movement share the Olympism philosophy. The IOC was created in 1894 in Paris and is the supreme authority that governs the Olympic Movement. It owns all rights to the Olympic symbols such as the five interlocking rings, coloured blue, yellow, black, green, and red on a white field, known as the 'Olympic rings' that represent 5 World continents, Africa, Asia, America, Europe and Australia as depicted in figure 16.2 (page 190).

The **IOC** is the **decision maker** (table 16.1), the supreme authority that governs the Olympic Movement. It is a non-profit organisation that receives no public funds. Next are the organisations recognised by the IOC, which comply with the Olympism principles and abide by the rules established by the Olympic Charter.

Table 16.1 – **the constituent parts of the IOC**

IOC		
International Federations (IFs)	National Olympic Committees (NOCs)	Organising Committees of the Olympic Games (OCOGs)
National sporting associations and clubs.	Sporting officials, coaches and managers.	Athletes.

The **International Federations**, such as the IAAF (the International Association of Athletics Federations), govern their own sports and ensure the promotion and development of that sport.

National Olympic Committees, such as the BOA (British Olympic Association - figure 16.3), have two principal roles:
* To **prepare** and **lead** our nation's finest competitors at the summer, winter and youth Olympic Games. Working with the NGBs, the BOA **selects** Team GB from the best sportsmen and women who will go on to compete in the summer, winter and youth Olympic sports.
* To **develop**, **promote** and **protect** the Olympic Movement within the UK in accordance with the Olympic Charter and the Olympic values.

The BOA is **independent**, privately funded and receives no annual funding from the lottery or government and has no political interests. Much of the Rio 2016 money went on the GB holding camp in Belo Horizonte - widely regarded to have been the best any team here enjoyed.

Organising Committees of the Olympic Games manage all practical aspects of the preparation of, the event, including local public impact and questions from the media.

The Paralympics

The **Paralympic Games** evolved from the efforts to rehabilitate soldiers wounded with serious back injuries during World War II. These Games took place at Stoke Mandeville Hospital, England. Games were developed for wheelchair users, leading to the 1948 International Wheelchair Games. Following this initial competition, overseas competitors, beginning with the Netherlands, added strength to the idea until the first official Olympic style games for athletes with a disability were organised in Rome in 1960.

In Toronto, 1976, as other disability groups were added to the programme, the modern Paralympic Games began to emerge. The first Paralympic Winter Games took place in Sweden in the same year. **Paralympic values** evolved in Toronto and were based on the tradition of fair play and honourable sports competition:

- **Determination** – the drive and motivation to overcome both physical and mental barriers in order to achieve your goals.
- **Courage** – having the self-belief and confidence to overcome adversity and face difficulty.
- **Equality** – showing respect and humility towards all those around you in the spirit of fair play.
- **Inspiration** – to be motivated by the achievements and actions of others and to be a positive example to others.

Political exploitation of the Olympic Games

The Olympics provide examples of the use made of sport by politicians who appreciate that sport has a **political** dimension to be **exploited** when they can. This topic is discussed further on page 202.

The '**shop window**' effect is the notion that the display of talent and excellence in both athletic **endeavour** and **organisation** of an event such as an Olympic Games, should be held up to demonstrate the high quality of **worthiness** of the national and political systems in which the games is held. This process was first promoted by Hitler for the 1936 Games in Berlin figure 16.4.

Berlin 1936, Third Reich ideology

In **1936**, Hitler decided to use the **Olympic Games in Berlin** (figure 16.4) of that year to highlight the excellence of the German state. The Olympic torch was a new feature, the opening ceremony was a display of military might, and the athletes had been coached to be the best display of Aryan superiority available. This display was somewhat downgraded by the supremacy of Jesse Owens (figure 16.5) in the 100 metres, 200 metres and long jump. Jesse Owens was competing in a country where the political beliefs of Hitler's party saw him as inferior because of his colour. Hitler refused to shake his hand during the award ceremony, but the rest of the games continued as a testament to the organisation of the German people.

Hitler was not part of the official awards ceremony and one view is that Hitler was trying to upstage the official IOC medal ceremony for his own propaganda purposes by linking himself with champion athletes. Jesse Owens and other black athletes had succeeded in discrediting Nazi ideology simply by what they did.

figure 16.4 – Berlin 1936

figure 16.5 – Jesse Owens

figure 16.6 – black power in Mexico 1968

Mexico City 1968 'Black Power' demonstration

On 16th October 1968, US athlete Tommie Smith won the 200 meter race with a World record time of 19.83 seconds. Australia's Peter Norman finished second with a time of 20.06 seconds, and the US John Carlos won third place with a time of 20.10 seconds.

After the race was completed, the three athletes went to the podium for their medals. The two US athletes received their medals shoeless, but wearing black socks, to represent **black poverty**. Smith wore a black scarf around his neck to represent **black pride**. Both US athletes intended to bring black gloves to the event, but Carlos forgot his, leaving them in the Olympic Village. It was Peter Norman who suggested Carlos wear Smith's left-handed glove. For this reason, Carlos raised his left hand as opposed to his right, differing from the traditional Black Power salute when the Star-Spangled Banner played (figure 16.6).

Smith and Carlos delivered the salute with heads bowed, a gesture which became front page news around the World. As they left the podium they were booed by the crowd. Smith later said, 'If I win, I am American, not a black American. But if I did something bad, then they would say I am a Negro. We are black and we are proud of being black. Black America will understand what we did tonight'.

In 2005, San Jose State University honoured former students Smith and Carlos with a 22-foot high statue of their protest which has become a globally recognised symbol of the Black Power movement that has helped to reshaped American culture.

The event is regarded as one of the most overtly political statements in the history of the modern Olympic Games.

figure 16.7 – terrorists in the Olympic Village

Munich 1972 Palestinian terrorism

In **Munich 1972**, The Black September Palestinian terrorist organisation (figure 16.7) organised and carried out the kidnap and then murder of 11 israeli athletes and coaches from the athlete village in Munich. One policeman was also killed. The German antiterrorist police attempted to release the hostages but failed at the airport as the group prepared to fly out.

The hostage-takers had demanded the release of 234 Palestinians and non-Arabs jailed in Israel, along with two German insurgents held by the German penitentiary system. Israel's official policy at the time was to **refuse to negotiate** with terrorists under any circumstances. In the wake of the hostage-taking, competition was eventually suspended for the first time in modern Olympic history, after public criticism of the Olympic Committee's decision to continue the games. On September 6th a memorial service attended by 80,000 spectators and 3,000 athletes was held in the Olympic Stadium.

The following day the Olympic programme resumed.

Montreal's Summer Olympics in 1976 was a turning point in Olympic history. It was the Games' first highly visible security operation in view of the terrorism act in 1972.

Moscow 1980 boycott led by US

The **Moscow Olympic Games in 1980** were reduced in significance by the USA and other countries' boycott of the games, organised by the then President of the USA, Jimmy Carter in reaction to the Soviet invasion of Afghanistan in December 1979. This was intended to reduce the shop-window effect sought by the Soviet Government for the Games. The Games went ahead without the USA, Japan, West Germany, China, the Philippines, Argentina and Canada. The governments of the United Kingdom, France and Australia supported the boycott, but left any final decision over the participation of their country's athletes to their respective NOCs and the decision of their individual athletes. The British associations that governed equestrian sports, hockey, and yachting completely boycotted the 1980 summer Olympics. But the United Kingdom sent 170 sportsmen and women to compete in all the other sports.

Los Angeles 1984 boycott by the Soviet Union

The boycott of the 1984 Summer Olympics in Los Angeles was after the US-led boycott of the 1980 Summer Olympics in Moscow. The Soviet Union declared it would not participate in the 1984 games, due to the commercialization of the games and lack of security for the athletes.

Deep down, it was undoubtedly the hurt and embarrassment of 1980 that lay behind the stunning Soviet decision. The boycott involved 14 Eastern Bloc countries and allies, led by the Soviet Union, which initiated the boycott on May 8, 1984. Nations not going included the Soviet Union, East Germany, Poland, Bulgaria, Mongolia, Vietnam, Laos, Czechoslovakia, Ethiopia, North Korea, Angola, Cuba and Iran.

The reasons given for the boycott were not just support of Soviet Russia, but issues in connection with Israel and 'US interference in middle east affairs'. China attended these games. The boycott affected a large number of Olympic events that were normally dominated by the absent countries. Boycotting countries organized another major event, called the Friendship Games, in July and August 1984.

Hosting global sporting events

Global events

The notion of International Competitions (or World Games) is broad and can be **multi-sport** or **single sport** and usually involves the **best competitors**, the **elite**, from around the **world**. Such games may be:

figure 16.8 – global games

* Multi-sport potentially involving all countries, for example, the Summer and Winter Olympic Games, and the Paralympic Games.
* Multi-sport involving several countries, for example, the Commonwealth Games, the African Games, and the Pan-American Games.
* Single-sport potentially involving all countries, for example, the Football FIFA World Cup, the World Athletics Championships, the World Hockey Championships, and the World Badminton Championships.

The characteristics of such global games are:
* They involve **elite performers**.
* Usually from the **whole world**, but can be regional.
* Usually require **qualification** from regional groupings or by standard.
* Most countries staging them will use them as a **shop window**.
* Often highly commercialised with **sponsorship**.
* Often with high **media** coverage (TV rights paid for as part of the finance for the event).
* Development of elite **facilities**, some or all of which will be a heritage for the future.
* Possibly involving large **spectatorship**.

Figure 16.8 outlines the factors involved in staging a global games.
* **Organisers**, the efficient handling of activities.
* **Participants**, the suitability, opportunity, comfort.
* **Spectators**, attendance provision, media provision.
* **Activities**, specified and provided.
* **Facilities**, highest standard with future potential.
* **Preparations**, ready on time.
* **Future use**, forward planning and extended value.
* **Media**, communication and commercial.
* **Travel**, convenient for training and competition.

There is frequently great competition to host international sporting events. Not everyone, however, believes that the price involved in hosting such events is worthwhile.

Government issues

Holding the 2012 Olympic Games was an obvious reason for Britain to join the USA, Australia and China in a drive to achieve sporting excellence. Issues connected with this could be:

- **National pride**, highlight political superiority, prestige and advertising for the host country (shop window effect).
- The British Government has a **political motive** for pouring money into sport in the UK.
- Improvement in sporting **facilities**, meeting society's demands for national sporting success.
- The **re-generation** of a whole London district.
- Improvements to trade, economy, tourism, **infrastructure** - transport, housing, hotels.
- A stimulus to a nation faced with excessive obesity.
- Encourages **mass participation** in sport.
- Enables individuals to **succeed** (due to increased provision).

Sporting impacts affecting hosting of global games

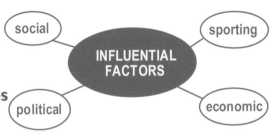

figure 16.9 – factors affecting hosting

social — INFLUENTIAL FACTORS — sporting — political — economic

Mass participation

Positive impacts

In Great Britain there was a sense of civic pride and national identity when GB athletes performed so well at the 2016 Rio games. These **outstanding results** (figure 16.10 - Laura Trott, Max Whitlock, Jack Laugher), 27 gold (in 16 different sports), 23 silver and 17 bronze medals, have raised the profile of many sports such as gymnastics, canoeing, diving, taekwondo, field hockey, alongside more established sports such as track cycling, rowing and track and field athletics.

figure 16.10 – team GB, Rio

After the success of GB's team in London 2012 and the 2016 Rio games, many sports have experienced an increase in participation rates, commonly known as the '**trickle-down effect**'. Having watched medal-winning performances by GBs athletes, young people have been inspired to be active and pursue sport. The UK marketing message in Rio was '**inspire a generation**' and it delivered.

Negative impacts

On the negative side studies have shown conflicting or mixed results that makes it impossible to conclude that mass participation increases as a result of hosting or excelling at major sporting events, since the trickle-down effect does not take into account the complexity of or the barriers to sport participation as illustrated with 'The Active People Survey 7', table 15.1 (page 184), which reveals mass participation trends over the past 10 years.

Volunteering

Positive impacts

70,000 Olympic volunteers ('games makers' - figure 16.11) gave their time and energy contributing towards the success of London 2012. This has provided a big boost to sporting infrastructure as witnessed by the oversubscription of volunteers for the Commonwealth Games in Glasgow 2014.

figure 16.11 - London 2012 Games makers

Elite athletes

Positive impacts

In London 2012 and Rio 2016 all UK elite athletes, not just the socially privileged ones, had the chance to achieve their potential, because of **organisation** and **funding** (provided by National Lottery funding and exchequer funding).
These two factors made possible the astonishing success of Team GB athletes (figure 16.12) who won a total of 65 medals in London and 67 medals in Rio – the greatest performances of GB teams at the Olympics to date.

Success in UK sport is measured by the medals won, the number of medallists developed, and the quality of the systems and processes in place to find and support the nation's most promising future champions. For example, UK rowing and track cycling receive the biggest annual budgets of £32m and £30m respectively, based on past and predicted future medal successes.

figure 16.12 – GB women's hockey, Rio 2016

Negative impacts

On the other hand, UK Sport decided to withdraw basketball's £7m funding package because there was no evidence it could win medals in 2016 or 2020. Withdrawal of funding reduces the sport's profile and may have a negative effect on mass participation rates for that sport.

Impact on the individual

Individuals are:

*   **Motivated** by high competitive drive (i.e. the will to be the best - intrinsic motivation).
*   Able to meet **personal goals** - to be number one in the World!
*   Able to develop a **career** and to gain recognition or sponsors - extrinsic motivation (rewards).
*   Inspired by **role models**.
*   **Encouraged** by peers or family.
*   Given the **opportunity**, **pride** or **satisfaction** to represent his or her own country.
*   Given the opportunity to **perform** at the **highest** level.

The disadvantages to the individual of this process are:

*   **High expectation** for individual to do well in future events.
*   **Increased pressure** on the individual to over-train and perform even whilst injured.
*   An individual may become **over-confident** or complacent with success.
*   There will be increased media attention and **intrusion** into individual's private life.

Table 16.2 – **summary of issues affecting global games**

the performer can obtain:	the spectator receives or develops:	commercial interests obtain:
celebrity status.	excitement.	money or revenue.
sponsorship deals.	entertainment.	advertising.
advertising deals.	escapism.	raised profile.
personal satisfaction.	fan base.	boosts to business.
high earning potential.	encouragement into sport.	association with elite performers.
recognition.		
respect.		

Facilities - a case study London 2012

Positive impacts

Construction for a major Games venue often involves considerable redevelopment. For example, the 200-hectare (490-acre) Queen Elizabeth Olympic Park (figure 16.13) was constructed on a former industrial site at Stratford, East London, and offered first class facilities for many of the Olympic events in London 2012. The athletes' village, a vast shopping mall and new transport links completed the picture.

Today the Queen Elizabeth Olympic Park is becoming a world class destination for people to live, work, play and visit (figure 16.14), hosting concerts, festivals, art installations and national and international sporting competitions.

West Ham United and UK Athletics are the primary tenants of the Olympic Stadium and the stadium will be used again for the 2017 World Athletics Championships, as well as the home ground for West Ham football fixtures.

The Olympic village has provided housing for over 8000 residents and the easy access to a shopping mall and public transport links – all positive legacies.

Negative impacts

Olympic facilities are often downsized, for example the colossal wings of the London Aquatic Centre and top tier seating in the Olympic Stadium have been removed.

Some sporting facilities are rarely used or are even closed down. For example, the 1991 Summer Universiade (also known as the World Student Games) took place in Sheffield. The athletics action was in Don Valley Stadium newly opened 1990. Unfortunately, due to austerity measures, this facility was demolished in 2013, despite protests from Jessica Ennis (Olympic heptathlon 2012) who trained there.

Sporting deviance and its negative impact

Sporting deviance covers a wide ranging list from:
Hooliganism which is characterised by unruly, violent, and destructive behaviour by overzealous supporters. Acts of hooliganism (figure 16.15) often overspill and impact local surroundings such as shops and bars, as witnessed between Russian and English football supporters in the 2016 European Championships in France.

Cheating which is manifested in drug taking. High profile cases include Ben Johnson, Marion Jones, Justin Gatlin and the Russian state doping scandal in 2016. Other forms of cheating include dirty play on the pitch, such as punching, biting and head butting in rugby, as exposed by the media.

figure 16.13 – facilities as a heritage

figure 16.14 – the Olympic Park

STUDENT NOTE

Some of the points below have already been discussed under sporting impacts.

figure 16.15 – Russian and England supporters brawling during Soccer Euro16

Sporting deviance and its negative impact

Corruption is evident at the very top of some games. It is notable in football, with bribery, and vote-rigging relevant to the election of FIFA ex-president Sepp Blatter and the organization's decision to award the 2018 and 2022 World Cups to Russia and Qatar. These allegations have led to legal prosecution in the USA and the increase in popular cynicism about the fairness and honesty of the whole international sport process.

Social impacts affecting hosting of global games

Positive impacts

Hosting Olympics boosts the **prestige** of a country. It is a '**once in a lifetime**' opportunity to provide a showcase to the world. Beijing 2008 provided us with the Bird's Nest (figure 16.16), and Tokyo's successful 2020 Olympic bid promises to be the most **compact** and **efficient** Olympic Games ever staged. Marketed as the 'green games' it aims to coexist in harmony with the natural environment, feature an array of eco-friendly systems such as solar and renewable energy, and aim for total waste recycling and reduced CO_2 emissions.

The London Olympic Parkland (see figure 16.14 page 197) has been created to leave a **legacy** for wildlife and the environment in the surrounding area that locals can enjoy, increasing civic pride and a nation-building identity.

Sport has the ability to inspire individuals to great things and change people's lives. A global event, such as the Olympic Games or **FIFA World Cup**, could have a positive impact by improving fitness standards and **reducing obesity** and the demand on health care services.

The **facility legacy** could encourage the local population to engage in sport.

Hosting a global games often involves the development of **new transport links**. For example, the Dockland light railway extension to the Queen Elizabeth Park in London, has helped to reduce congestion and increase productivity.

Impact on **local infrastructure** – for example, the London 2012 Olympic athletes' village has provided housing for over 8000 residents and other social facilities such as bars, restaurants, shops and schools.

A FIFA World Cup event is staged throughout the host country, using existing stadia and so most parts of the host country benefit from improvements in facility upgrades and tourism.

Negative impacts

Building an Olympic Park does have its drawbacks, since regeneration plans may adversely affect housing and local facilities. For example, in Beijing two million people were **evicted** or displaced as a result of houses being demolished to make way for transport infrastructure and facilities for the 2008 Olympic Games (see the Bird's Nest in Beijing, figure 16.16).

While sports' tourism can bring money into an area, it can also bring **overcrowding**, **social deviance** in the form of **criminal activity,** excess **alcohol** consumption, and limited community support for residential rights.

Local residents have to cope with **congested roads and railways**, **noise** disturbance and their impact on local businesses.

During the Rio Olympic Games pickpockets did well from unsuspecting tourists.

figure 16.16 – the Bird's Nest - courtesy of Anwar El Bizanti

Economic impacts affecting hosting of global games

figure 16.17 – Montreal

Negative impacts – national debt

The **commercialisation** of a major sporting event, such as the Olympic Games, can be explained in terms of funding and sponsorship. The funding of the Olympic Games up to 1980 was largely the responsibility of the host state or city, which raised money out of local taxation. This nearly caused the bankruptcy of the City of Montreal following the 1976 Games. It took 30 years to pay off the debt. This is not quite the same with communist countries, where more general state funding and planning are made available.

The economic investment may be perceived as short term. Many facilities can only be used for the three week duration of the Olympics. After that there is a danger of 'white elephant projects' - facilities that cannot be effectively reused, similar to the Millennium Dome. Many sceptics would rather have the money spent on alternative investment schemes such as health and education.

Bidding for a major global sporting event

There is an increasingly apparent problem of a lack of bid cities for major sporting events, in particular the Olympics, which is seeing more and more cases of potential bidders put off due to political and economical arguments.

For example, there are only 2 realistic bids for the 2024 Olympic Games - Paris and Los Angeles, and the other three contenders Budapest (so far five unsuccessful bids), Rome (austerity measures) and Hamburg (political pressures) had already withdrawn at October 2016. Note that there are no developing countries in this short list.

figure 16.18 – Rio empty seats

The bidding process can be hijacked by private interests, including corruption (refer to page 198), and as the bidding process proceeds, the plans become more and more detailed and expensive. For example, England 2018 was the Football Association's unsuccessful bid for the right to host the 2018 FIFA World Cup. The total expenditure over two years was £21m.

Empty seats were a big problem for most organisers as illustrated during the 2016 Rio Olympic Games figure 16.18, in contrast to the packed crowd who watched the Olympics and Paralympic Games in London 2012, and the Commonwealth Games in Glasgow 2014. Poor ticket sales in Rio, represented lost revenue and frustration to locals who could not afford to buy tickets and to local tourism which was unable to capitalise fully from the expectation of overseas visitors. Increased spectatorship for the Paralympic Games was due to cheaper tickets for the locals.

figure 16.19 – Atlanta 1996

Positive impacts

By 1984 and the Los Angeles Summer Games, the IOC and the organising committee of these Games had realised that sales of anything in connection with the Games could bring in a huge income, and that global commerce would willingly pay large amounts in direct sponsorship of the Games. TV rights, clothing, logos, advertising at the venues and special edition postage stamps were all sold to bring in revenue for the games.

The Atlanta Games 1996 (figure 16.19), generated 34 sponsors and licensed 97 companies to sell products carrying the Olympic 'logo'. **The Olympic Programme** (TOP) was created to ensure that the main TOP sponsors are unchallenged in their category of merchandise. All TOP sponsors are multi-national companies and have the use of all Olympic symbols, exclusive hospitality at the Games and direct access to an advertising and public relations programme. Hence many global companies, Cocoa Cola, Kodak, McDonalds, Xerox, Swatch and Adidas, give money to the Games organisers, so that their names can be displayed prominently at the various venues.

Economic impacts

Positive impacts

A major problem with these arrangements is that commerce and commercials tend to dictate when events are held. Major sponsors, particularly American TV networks, want some say in how things are run in return for their massive investment. In some cases events are held so that TV exposure is maximised rather than the best time of the day for the athletes.

From 1984 up until today, these commercial ventures have created a surplus income which the IOC has used by investing in projects. For example, the 'Sport for Hope Programme' (figure 16.20) targets developing countries and provides young people and local communities with positive sports development opportunities.

figure 16.20 – Sport for Hope

The building of sporting facilities, accommodation and transport infrastructure creates jobs for locals and therefore has a direct impact on the local economy, reducing crime and improving skills. For example, the UK economy saw a £9.9bn boost in trade and investment from hosting the 2012 London Olympic and Paralympic Games, resulting from factors such as improvements to trade, boost to tourism and travel and their impact on economic benefits during and following the games. East London has new rail lines (Dockland light railway extension) and improved public transport, including an improved international rail station at Stratford. This helps to reduce congestion and increase productivity.

Political impacts affecting hosting of global games

As previously mentioned the '**shop window**' effect provides the ideal opportunity to showcase the very best that a country can offer. The Olympics can be a fantastic global shop window for sport. Early on in this chapter (page 192) there are examples where the Olympic Games has been used as a political tool with both **positive** and **negative** impacts.

Berlin 1936 - Hitler and Jesse Owens - Jesse Owens and other black athletes had succeeded in discrediting Nazi ideology. Adolf Hitler unsuccessfully used the event as a platform to prove his theory of racial superiority.

Mexico City 1968 - the Black Power salute – at the time this gesture rocked the Olympics and the world. Thirty years after their protest, the two men were honoured for their part in furthering the civil rights movement in America.

Munich 1972 Palestinian terrorism - the massacre led the German federal government to re-examine its anti-terrorism policies.

Moscow 1980 - boycotts due to the Soviet invasion of Afghanistan -the Cold War came to the Olympics as the US led the way in a mass boycott of the Moscow Games in protest at the Soviet invasion of Afghanistan. The Lenin Stadium in Moscow had plenty of empty seats available due to the US-led boycott.

Los Angeles 1984 - the Soviet Union boycott in return for 1980.

Another example of a successful global sporting boycott occurred in South Africa.
Apartheid was a political and social system in South Africa while it was under white minority rule. Apartheid **boycotts** (South Africa was not allowed to compete at the Olympic Games from 1964 to 1988) were used to isolate South Africa and bring about a major overhaul in the country's social structure.

More examples of Political **negative** impacts

Public protests can be embarrassing for the host nation, particularly when the host country has a poor record on **human rights**. For example, prior to the Beijing Olympic Games in 2008, 40,000 protesting Chinese were imprisoned. Many of the prisoners were supporters of the Tibetan freedom movement who demonstrated during the journey of the Olympic Torch around the world. These negative events tarnished the PRC's image in advance of the Games.

The **cost** of the event can exceed the budget. For example, **security costs** for the London 2012 Olympic and Paralympic Games exceeded £1bn, with the in-venue security element costing £553m alone. This expense was met from the public purse. 23,700 security personnel and 500 MI5 officers were assigned exclusively to keep the games safe from extremist **terrorist attacks**.

More examples of Political **positive** impacts

The 'shop window' effect. For example, China ensured that their organisation, standard of participation and number of gold medals demonstrated how wonderful the Chinese Government and people were throughout the Olympic and Paralympic Games in 2008 and used these Games to highlight its **economic rise** and emergence as a **world power** that works under communism.

Another example is that team GB's results in both Olympic and Paralympic Games in London 2012 and Rio 2016 enabled British sport to move forward and improve on the fantastic results of 2008. These results highlight **political superiority**, **prestige** and **advertising** for the UK and will continue to bolster financial support to Team GB and improvement in sporting facilities to meet society's demands for national **sporting success**.

When the authorities **plan carefully**, they can use the occasion of the sporting event to help finance public works that benefit the whole population in the long term to provide a sporting legacy for future generations.

Practice questions

1) Modern technologies and social media are transforming sports in the 21st century.
   Which one of the following choices does not offer best practice in global sports communication?
   a. data collection on mass sports participation.
   b. understanding of the current online practices.
   c. use of multi media such as internet, television, radio and printed publications.
   d. newspaper reports on smoking.

2) What was the main reason for the commercialisation of the modern Olympic Games after 1980?
   a. all previous games were in debt.
   b. corporations wanted to advertise their goods.
   c. media wanted improved TV rights.
   d. finance was needed to increase security.

3) Which one of the following does not represent an Olympic value?
   a. do your best in everyday life.
   b. fair play.
   c. get on well with team members and opponents.
   d. win games by using various ploys and tactics.

4) Which one of the following does not describe the 'shop window' effect?
   a. develops national pride.
   b. portrays worthiness of political systems
   c. empowers local residents.
   d. tarnishes national image through demonstrations.

5) Which one of the following is an example of a National Governing Body (NGB)?
   a. British Olympic Association.
   b. UK Sport.
   c. Lawn Tennis Association.
   d. International Olympic Committee.

6) Describe the limitations which existed in the early Modern Olympic Games.   4 marks

7) Discuss the characteristics of World Games, and explain how participation in such a games
   will affect the competitor.   8 marks

8) In the 1980 Moscow Olympic Games it was left up to the politicians to decide whether or not to send
   national teams to these Olympic Games. Discuss arguments for and against a boycott of these games.   8 marks

9) State three ideals that the Olympics aim to promote.   3 marks

Practice questions

10) A Level. In 1896 the modern Olympic Games were established around the principle of the 'amateur ideal'. Discuss whether this principle is still relevant to Olympic performers in the twenty first century.   20 marks

11) a) Identify three goals of the Olympic movement that together define Olympism.   3 marks

    b) Suggest two ways in which the Olympic ideal is no longer apparent today.   2 marks

12) Describe three functions of the British Olympic Association (BOA).   3 marks

13) a) In relation to global sporting events, what is meant by the phrase 'the shop window effect'?   2 marks

    b) Using examples from past major global games highlight some of the positive and negative impacts that the 'shop window' effect may have had on national and political groups.   6 marks

14) Explain how sporting success at an Olympic Games can be used as a vehicle for nation building.   4 marks

15) Team GB won 27 gold (in 16 different sports), 23 silver and 17 bronze medals during the Rio Olympic Games, finishing second in the meal table ahead of China. Suggest the positive and negative impacts that participating in a global sporting event can have on the elite athlete and society.   10 marks

16) The London 2012 Olympic Legacy is described as the longer-term benefits and effects of the planning, funding, building and staging of the Olympic and Paralympic Games in the summer of 2012. Evaluate the success of this legacy.   6 marks

17) Many people want their country to host an international sporting event. Others believe that international sporting events bring more problems than benefits. Discuss both views and state your opinion.   6 marks

18) A Level. Explain how social factors and the support programmes in the UK encourage development of elite athletes and increase the chance of winning medals.   20 marks

19) The 19th century English public schools had a major impact on the development of rational recreation and the sporting values of the modern Olympic Games. What are the similarities between the sporting values of the 19th century English public school and the modern Olympic Games?   4 marks

20) At the Rio 2016 Olympics, billions of people watched both amateurs and professionals competing in 42 sports. Suggest reasons why the International Olympic Committee (IOC) has allowed professional performers to compete at the Olympic Games.   5 marks

21) Suggest reasons why there have been few instances of spectator violence at the modern Olympic Games compared with the FIFA World Cup.   4 marks

Answers link: http://www.jroscoe.co.uk/downloads/as_a1_revise_pe_ocr/OCRAS_A1_ch16_answers.pdf

Instruction/terms used in examination papers

Advantages and disadvantages

Clear statement of why one condition is better that another. Would normally need justification and/or qualification relevant to the question.

Characteristics

Common, agreed factors for a situation, structure or process.

Define/What is meant by....?

Formal and precise description frequently of a technical term/less formal by definition.

Describe

Use of quantitative or qualitative information to explain a statement or a relationship between factors. This term is maybe qualified as 'briefly describe'. Examples are frequently used.

Differences

A comparison between two states in the question. You should be precise and not be tempted to wander.

Discuss

Presentation of both sides of an argument, seeking an opinion based on knowledge and analysis with a justified conclusion.

Explain

Justification beyond simple statement or descriptions required (the why). Will frequently require examples, sometimes qualified as explain briefly. Consider number of marks allocated.

Identify and explain

Linking of cause/problem and effect/solution. Marks awarded only if links are made.

List

A number of points or features, frequently only a single word. No description required.

Name

No explanation required or credited. Will normally require use of a degree of technical language. One or two words.

Plot, Sketch and Label

Used for graphical presentation. For a sketch, graph paper is not required. Important factors are correct labelling of axes and shape of graph. Plotting requires the use of appropriate scales on axes and accurate plotting points.

Principle

Theoretical concept underpinning a practical example.

Suggest

More than one option available which require a justification linked to a question. Not to be answered from pure recall.

Assessment objectives for AS/A1 and A Level OCR Physical Education examination papers.

OCR's 'A' Level in Physical Education consists of three components that are externally assessed. These are physiological and psychological factors affecting performance and socio-cultural issues in physical activity and sport, as exemplified within this student text.

Assessment is achieved by using a mixture objective response, short and medium length questions and extended questions that may also test synoptic understanding within different parts of the 'A' Level syllabus. Also included are multi-choice questions. You will find examples of all these types of questions throughout this revision text.

A synoptic element of learning will enable you to develop knowledge and understanding of subject specific skills. This type of assessment is often examined in the 10 mark AS/A1 and 20 mark 'A' level questions. Again there are examples of synoptic questions within the student text.

Quantitative skills are examined during the interpretation and analyse of data and graphs in both chapter content and questions.

There are 3 assessment categories AO1, AO2 and AO3 that are used to examine question content.

Where questions carry more than a few marks, the **indicative content** for your answer is marked up to three levels that are categorised as follows:

AO1 – is marked on recall information, and so you will be expected to demonstrate knowledge and understanding of the factors that underpin performance and involvement in physical activity and sport.

AO2 – is marked on application of theory, and so you will be expected to apply knowledge and understanding of the factors that underpin performance and involvement in physical activity and sport.

AO3 – is marked on analyses and evaluation, and so you will be expected to analyse and the factors that underpin performance and involvement in physical activity and sport.

When answering a question, consider the weighting and ensure that you have sufficient indicative content, particularly for the AO3 level. For example, a 10 mark question may consist of 5 marks for AO2 and 5 marks for AO3. An A Level 20 mark question may consist of 5 marks for AO1, 5 marks for AO2 and 10 marks for AO3. If the question is to analyse and evaluate, then the indicative content would fall into the AO3 category. So you need read the question carefully and decide how the marks fall into these three categories.

For further examples of mark allocation to questions, please refer to 'A' Level GCE OCR Physical Education - H155, H555.

INDEX